The Sydney Morning Herald

good food
guide 2009

Simon Thomsen & Joanna Savill

PENGUIN BOOKS

The editors would like to serve a veloute of thanks to the following degustation of delicious people, plus a side dish of slow-roasted appreciation: our insightful and enthusiastic reviewing team; resident Google, eagle eye and life support system, Paul McLean; Capt. Kevin Stokes and the crew of the good ship Enterprise for letting us boldly spend like no one has done before; our understanding Melbourne compatriots Necia Wilden and John Lethlean; our supportive and patient Fairfax editors, especially Sue, Lauren and Anthony; Mark Polden and Richard Coleman for keeping our noses clean; Shane 'upper or lower case?' Brady for making it so much easier; Scott 'have you heard?' Bolles; photographers Earl Carter for the cover shot and Richard Birch for the internal pics; Virginia Birch, Megan Baker, Claire de Medici and all the other Pinguini; Les Schirato and Tania Moroko of Vittoria Coffee for their unstinting support and encouragement; and the fabulous, untiring regional editor Angie Schiavone, who's worth her weight in wedding rings. Most of all, our love and admiration go to our tolerant, gorgeous and understanding families: the luscious, wise and forthright Sally Webb and the inevitably hungry Archie and Lulu; and the equally wise and wonderful Giuliano Dambelli, he of the palate and (mostly) patience, and Milena and Lily Rose for their (mostly) discerning eating skills.

PENGUIN BOOKS

Published by the Penguin Group
Penguin Group (Australia)
250 Camberwell Road, Camberwell, Victoria 3124, Australia
(a division of Pearson Australia Group Pty Ltd)

Penguin Books Ltd, Registered Offices: 80 Strand, London, WC2R 0RL, England

First published by Penguin Group (Australia), 2008

1 3 5 7 9 10 8 6 4 2

Cover design by Megan Baker © Penguin Group (Australia)
Text design by Ann Loveday, *The Sydney Morning Herald*, and Megan Baker, Penguin Group (Australia)
Cover photograph by Earl Carter of Universal Restaurant, Darlinghurst
Internal photographs by Richard Birch, except page 306 by Arsineh Houspian
Photographs taken at Apple Bar, Blue Bar and Restaurant, Bodega, Fishmongers, Glacé, Leura Gourmet, Madame Fling Flong, Manly Wharf Hotel, Marigold, Pizza Mario @ St Margaret's, Rockpool (fish), Sister Bella, Solitary
Mural on page 179 designed by Ken Lambert of Ink Project and used with permission of Bodega Restaurant Pty Ltd.
Fabric on page x–xi from Rockpool (fish) designed by Hella Jongerius and used with permission of Maharam
Maps by Country Cartographics
Hat logo design by David Band. The Hat logo is the registered trademark of Fairfax Media Publications Pty Ltd
Typeset in Frutiger Light by Post Pre-press Group, Brisbane, Queensland
Colour reproduction by Splitting Image, Clayton, Victoria
Printed and bound in Australia by BPA Print Group Pty Ltd

Managing Editor, Fairfax Books: Michael Johnston
Project Co-ordinator, Fairfax Books: Paul McLean
Publishing Manager – Operations, Fairfax Books: Stephen Berry
Publishing Manager – Commercial, Fairfax Books: Linda MacLennan
Group General Manager, Fairfax Enterprises: Kevin Stokes

For advertising enquiries for *The Sydney Morning Herald Good Food Guide 2010*
please contact Fairfax Books on (02) 9282 2514.

Contents

Meet the Editors

Simon Thomsen, co-editor

Simon is chief restaurant reviewer for *The Sydney Morning Herald*, where his reviews appear in 'Good Living' every Tuesday. This is his fifth year as co-editor of *The Sydney Morning Herald Good Food Guide*. Simon once travelled the world working as a chef and waiter but now the thing he makes most often for dinner is reservations. He believes that while food matters, the most important part of a meal is sharing it with good company and conversation that sparkles like champagne and flows like a good pinot noir. He loves his wife Sally's homemade muesli and baking almost as much as he loves her.

Joanna Savill, co-editor

Joanna is a journalist, linguist, traveller and food tragic. This is her second year as co-editor of the *Guide*, but she's been on the food trail ever since discovering toad-in-the-hole at kindergarten school-dinner in England. Her big epiphany came while living and eating in Bologna, Italy's gastronomic heartland (or so the Bolognesi say). As a current affairs reporter and TV presenter, she co-created SBS TV's *The Food Lovers' Guide to Australia*, and told Sydneysiders about wood-fired pizza and secret Italian food spots like Haberfield(!) way back in 1992 for the very first *SBS Guide to Ethnic Eating*. These days she continues her food explorations weekly for her Three of a Kind column in 'Good Living'. She sometimes feels it's time she did more about world peace.

Angie Schiavone, regional editor

Angie knows the *Guide* inside and out, both as a former production co-ordinator and reviewer and now as regional editor. She has been part of the team for five years, and has been eating all her life. This year she spent more time in transit than anywhere else but still managed to find the time to get married to Clive. Her favourite place to dine is at her nonna and nonno's (they take bookings, and everything is homemade with love). Angie also reviews children's books for 'Spectrum' in Saturday's *Sydney Morning Herald*.

Other reviewers

Keith Austin, Sue Bennett, Jeanine Bribosia, Victoria Cosford, Anthony Dennis, Kate Duthie, Bruce Elder, Hugh Fitzhardinge, Molly Foskett, Akiko Mori Ganivet, Helen Greenwood, Guy Griffin, Kendall Hill, Amanda Hooton, Anthony Huckstep, Belinda Jeffery, Catherine Keenan, Sally Lewis, Elizabeth Love, Les Luxford, James Mayson, Lyndey Milan, Roberta Muir, Lynne Mullins, Sarah Nicholson, Helen O'Neill, Danielle Oppermann, Philip Putnam, Lauren Quaintance, John Saxby, Rosemary Stanton, Paul van Reyk, Stephanie Wood.

Introduction

It is the best of times and the worst of times. Despite terrifying oil price hikes and interest rate rises, as well as skyrocketing commodity prices (who'd have guessed rice would treble in cost during the first half of 2008?), it's never been a better time to eat out.

Sure, menu prices have gone up – hello $30+ entrees and $50+ mains – but not as much as restaurateurs would hope or like, and not nearly as much your supermarket shopping bill. Right now though, restaurant owners are worried that dining out may become a luxury you can no longer afford. Then there's the amped-up competition in a city blessed with a surfeit of fantastic eating destinations. The end result is that your meal has never been better value.

But while restaurants are feeling the pinch, the biggest burden is on the farmers and fishers who, in some instances, are now spending more to produce the food than we're prepared to pay at the markets. We keep our fingers crossed that 2009 will see everyone receiving a fairer slice of the financial pie.

In the meantime, enjoy the bounty on offer. 2008 has seen some inspiring openings, from the return of spice queen Chris Manfield at Universal Restaurant to Dietmar Sawyere's revival of the iconic Berowra Waters Inn. We welcome back Peter Conistis at Civic Dining (and his mum, Eleni, downstairs), and bow in gratitude to a slew of well-priced suburban eateries.

Italian remains an old favourite but it's good to see more Asian flavours, such as Malaysian and Japanese, joining the charge. The year ahead looks just as impressive (see Stop Press), so it seems there's no shortage of industry confidence about enticing us to open our wallets.

So, here's our wish list for the year ahead:

• Scallops and cauliflower puree – these two have been dating for a long time but the romance has gone. It's time one of them moved on (but preferably not straight back into bed with pork belly, please).

• Bananas – yes, the price is a sixth of last year's post-hurricane cost, but just how many banana tarte Tatins can a dessert-lover consume?

• Wagyu – we love it, but it's getting harder to justify on sustainability grounds and there are lots of other interesting cattle breeds out there.

• Avruga 'caviar' – it's not caviar; it's Spanish herring, reformed to look like sturgeon roe. You wouldn't call a sausage a fillet steak, so don't call this caviar.

• Jamon – adore it, but really, if you're running an Italian ristorante, cheer for the home side and serve prosciutto, rather than follow the food-fashion crowd.

• Pepper grinders – why can't we be trusted with our own? And what's the point of offering one before we've tasted a dish? Doesn't the chef season the food?

• Grotty loos – say no more.

• Expensive wines – nine times out of 10, a Cotes du Rhone is not worth $80. We're all for more foreign wines on the list, but not so that restaurants can charge a 300 per cent mark up and think we won't notice because we won't be able to compare prices at the local bottle shop.

• Mineral water – we drink it too sometimes, but rather than just "still or sparkling?" (kerr-ching! goes the cash register), restaurants should offer tap water too, as a matter of course.

Enough quibbling. We've really had a lovely time. Sydney remains one of the best-value cities in the world in which to eat out. The produce just keeps getting better and we can see a lot of true professionals trying hard to deliver good service. We applaud them and hope this book gives them some recognition for their efforts.

This year we've introduced an exciting new section, Global Gems. These are places we love for the passion and authenticity of their food but which may not quite rate on a fine-dining scale. It might be because the setting is too casual or the surrounds less than salubrious, but if good, simple eating is what matters most to you, seek them out. It's one of the best ways to take your palate around the world and (in many cases) still have change from a $50 note.

Also with an eye to the wallet (but without forgetting the stomach), we've expanded our Ten of the Best section to include pub food – places where you rock up to the counter, order and pay up front, then look for a table – in recognition of some great, nourishing and affordable grub. Sydney's latest shared-plate craze, tapas, is also included, along with an old brunch-to-lunch favourite, yum cha. Pizza, ice-cream and fish and chips are there too. Because we love them and so do you.

Meanwhile, our indefatigable regional editor Angie Schiavone and her team have scoured the state for new, and older, places to dine, both up and down the coast and on or across the Great Divide. The regional section also includes the finest provedores and other simpler eating spots to make out-of-town trips (and edible-souvenir shopping) even more fun.

So now it's up to you. Put this *Guide* to work. Make a booking. Go eat! We hope you have the best of times. Buon appetito.

Simon Thomsen & Joanna Savill
July 2008

About the book

How we review

Every scored restaurant in the *Good Food Guide* has been visited anonymously in the past 12 months by at least one of our experienced reviewers. We pay for our meals in full and sample at least two courses, usually three. Every three-hat candidate has been visited numerous times by various reviewers over the year; likewise many of the two-hatters. We eat at many more restaurants than will fit into this book to give you a guide to the best we can find. If we wouldn't feel comfortable recommending a restaurant to a friend, we don't include it. In total we visit more than 550 restaurants throughout New South Wales to publish more than 400 reviews.

We've updated our Cafes section to explore all points of the Sydney compass. The Bars guide lets you kick on or wind down, and we've listed Ten of the Best for everything from pizza to ice-cream. Our new Global Gems section comprises around 50 interesting and exciting eateries across the city and suburbs that may not necessarily rate on the fine-dining scale, but more than make up for it with their real-deal food...and prices.

Our regional editor Angie Schiavone and her team have scoured the state for the best places to dine, shop and get a decent coffee or holiday supplies. And if you're heading interstate, there's a list of the best from capitals around Australia as well as further afield.

Feedback

We welcome your recommendations and comments. Email us at goodfoodguide@smh.com.au or write to *The Sydney Morning Herald Good Food Guide*, GPO Box 506, Sydney, 2000.

Bill

We want to let you know how much eating out will cost but recognise that not everyone will eat three courses, or possibly even two, so we've listed the range of prices for entree (**E**), main (**M**) and dessert (**D**). Some places have set prices, higher prices on weekends or degustation menus, so we've tried to include those too. Remember, though, that this is only an indication. Prices rise (and very occasionally fall) but all details are provided by the restaurants themselves and confirmed by our team before we go to press.

Wine

Wine is a very important part of dining out, so we've given you a user-friendly description of the wine list for each restaurant as well as the cost of BYO. Corkage is either per person (e.g. $2 pp) or per bottle. Most of the restaurants in this *Guide* are BYO for bottled wine only – no beer, spirits or casks. A wine glass symbol (Υ) indicates a particularly good wine list.

Wheelchair access

Using information supplied to us by the restaurants, we indicate wheelchair access only if accessible toilets are also provided. Many restaurants have side or back access for wheelchairs; so, if in doubt, call ahead.

Child friendly

Eating out shouldn't stop just because you don't have a babysitter. We're keen to encourage the next generation of diners and most restaurants welcome (well-behaved) children. Some go to an extra effort with kids' menus, highchairs and things to entertain, so we want to let you know by listing them as 'child friendly'. However, if we don't mention 'child friendly' it doesn't necessarily mean they *don't* welcome kids – just ring and check to see if the restaurant suits your family.

Bookings

Bookings are recommended for all restaurants that take them. We mention it only if the restaurant regards bookings as essential or if they are not accepted at all.

Vegetarian

Not everyone wants to eat meat, so this year we've introduced a new category for vegetarians, noting menus with more than just a couple of non-meat options. Most restaurants offer at least one meat-free entree and main – but we've singled out places that make an extra effort. In every case, though, we encourage vegetarians and those with other dietary requirements to phone a restaurant ahead of time to ensure their needs can be met. With notice, some places will offer a full vegetarian, vegan or even gluten-free degustation.

And...

Because we want to provide as much information as we can, the final line on every restaurant entry is designed to let you know something incidental, interesting and hopefully useful, but not necessarily essential, about the experience.

Accuracy

We check the information in the *Guide* numerous times. First, the restaurant fills out a questionnaire; then our team of reviewers gathers the information; and later, as close to publication as possible, phone checks are made for every entry. However, things can still come unstuck if a restaurant closes suddenly or changes its pricing, chef or opening times. This is, unfortunately, beyond our control.

The scores

Apart from our chef's-hat ratings, we score restaurants out of 20 to give you a more useful sense of their merits. The score comprises 10 points for food, 5 for service, 3 for ambience, with an extra 2 points possible for a sprinkling of magic, whether it be the great location, stunning service or food that is sublime beyond belief. Places scoring less than 12/20 are not included.

This year we have raised the bar for the coveted chef's hats. A restaurant needs to score at least 15 to be awarded one hat, 16 for two hats and 18 for three hats.

12	Reasonable
13	Some respectable highlights
14	A solid, enjoyable experience
15	♙ Reliably good
16	♙ ♙ A bit of that WOW factor
17	♙ ♙ Amazingly good
18	♙ ♙ ♙ World class
19	♙ ♙ ♙ Truly spectacular
20	♙ ♙ ♙ Perfection on a plate

Awards

Along with our chef's-hat awards, we also have other ways of recognising greatness in various fields. Some are self-explanatory; the others are listed below.

Restaurant of the Year – a place that has shown remarkable energy and consistency and sets a standard others should aspire to.

Chef of the Year – an individual who shows not only talent and dedication to his or her craft but whose work continues to excite and evolve.

Best Regional Restaurant – the best in the bush or on the beach, but certainly beyond Sydney.

Editors' Picks – restaurants we love to eat at for the simple joy of dining out (and spending our own money).

Award for Professional Excellence – for a long-term contribution to the restaurant industry.

Silver Service Award – for defining, redefining or showing the ultimate level of service.

Sommelier of the Year – a great wine list needs someone to help diners navigate it and make their choice. This award recognises a wine waiter who makes drinking a pleasure.

Wine List of the Year – it's not about size, but how well a list matches the setting and food, offering accessible excitement and adventure.

The Josephine Pignolet Best Young Chef Award – chosen by some of Sydney's leading chefs in memory of a great chef, this is the ultimate accolade for a passionate, talented young cook. The young chef receives a return international flight, courtesy of Qantas, the chance to work in leading European restaurants, a substantial cash prize from Sydney's leading food suppliers and chefs, and a set of Furitechnics knives.

The Vittoria Legend Award – chosen by Les Schirato of Vittoria Coffee, for an individual's outstanding contribution to the industry.

Symbols

★	An award-winning restaurant
♗	A particularly good wine list
NEW	A new listing in this *Guide*, but not necessarily a new restaurant
AE	American Express
DC	Diners Club
MC	MasterCard
V	Visa

Awards

Vittoria Coffee Restaurant of the Year
Quay

All-Clad Chef of the Year
Justin North at Bécasse

Best New Restaurant
Berowra Waters Inn

Best Regional Restaurant
Rock (Pokolbin)

**The Sydney Morning Herald Award
for Professional Excellence**
Rob Hirst and the late Judy Hirst of Fine Wine
Partners, for their efforts in educating and
raising the standards and professionalism of
wine service and championing quality wines,
especially boutique Australian producers.

Silver Service Award
Lucio Galletto of Lucio's, for his charm, warmth
and discretion, and for making Lucio's a unique,
distinctive marriage of food, wine and art.

Sommeliers of the Year
Stuart Halliday and Jerry Jones of Tetsuya's, for
making wine fun, adventurous, exciting and
accessible and taking the time to explain why.

Wine List of the Year
ARIA

Regional Wine List of the Year
Rubicon (Canberra)

The Josephine Pignolet Best Young Chef
James Parry, second chef at Oscillate Wildly

The Vittoria Legend Award
Maurice Terzini of Icebergs Dining Room and Bar

Editors' Picks
Favourite Bistro – Tabou (Surry Hills)
Favourite Mediterranean – Cafe Sopra (Waterloo)
Favourite Asian – Mamak (Haymarket)
Favourite Global Gem – Al Aseel (Greenacre)
Favourite Bargain – Eleni's at Civic (Sydney)
Favourite Extravagance – Sardinian tasting
menu, Pilu at Freshwater (Freshwater)
Favourite Food-with-a-view – North Bondi
Italian Food (North Bondi)
Favourite Cafe – Single Origin (Surry Hills)
Favourite Pizza and Ice-cream – Pompei's
(Bondi Beach)
Favourite Tapas – Bodega (Surry Hills)

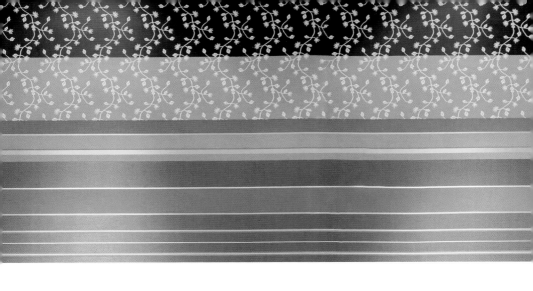

City

Bilson's, Claude's, est., Marque, Pier, Quay, Tetsuya's

ARIA, Bécasse, Bentley Restaurant & Bar, Berowra Waters Inn, Bistro Ortolan, Buon Ricordo, Forty One, Guillaume at Bennelong, Icebergs Dining Room and Bar, Lucio's, Pilu at Freshwater, Restaurant Balzac, Rockpool (fish), Universal Restaurant, Yoshii

Assiette, Astral, a tavola, Azuma, The Bathers' Pavilion Restaurant, Bird Cow Fish, Bistro CBD, Bistro Moncur, Bistrode, The Boathouse on Blackwattle Bay, The Burlington Bar and Dining, Catalina, Civic Dining, Fish Face, Flying Fish, Four in Hand Dining Room, Foveaux Restaurant + Bar, Glebe Point Diner, Grand National, Jonah's, The Light Brigade, Longrain, Milsons, Oscillate Wildly, Otto Ristorante, Ottoman Cuisine, Perama, Pier Tasting Room, Restaurant Arras, Sailors Thai Restaurant, Sean's Panaroma, The Wharf Restaurant

Regional

Darley's (Katoomba), FINS (South Kingscliff), Rock (Pokolbin), Vulcans (Blackheath)

Artespresso (Canberra), Bamboo (Casuarina Beach), Bells at Killcare (Killcare), Caveau (Wollongong), Courgette (Canberra), Eschalot (Berrima), Katers (Sutton Forest), Lochiel House (Kurrajong Heights), Neila (Cowra), No. 2 Oak Street (Bellingen), The Old George & Dragon (East Maitland), Ottoman Cuisine (Canberra), Pacific Dining Room (Byron Bay), Restaurant II (Newcastle), Restaurant Como (Blaxland), The School House (Orange), Tonic (Millthorpe), Zest Restaurant (Nelson Bay)

We would like to thank Vittoria Coffee for their generous support of The Sydney Morning Herald Good Food Guide *launch.*

Stop Press

Changes due as we go to press.

Ash St Cellar
Ivy, 330 George Street, Sydney
Tel 9240 3000
Former Lotus chef Lauren Murdoch takes charge of a European-style bistro and wine bar at the base of Ivy's large staircase. Open weekdays for lunch and dinner, it has a communal table and plenty of outdoor seating with a large menu of shared plates and a la carte fare. No bookings.

The Beresford
348 Bourke Street, Darlinghurst
Tel 9357 1111
Peripatetic chef Danny Russo (ex l'Unico and Aqua Luna) does Italian, in trattoria mode, at this Taylor Square 1920s New York-style pub and beer garden. Expect classic caprese and stuzzichini (Italian tapas) through to serious chargrills.

dish
Cnr Jonson & Marvel streets, Byron Bay
Tel 6685 7320
New owners, a new chef and a makeover mean a new beginning for this popular Byron diner. Ross Skinner and Michael Delaurence, the duo behind Bangalow's Utopia, will stamp their own style on this smartly casual setting.

Hungry Duck
85 Queen Street, Berry
Tel 4464 2323
The Book Kitchen's David Campbell goes bush, with a kitchen garden and a modern Asian focus. No surprise that duck's on the menu – in a red curry, a salad and cooked three ways – or try house-made pork buns, plenty of seafood, and, just in case, oxtail bolognese.

Rockpool Bar & Grill
66 Hunter Street, Sydney
Neil Perry brings his Melbourne steakhouse to Sin City in an elegant art deco building. Expect dark leathers and solid timbers, a 2000-bottle wine list and several cuts of the very best beef from the in-house ageing rooms. There's sustainable fish and live shellfish, or a wagyu burger at the bar. Opening January 2009.

Sean's Kitchen
Star City Casino, Pyrmont
Tel 1800 700 700
Astral's Sean Connolly goes casual for steak, seafood and comfort food, from French onion soup to wagyu sausages with borlotti bean casserole. Claypot chicken is a signature,

and you can try six different Spanish hams in the jamon bar. Opens September '08.

Spice Temple
66 Hunter Street (entry on Bligh Street), Sydney
In this basement space, Neil Perry goes modern Chinese with lively, spice-driven flavours drawn from five key food regions beyond the usual Cantonese realm. He promises a new and playful way of dining, with a bar and colourful, temple-like dining room. Opens November '08.

Steel
60 Carrington Street, Sydney
The team behind Pony – designer Michael McCann and chef Damian Heads – have set their sights on a theatrical 180-seat CBD brasserie with a central open kitchen, fish tanks and a glass cool room as part of the show, not to mention a 3000-bottle wine wall. Expect steaks on a wood fire, sharing plates and bar food, granite kitchen counter dining, a large communal table and a white onyx deck. Opens September '08.

Sushi Choo
Ivy, 330 George Street, Sydney
Tel 9240 3000
Thomas the Tank Engine turns Japanese, with former sushi e and Nobu chef Shaun Presland blowing the whistle on a pair of upmarket sushi trains. A further dozen dishes will come from the kitchen behind, including mixed tempura, teriyaki and tataki, plus a sashimi pizza. No bookings for weekday lunch and dinner, or Saturday night.

Uccello
Ivy, 330 George Street, Sydney
Tel 9240 3000
Roman chef Massimo Bianchi (ex Buon Ricordo) serves up traditional Italian cucina in a poolside setting, complete with cabanas and a pizza oven. Expect a large antipasto table and much of the 200-bottle wine list to be Italian. Open nightly for dinner and lunch Sunday to Friday.

Water's Edge
Parkes Place (North), Parkes, Canberra
Tel 6273 5066
James Mussillon (of Sabayon and Courgette) wants to restore this waterfront setting to the top of Canberra dining, as a casual bistro and alfresco cafe by day and fine diner by night. Canberra's answer to Icebergs, he says, with a strong seafood focus and a cocktail bar.

City + Suburbs

Abhi's

163 Concord Road, North Strathfield
Tel 9743 3061   Map 6

Indian

Score 14/20

Sandwiched between a bottle shop and a pharmacy on a busy main road, Abhi's could be mistaken for just another suburban Indian. One glance at the menu, however, and you'll know that Abhi's breaks the mould, cleverly fusing contemporary Western cooking and presentation style with time-honoured combinations of Indian spices and ingredients. It's there in an entree of blue swimmer crab flesh, tangy with tomato, turmeric and green chilli, accompanied by a cooling scoop of porial – just-wilted shredded spinach tossed with coconut, mustard seed and black lentils. Mirapakai kodi combines chunks of boneless chicken with whole red and green chillies, ginger and curry leaves, accomplishing satisfying heat without sacrificing the delicacy of the sparse spicing. Mirchi baingan ka salan tempers the slightly bitter caramel of fried whole small eggplant with a sweetish sauce of peanut, sesame and roasted coconut. Inlaid wooden tables, subdued lighting, restraint in decoration and zealous and courteous staff round off the not-just-another-suburban-Indian experience.

Hours Lunch Sun–Fri noon–3pm;
Dinner daily 6–10pm; bookings essential
Bill E $10.80–$18.80 **M** $16.80–$22.80 **D** $9.80–$11.80
Cards AE DC V MC
Wine Decent range, plus good beers;
11 by the glass; BYO (corkage $2.50 pp)
Chefs Kumar Mahadevan & Ranjan Choudhury
Owners Kumar & Suba Mahadevan
Seats 180; private room; wheelchair access
Vegetarian Nine dishes
www.abhisindian.com.au
And...double ke meetha, heavenly bread pudding

Aki's

Shop 1, 6 Cowper Wharf Road,
Woolloomooloo
Tel 9332 4600   Map 2

Indian

Score 13/20

This is quintessential Sydney: a wide, wooden wharf where the beautiful people stroll and a shimmering city skyline provide a glorious backdrop. As the first cab off the rank on the Woolloomooloo boardwalk, Aki's is the ideal people-watching spot, especially with a long Old Raj cocktail of basil and lemongrass-infused gin to sip on. Entree or small plates include palak patta chaat – spinach leaves set in thick, fried lentil batter and slathered with sweetened yoghurt, ribbons of tamarind, chilli and mint sauces. Lightly seared scallops tamateri are a better, and lighter, choice, served with a spicy dollop of minced tomato and ginger and curry leaf-infused olive oil. A jumble of quail pieces, each in a fragrant crust of ginger, lime, toasted black pepper, cassia bark and fennel, is a main course highlight. Railway goat curry sounds intriguing but tasted rather more pedestrian. While service can be shaky to the point of indifference, pistachio kulfi for dessert will lift the mood, as will the smart revamp of the decor.

Hours Lunch Sun–Fri noon–3pm;
Dinner daily 6–10pm
Bill E $10–$23 **M** $19–$34 **D** $10–$13
Cards AE V MC
Wine Excellent, well-priced list; 16 by the glass
Chefs Kumar Mahadevan, Vikram Arumugam & Vijayan Ramasamy
Owners Kumar & Suba Mahadevan
Seats 150; outdoor seating
Vegetarian One in every four dishes
www.akisindian.com.au
And...visit Aki's older brother, Abhi's in North Strathfield

Alchemy 731

731 Military Road, Mosman
Tel 9968 3731   Map 7

Modern European   ♀
                                    Score 13.5/20

Brit chef Derek Baker must have a thing
for science. Take his restaurant name, for
starters. Next, there's a menu reading as
though his kitchen were a lab – peanut
brittle with duck prosciutto; scallops with
pickled ox tongue. An amuse bouche of
potato soup in a test tube, set in a test-
tube rack, completes the image. And while
the RSL next door may not be feeding
him patrons, it's clear his experiments are
bringing in the locals, as he has lasted
longer than most in this spot. (Or maybe
it's the safe decor – real linen tablecloths
and a padded linen wall.) Food-wise, some
concepts succeed better than others, such
as a lozenge of perfectly poached ocean
trout framed by beetroot puree, or juicy pork
belly with spiced black pudding. Others may
need a little more testing. Chicken rillettes
were too dry, and a side of broccoli with
lemon and almonds inexplicably bland. But
a chocolate millefeuille with white chocolate
sorbet has plenty of mad-scientist magic.

Hours Lunch Fri noon–2pm; Dinner
Tues–Sat 6–9pm; bookings recommended

Bill 2 courses $55 pp, 3 courses $65 pp, 6-course
tasting menu $80 pp, menu surprise $100 pp;
Friday lunch 2 courses $30 pp, 3 courses $40 pp

Cards AE V MC Eftpos

Wine Some left-field, some tried-and-true, mainly
domestic labels; 12 by the glass; BYO Tues–Thurs
& Fri lunch (corkage $7 per bottle)

Chef/owner Derek Baker

Seats 50; private rooms

Child friendly Kids' menu

Vegetarian Good options, six-course tasting menu

www.alchemy731.com.au

And...peanut brittle, jams and fudge for sale

Alhambra

Shop 1, 54 West Esplanade, Manly
Tel 9976 2975   Map 7

Spanish/Moroccan
                                     Score 13/20

If Morocco is on your must-visit list, a ferry
to Manly is a good primer for a rewarding
culinary adventure in Moorish and southern
Spanish classics. This bright, terracotta-tiled
space right opposite Manly Wharf may be
a far cry from Fez but its exotic menu will
soon transport you. Entrees (also served as
tapas) offer more than 30 tantalising choices,
such as pan-fried chermoula sardines served
with tomato salsa. Then there's warm zaalook
salad – roasted eggplant paired with olives
and preserved lemons, with a cumin and
coriander dressing. Aromatic, slow-cooked
tagines and paella, prepared to order, are
both favourites. Bastilla – the Moors' ultimate
medieval dish – is a generous, heavenly parcel
of paper-thin pastry dusted in powdered
sugar, filled with delicately spiced chicken,
almonds, orange blossom water, cinnamon
and saffron. Desserts keep the dream alive
with pears poached in red wine, cinnamon
and cloves, served with sweet anise couscous.

Hours Lunch Wed–Sun noon–3pm;
Dinner daily 6–10pm; bookings essential

Bill E $9–$18 **M** $22–$29 **D** $13–$16;
10% surcharge on public holidays

Cards AE DC V MC

Wine Snappy list of Australian and Spanish labels;
4 by the glass; BYO (corkage $3.50 pp)

Chef/owner Aziz Bakalla

Seats 110; wheelchair access; outdoor seating

Child friendly Highchairs; books

Vegetarian Numerous entree and tapas choices

www.alhambra.citysearch.com.au

And...take friends to share dishes and enjoy
the weekend flamenco

Alio

5 Baptist Street, Redfern
Tel 8394 9368   Map 3b

Italian

Score 13/20

Although Alio looks, feels and sounds about as Italian as the incumbent Pope, the menu is reassuringly true to theme. The commendably spacious dining room can feel a bit solemn, but not once the crowds arrive, as it remains a popular local haunt away from the Crown Street hubbub. Siblings Tracey and Ashley Hughes boast London's famed River Café on their CVs, and that experience shows in the southern Italian menu. After a welcome quartet of antipasti comes a well-balanced range of fish, meat and pasta – even snails for added interest. Dishes can include fritto of squid, chilli, rosemary and garlic; ravioli of prawn, blue swimmer crab and dill with a prawn bisque; and chargrilled veal cutlet with pea, prosciutto and gorgonzola. A little more Latin zeal, both on the plate and the floor, and this would be a great, rather than good, Italian eatery. But summer berries with vanilla mascarpone and caramel wafers, and the stalwart Locatelli-family tiramisu are right on track.

Hours Dinner Mon–Sat 6–10pm; bookings essential

Bill E $19 **M** $27–$31 **D** $14

Cards AE DC V MC Eftpos

Wine Affordable, concise and international selection; 15 by the glass; BYO (corkage $7 per bottle)

Chef Ashley Hughes

Owners Tracey & Ashley Hughes

Seats 90; private room; wheelchair access

Vegetarian Degustation and good a la carte options

www.alio.com.au

And...arrive early and have a drink at the attractive cocktail bar

Almond Bar

NEW

379 Liverpool Street, Darlinghurst
Tel 9380 5318   Map 2

Middle Eastern

Score 13/20

Sisters Carol and Sharon Salloum are mad about almonds. The decor of their Darlinghurst bolthole (formerly Ristorante Riva) channels the brown and green hues of this fruit (yes, technically, it is…) into ottomans, tables and cushions. Guests are greeted with a tiny tray of sugared, chilli, plain and salted nuts. The Salloums, like the almond, have descended from the Middle East – Syria, in fact – and their food reflects those origins. The menu comprises dozens of mezze or tasting plates, from the muhammara-like "red" dip of zingy capsicum, walnut and pomegranate to pleasing vegetarian dolmades (made by mum Violet from home-grown vine leaves) and juicy haloumi topped with oregano and diced tomatoes. Traditional Syrian sumbusic pastries stuffed with minced lamb, onion and pine nuts are melt-in-the-mouth sensations, while a fattoush of grilled pita, salad vegetables, garlic and sumac was satisfying but unremarkable. A tiny wedge of sticky baklava and a glass of mint tea make a delicate, Middle-Eastern finish.

Hours Lunch Fri noon–3pm; Dinner Tues–Sun 5–10.30pm

Bill Shared plates $6–$15, tasting plates $20

Cards AE DC V MC Eftpos

Wine Smart, succinct list of Australian and European varieties; 13 by the glass

Chef Sharon Salloum

Owner Carol Salloum

Seats 50

Vegetarian Set menu and tasting plate, plus 10 mezze dishes and dips

www.almondbar.com.au

And...if the menu options overwhelm, order a tasting plate

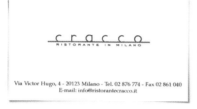

To enhance great foods
they choose great waters.

The delicate complex flavours of the finest cuisine are best appreciated by an educated palate.
And in the same way that the right wine can release the nuances of a dish, the right water
can subtly cleanse the palate, enhancing the pleasure and experience of both. To discover why
S.Pellegrino and Acqua Panna are seen on all the best tables, go to WWW.FINEDININGWATERS.COM

ACQUA PANNA AND S.PELLEGRINO. FINE DINING WATERS.

Altitude

Level 36, Shangri-La Hotel,
176 Cumberland Street, The Rocks
Tel 9250 6123   Map 1

Contemporary

Score 13.5/20

Panoramic and breathtaking, the view from this eyrie is just the place to introduce an out-of-towner to the theatre of Sydney – stage left, the Opera House, stage right, the Harbour Bridge. Chef Steven Krasicki, whose CV includes time at Banc and Restaurant Balzac, displays a Eurocentric leaning across the menu. Occasional "hotel food" traits blunt his ingenuity – three choices of complimentary bread barely distracted from the sizeable wait between courses, while twice-cooked quail was disappointingly dry. Other dishes were overcomplicated – confit chicken wing and cockscomb seeming superfluous to a luscious roast snapper with celeriac puree. Yet others are a match for the view: seared scallop risotto with pungent shellfish bisque, and succulent Bangalow pork rack with wicked crackling are both picture-perfect. Service is well rehearsed, while the charming sommelier manages simultaneously to break the ice and, perhaps, your budget.

Hours Dinner Mon–Sat 6–10.30pm; bookings essential

Bill E $25–$28 **M** $32–$42 **D** $18; 10% surcharge on public holidays

Cards AE DC V MC Eftpos

Wine Stiff mark-up on an outstanding range of Australasian wines with a select international list; 23 by the glass

Chef Steven Krasicki

Owner Shangri-La Hotels & Resorts

Seats 80; private room; wheelchair access

Vegetarian Separate menu

www.36levelsabove.com.au

And...7-course "Epi-curious" dinner for $135

a'Mews

99 Glebe Point Road, Glebe
Tel 9660 4999   Map 5b

Anglo–French

Score 13.5/20

Blink and you'll miss the entrance to this shopfront terrace but inside, a warm and inviting environment unfolds. Split over four levels, it has cosy and private areas that allow for real intimacy. Service is caring and knowledgeable about Richard Moyser's upmarket Brit-pub food with Euro influences. The well-priced menu delivers substantial portions, so moist rabbit rillettes are made to share, enhanced by sides of zucchini and lemon chutney and salty olive tapenade. Wagyu beef, braised overnight, didn't melt as much as hoped, but the accompanying peas and sweetbreads more than satisfy. Poached chicken with truffle and leek stuffing is a standout; creamed cauliflower, lentils and salty smoked ham hock packs a similar punch. For dessert, Cointreau and lemon sponge comes to life with white nectarine, although pistachio ice-cream seemed a little misplaced. No matter, because dining here has all the comfort of a duck-down Doona.

Hours Lunch Fri noon–2.30pm (bookings only); Dinner Tues–Sat 6.30–9.30pm; bookings essential

Bill E $19–$22 **M** $29–$34 **D** $15; 8-course degustation $72 pp

Cards AE DC V MC Eftpos

Wine Eclectic, well-priced list with Euro options; 18 by the glass; BYO Tues–Thurs only (corkage $9 per bottle)

Chef Richard Moyser

Owners Richard, Dani & Ian Moyser

Seats 55; private room; outdoor seating

Vegetarian Degustation

www.amews.com.au

And...decent Australian & European cheese plate

Amici

465 Miller Street, Cammeray
Tel 9922 2222   Map 5a

Italian

Score 13/20

It won't challenge gastronomic boundaries but this energetic little local is always full to the brim, for good reason. In the slender downstairs room, diners practically sit on each other's laps, while guests upstairs squeeze into a lovely little alfresco setting or a larger room for big groups. Waiters can get a bit lost in the crush, but their vivacious energy wins through. A simple pizza margherita with a sexy tomato sauce would please a princess, but it's not just about the toasty discs flying from the wood-fired oven. Baked fig antipasto, neatly wrapped in crisp prosciutto, lolls in a gorgonzola puddle. Bresaola (cured beef), drizzled in lemon juice and olive oil, comes to life with rocket, artichoke and parmesan. Two thick veal cutlets dominate a plate of sauteed green beans and wild mushrooms doused with black truffle oil. A porcini and wild mushroom risotto also (regrettably) gets the truffle-oil treatment. The coffee, as you'd expect, is damned good and the desserts are familiar classics.

Hours Dinner daily 6pm–late; bookings essential

Bill E $14.50–$16.50 **M** $17.50–$31.50 **D** $8.50–$12.50; 10% surcharge Sundays & public holidays

Cards AE V MC Eftpos

Wine Short list, best bring your own; 9 by the glass; BYO (corkage $3 pp)

Chefs El Mostafa Solaihan & Francesco Spataro

Owners Jac Soghomonian, Antonio Castelnuovo & Marco Pietrobon

Seats 95; private room; wheelchair access; outdoor seating

Child friendly Kid-sized pizza and pasta

Vegetarian Several choices, from pizza to salads

And...monthly menu focusing on Italian regions

Aperitif

7 Kellett Street, Potts Point
Tel 9357 4729   Map 2

Mediterranean/French

Score 13/20

Much has been made of Sydney's love of cavernous booze barns – apparently we don't do small, civilised bars nearly as well as our southern rival. That must make Aperitif in the Cross one of this town's best-kept secrets. It's surprisingly easy to secure one of the red suede seats in the dimly-lit back room on a Saturday night, although the leafy terrace is busier. Service is brisk and well-informed about the North African-influenced Med fare and sommelier Charles Leong's terrific list of mainly European wines. A wedge of lime offers a burst of citrus relief in a dish of prawns with a rich chilli sauce. North African spices dominate – but never quite overwhelm – a skewer of tender lamb. More delicately flavoured dishes include discs of raw ocean trout rolled in dill, and scallops on a bed of fennel-laced mushrooms with a smattering of roe (although two for $15 seems miserly). With a choice of small or large plates, famished late-night diners should order up big.

Hours Dinner Mon & Wed–Sat 5.30pm–3am, Sun 5.30pm–midnight

Bill E $9–$15 **M** $25–$29 **D** $12

Cards AE DC V MC Eftpos

Wine Extensive list of European wines, including some rare labels; 22 by the glass

Chef Laurent Curvat

Owners Elie Griplas & Charles Leong

Seats 80; wheelchair access; outdoor seating

Vegetarian A handful of options

And...try the "chi chi" or churros (finger-like Spanish donuts) with chocolate dipping sauce

Aqua Dining

Cnr Paul & Northcliff streets, Milsons Point
Tel 9964 9998   Map 5a

Contemporary   ♀
                              Score 13/20

Bring a new arrival to Sydney here and they'll be in thrall to the city for life. Every which way a view: the bridge and its trusses framing the Opera House; Anzac Bridge to the south; Luna Park at your shoulder; and below, the Olympic Pool, all sparkling lanes and dogged lappers. Concentrate your focus and you'll find a menu as safe as the brown-hued contemporary space – plenty of seafood dishes, zeitgeist ingredients (jamon iberico, buffalo mozzarella), and one or two daring flourishes, such as seared black pudding with rabbit. For the most part, dishes are pleasant, if not exceptional: you may be dazzled by a frothy, creamy, white asparagus "broth" amuse bouche or a superb roasted saltwater barramundi fillet, but we felt a bit let down by the squashed basil gnocchi under the fish and by an indifferent chunk of Tasmanian crayfish in yet another creamy white foam. All is forgiven though, by dessert – perhaps a milk-chocolate brownie with cherry ripple ice-cream – and by a view that few can beat.

Hours Lunch daily noon–2.30pm; Dinner Mon–Fri 6.30–9.30pm, Sat–Sun 6–9.30pm

Bill E $26–$35 **M** $38–$49 **D** $15–$19; 15% surcharge on public holidays

Cards AE DC V MC

Wine A strong list with a good old-world selection and interesting champagne offerings, including good back-vintages; 12 by the glass

Chefs Jeff Turnbull & Daniel Bonello

Owner Bill Drakopoulos

Seats 120; wheelchair access; outdoor seating

Child friendly Kids' meals

www.aquadining.com.au

And...best book early if you want a table on the deck overlooking the pool

ARIA ★

1 Macquarie Street, East Circular Quay
Tel 9252 2555   Map 1

Contemporary   ♛♛♀
                              Score 17.5/20

WINE LIST OF THE YEAR

As the sun drops over the harbour, so do the lights over ARIA's comfortable dining room, allowing the Opera House to shine. Inside, it is the service that gets our attention, delivered by knowledgeable, obliging, black-suited waiters. A remarkable entree of double-cooked Kurobuta sweet pork belly paired with black pudding is lifted by apple and elderflower puree. A special of lobster ravioli is rich and decadent but, at $48 for an entree, is as memorable for its price tag as its flavour. Mains are hearty rather than showstopping. Glenloth chicken with gnocchi, treviso mushrooms and jus gras is tender and generous. Blue-eye roasted with a salt cod brandade is pert and abundant in flavour, matched with a chimichurri sauce. The evening glides. A shared dessert of mango and passionfruit turnovers with banana ice-cream stays with us long after we have left. And we haven't even mentioned the bridge...

Hours Lunch Mon–Fri noon–2.30pm; Pre-theatre dinner daily 5.30–7pm; Dinner daily 7–11.30pm; bookings essential

Bill E $36–$46 **M** $44–$56 **D** $22–$28; pre-theatre menus $42–$85; 10% surcharge on Sundays & public holidays

Cards AE DC V MC

Wine A spectacular tome of Europeans and benchmark Australians; 19 by the glass

Chef Matt Moran

Owners Matt Moran & Peter Sullivan

Seats 180; private rooms; wheelchair access

www.ariarestaurant.com

And...gather seven friends and treat yourselves to the exclusive kitchen table

Art Gallery of NSW Restaurant

Art Gallery of New South Wales,
Art Gallery Road, The Domain
Tel 9225 1819   Map 2

Contemporary

Score 13/20

This is a room that sparkles as brightly as
its breathtaking harbour view: all white-on-
white, vibrant red carpet and floor-to-ceiling
windows. The modern space is popular
with art lovers and a handful of lunching
corporates. Weekends bring families keen
to enjoy the gallery, brunch or high tea.
The short, sophisticated lunch menu offers
an appealing entree of jamon serrano strips
tossed with fresh figs and buffalo mozzarella,
dressed with a pungent, aged balsamic.
A main of pea and broad bean cannelloni
is served simply with sweet and sour onion,
the texture and flavour satisfying rather
than exciting. Crisp-skinned snapper fillet
is remarkably good, but didn't need a dollop
of bland skordalia on top; it combines well
with roasted eggplant, baby tomatoes
and olives. Service can stumble – or go
missing altogether – and can lack the magic
that awaits in the gallery. Before heading
there, savour a tumbler filled with divine
mascarpone sorbet, topped with fresh
cherry granita.

Hours Breakfast Sat–Sun 10–11.30am;
Lunch daily noon–3pm; High tea daily 2–4pm
Bill E $16–$20 **M** $23–$32 **D** $15–$16;
2 courses plus glass of wine $45
Cards AE DC V MC
Wine Good, medium-sized list; 8 by the glass
Chef John McFadden
Owner Trippas White Catering
Seats 220; private room; wheelchair access
Child friendly Highchairs
www.trippaswhite.com.au
And... Art Gallery members enjoy a discount

Arun Thai

28 Macleay Street, Potts Point
Tel 9326 9132   Map 2

Thai   ♀

Score 13/20

Beyond Arun Thai's teak "sala", or entrance
pavilion, lies a raffishly elegant dining
room modelled on the noble houses of
18th-century Thailand. Upholstered silk
seats and hand-painted plates set the scene
for a cuisine that blends royal Thai dishes
with all-time favourites (the chicken satay
is always dependable) and fiery creations
from Thailand's south. Bite-sized betel leaves
layered with chilli, peanut, dried shrimps,
ginger and toasted coconut prime the
tastebuds before launching into the crisp
flavours of steamed barramundi seasoned
with lemongrass, chilli and lime. An organic
Barossa chicken special sounds tantalising, but
arrived as a crisp-skinned chook splayed on
noodles doused in a cloyingly sugary tamarind
sauce. Much better is gaeng garee phetkae,
tender lamb shank meat cooked massaman-
style but deftly spiced to offset the sweetness
of coconut milk. Dessert offerings are limited
and service can be hyper-attentive, yet staff
are always willing to recommend menu
selections to enhance your royal Thai evening.

Hours Lunch Thurs–Fri & Sun noon–3pm;
Dinner daily 6–10.30pm
Bill E $13–$18 **M** $15–$31 **D** $10–$12;
$2.50 pp surcharge on public holidays
Cards AE DC V MC Eftpos
Wine Vast, sophisticated list; 20 by the glass
Chefs Chaiwat Tanti-Arphaphong
& Supot Rattanakomol
Owner Khamtane Signavong
Seats 200; private rooms
Child friendly Highchairs
Vegetarian menu available
www.arunthai.com.au
And...try khua kling, a fiery dry curry

Assiette

48 Albion Street, Surry Hills
Tel 9212 7979   Map 3b

Contemporary

Score 15.5/20

Warren Turnbull turns out modern, whimsical, classy food that doesn't skip a beat – from a transparent amuse bouche of tomato consomme to a sumptuous hazelnut dacquoise with white chocolate ice-cream. That he does it from a tiny open kitchen in a small, white-walled room with simple bistro decor and somewhat casual staff makes the experience all the more amazing. Pan-fried scallops come with a winning curried parsnip puree and onion bhaji that beg for more Indian influences in menus. Carpaccio of wagyu beef with baby beetroot, jammy port jelly, the lift of horseradish and crunchy little shoestring potatoes shows off his skills with texture and balance. Rabbit is deconstructed into an assiette of pleasurable morsels. Flounder is sweet with spanner crab and dainty zucchini beignets. A pre-dessert of strawberry jelly with creme fraiche and lime sorbet is swoon-inducingly decadent, and a tarte fine of spiced fig and honey ice is very fine indeed.

Hours Lunch Fri noon–3pm; Dinner Tues–Sat 6–10.30pm; bookings essential

Bill E $22 **M** $33 **D** $16; 10-course degustation $90 pp

Cards AE DC V MC Eftpos

Wine Thoughtful French and Australian choices at good price points; 15 by the glass

Chefs Warren Turnbull & Soren Lascelles

Owner Warren Turnbull

Seats 50

www.restaurantassiette.com.au

And...great-value, $30 three-course Friday lunch

Astral

Level 17, 80 Pyrmont Street, Pyrmont
Tel 9657 8767   Map 5b

Modern European

Score 15/20

Although far from the madding crowds of the casino below, Astral's spacious dining room isn't exactly bereft of its own bright lights and drama, with dazzling 270-degree city views. Elegant touches, such as luxurious high-backed chairs, may make you too relaxed to contemplate a la carte choices, instead opting for the sophisticated tasting menu (it's your only option on Friday and Saturday). A moussaka of cumin-spiked eggplant and tomato hits the jackpot, arriving in a glass tube that's unexpectedly raised, allowing a layer of featherlike bechamel foam to envelop the dish. The pay-out is just as big on a warm vegetable soup with delicate cubes of smoked ocean trout, a touch of tart yoghurt jelly and bursts of roe. Beef tenderloin, perfectly pink as promised, sits atop slinky slices of confit mushroom, but much more assertive flavours abound in a dessert of mouth-puckering passionfruit sorbet with a trail of tomato pulp and soothing vanilla panna cotta. A glorious cheese trolley makes this your lucky night.

Hours Lunch Fri noon–2pm; Dinner Tues–Thurs 6–10pm, Fri–Sat 6–10.30pm; bookings essential

Bill Degustation menu $125–$260; 3-course menu (Tues–Thurs only) from $105; pre-theatre menu daily (6pm) 2 courses $70, 3 courses $85; 10% surcharge on public holidays

Cards AE DC V MC Eftpos

Wine Impressive list with a global reach; 27 by the glass

Chefs Sean Connolly & Tony Gibson

Owner Star City

Seats 100; private room; wheelchair access

Vegetarian Degustation available

www.astralrestaurant.com.au

And...outdoor terrace dining is coming

a tavola

348 Victoria Street, Darlinghurst
Tel 9331 7871   Map 2

Italian

Score 15/20

Eugenio Maiale has tunnelled a perfectly proportioned dining room out of a narrow, long space and warmed it with a glowing pink marble communal table and coppery lights, a bowl of lemons and a curtain of backlit angel hair pasta dangling over the kitchen window. A winsome waitress recites the specials that complement the concise menu of two spuntini, or snacks, three entrees, three pasta dishes and three salads. Focaccia is house-baked and served with olive oil infused with chilli. Fried salami Veneto nestles in parmesan-dusted polenta. A pink, tender pork fillet is fanned over soft lentils in balsamic. Triangles of al dente ravioli, stuffed with rabbit and morsels of mustard fruits, wallow in golden-brown butter. Desserts continue Maiale's high-class balancing act. Polenta and orange cake combines a citrussy bite with sweet spongy lightness and comes with organic honey ice-cream. Creamy, dreamy limoncello panna cotta is matched with strawberries and lemon syrup, and poppy seeds for crunch. Perfectly proportioned, indeed.

Hours Lunch Fri noon–2.30pm; Dinner Mon–Sat 6pm–late

Bill E $15–$20 **M** $22–$38 **D** $10–$12

Cards AE V MC Eftpos

Wine Compact, totally Italian and charming; 7 by the glass; BYO (corkage $15 per bottle)

Chef/owner Eugenio Maiale

Seats 65; private room

www.atavola.com.au

And...you can get a simple bowl of spaghetti, too

Azuma

Level 1, Chifley Plaza, 2 Chifley Square, Sydney
Tel 9222 9960   Map 1

Japanese
Score 15/20

When Japan's Crown Prince and Princess visited Sydney, Azuma was their chosen place to dine. And so it should be. Served on exquisite ceramics by acclaimed artist Mitsuo Shoji is a procession of authentic Japanese dishes highlighting the finest Australian produce. Lunch buzzes with regulars in suits, while the room is seductively lit for dinner service. The decor is restrained, mirroring the cuisine. Chef Kimitaka Azuma's grilled silver cod fillet marinated in prized Saikyo miso (imported from Kyoto) is a knockout, while his braised Bangalow sweet pork is tender and more-ish. A nigiri of quickly seared kingfish belly is a must, lightly salted and fragrantly charcoaled. Fresh Tasmanian abalone is a winner, accompanied by a sake tasting set or the refreshingly sweet Azuma cocktail of limoncello. Azuma's wife, Yuki, admirably leads a team of efficient floor staff, while the friendly sushi masters happily answer queries over the counter. A 10-course chef's degustation is profoundly luxurious but, for a quickie, a bento box lunch is brilliant.

Hours Lunch Mon–Fri noon–2.30pm; Dinner Mon–Sat 6–10pm

Bill Set lunch $36–$42, degustation lunch $70 pp; Dinner sushi bar set $88 or $120 pp, degustation $110 pp, a la carte $15–$66; **D** $14.50–$20

Cards AE DC V MC Eftpos

Wine Medium-sized list of Australian and French wines; 8 by the glass; good sake list

Chef Kimitaka Azuma

Owners Kimitaka & Yuki Azuma

Seats 85; private rooms

www.azuma.com.au

And...free parking for diners under Chifley Tower after 5.30pm

Bai Yok

Shop 2A, 122 Edinburgh Road, Castlecrag
Tel 9967 3433   Map 7

Thai
Score 12.5/20

Smartly decorated and with beautifully presented food, Bai Yok obviously cares about doing Thai well. A charming welcome sets the scene for ever-obliging and smiling service and cooking that is a cut above your average neighbourhood Thai. There's plenty that appeals on the extensive menu. Start with the usual selection of crunchy entrees, and while vegetarian spring rolls didn't shine, the more interesting hoy jor with crabmeat, pork and water chestnut is juicy and crisp. You'd be wrong to ignore pad thai with king prawns – perfectly moist noodles with the right combination of sweet, salt, tang and crunch make this an addictive if predictable choice. Nam Tok lamb was a little subtle in its marinade; opt instead for a whole deep-fried fish done salt-and-pepper Thai-style. Care and consistency carry through to dessert. A palate-cleansing coconut ice-cream with chewy sweet palm fruits is irresistible.

Hours Lunch Fri noon–3pm; Dinner Tues–Sat 6–10pm, Sun 5.30–9.30pm

Bill E $8–$14 **M** $13–$28 **D** $5–$10; $2 pp surcharge on public holidays

Cards AE V MC Eftpos

Wine Simple list of well-known Australians; 4 by the glass; BYO (corkage $3 pp)

Chef Warangkana Lui

Owner Michael Lui

Seats 75; outdoor seating

Child friendly Highchairs and milder dishes

Vegetarian Several options, from soups to stir-fries and steamed dishes

And…Thai Nine in Mosman is its sister restaurant

Bambini Trust

Ground floor, 185 Elizabeth Street, Sydney
Tel 9283 7098   Map 1

Modern European   ♀
Score 14/20

For consistency and consistent excellence, there are few Sydney bistros to top Bambini. We love its elegant, intimate European style, soft lighting, dark timber and marble surrounds, the waiters' panache, specials written on the mirror and a wine list that dissipates any concerns from the outside world. Most of all, we love the brassy yet polished menu of clever comfort food – whether the masculine reassurance of house-made black pudding with braised red cabbage and the relief of an apple, watercress and frisee salad, or a risotto freckled with broad beans, peas and fresh herbs. A special of poached veal with sauteed wild mushrooms, sweetbreads and thyme-infused red wine jus is as assured as a crisp-skinned barramundi fillet with crushed peas, tomato and saffron vinaigrette. House-made seasonal sorbets and ice-cream are always a fine finish, but there's nothing like lingering over prime European and Australian cheeses with an affordable glass of French wine.

Hours Breakfast Mon–Fri 7–11am; Lunch Mon–Fri noon–3pm; Dinner Mon–Sat 5.30–10.30pm; bookings essential

Bill E $19–$27 **M** $34–$36 **D** $12–$15

Cards AE DC V MC

Wine Long, lovely mix of international and domestic drops; 15 by the glass; BYO (corkage $20 per bottle)

Chef Oliver Carruthers

Owners Michael & Angela Potts

Seats 80; private room; wheelchair access; outdoor seating

www.bambinitrust.com.au

And…fine and hearty breakfasts to start the working week

The Bathers' Pavilion Restaurant

4 The Esplanade, Balmoral
Tel 9969 5050   Map 7

Contemplorary

Contemporary

Score 15/20

Dusk brings a warm glow to the view to Sydney Heads. The tide tugs gently at the sand. The last bathers promenade. Diners settle into leather banquettes and blue-cushioned chairs at tables arranged so that everyone shares the vista. Serge Dansereau is the champion of market produce, and his intricately detailed, confidently crafted menus reflect this. His food is prettily presented, artfully composed elements dotting the plates. There are divine moments: potato roesti layered with minced mushroom; wisps of rice-flour tempura clinging to clumps of juicy Bribie Island soft shell crab; firm-fleshed, salmon-like Arctic char stroked with coriander pesto; a wagyu beef cheek, sublime in taste and texture. Honey-poached figs, fresh pistachios, baby basil and icy lozenges of mascarpone combine gloriously. After dark, the long, low-ceilinged roof has a warm, relaxed ambience that even occasional lapses in service cannot disturb: serendipity.

Hours Lunch daily noon–2pm; Dinner daily 6.30–9pm; bookings essential

Bill 2-course dinner menu $95 pp, 3 courses $115; less for weekday lunch

Cards AE DC V MC

Wine Sally Harper has built a long, marvellous list; 15 by the glass; BYO Mondays (corkage $10 pp)

Chefs Serge Dansereau & Simon Bestley

Owner Serge Dansereau

Seats 80; private rooms; wheelchair access

Child friendly Under–10s, and 10–16-year-olds' menus; highchairs

Vegetarian A la carte and degustation menus

www.batherspavilion.com.au

And...produce-based menus can change daily

Bayleaf Brasserie

Shops 12–14, 103–111 Willoughby Road, Crows Nest
Tel 9906 6080   Map 5a

Indian

Score 14/20

It's a cafe space in a shopping arcade food court, so rising to restaurant level is a challenge. Bayleaf achieves it with food that really demands a visit. Alongside the usual suspects of all-India cuisine there are individually distinctive, palate- and eye-pleasing dishes. An entree of Malabari scallops has the firm, succulent, seared bivalves dusted with cinnamon and curry leaves, perched on a luridly red fresh apple chutney, all on small banana-leaf mats. Baingan caldeen presents fat, iridescently purple snap-fried baby eggplants in a verdant green coconut milk gravy, strong on coriander, peppercorns and mint. Nali ka gosht brings together meltingly soft slices of dum-cooked (pot-baked) lamb with a sauce nicely balancing cinnamon, cloves and saffron with the crunch of nuts. The bone is presented on the side – for indulging in osseous pleasures. Five choices of kulfi make for a creamy, perfumed dessert.

Hours Lunch Mon–Fri noon–3pm; Dinner daily 6–9pm

Bill E $8–$12.50 **M** $15–$19.50 **D** $5

Cards AE DC V MC Eftpos

Wine BYO (corkage $1.50 pp)

Chef/owner Rohit Chaudhary

Seats 70; private room; wheelchair access

Child friendly Kids' menu; highchairs

Vegetarian Good range, plus monthly menus

www.bayleafindian.com

And...go later in the evening when the noise level from kids and hard surfaces drops

Italian Bluebottles
hit our shores

SANTA VITTORIA
ACQUA MINERALE

Italian mineral water bottled at the source.

Bayswater Brasserie

32 Bayswater Road, Kings Cross
Tel 9357 2177   Map 2

Contemporary

Score 13/20

Recalling a Parisian bistro, the dining room and conservatory buzz with activity. Diners shout above the din, and waiters rush about under subdued lighting, delivering dishes and topping up water glasses. The Bayz seems like it's been around forever, but that doesn't mean it can rest on its laurels. An entree special of tempura zucchini flowers stuffed with prosciutto, fig and goat's cheese failed to excite with soggy batter, while the cheese overwhelmed the other ingredients. Twice-cooked pork belly could have left the oven sooner but is well paired with apple and pickled red cabbage. The main course calf's liver with mash is perfect with crisp fried onion and balsamic jus, but best is a succulent, flavour-packed ballottine of corn-fed chicken and rabbit farce with fondant potato and spring onion. Dishes are well priced and portions generous, but we somehow manage to find space for a super sweet raspberry bombe Alaska.

Hours Lunch Fri noon–3pm;
Dinner daily 6–10.30pm

Bill E $17–$21 **M** $27–$38 **D** $14–$15

Cards AE DC V MC

Wine Wide selection of home-grown and New Zealand varietals with a handful of French and Italian choices; 13 by the glass

Chef Jeff Schroeter

Owners Nigel Lacy & Robert Smallbone

Seats 150; private rooms

Child friendly Kids' menu; highchairs

www.bayswaterbrasserie.com.au

And...sample the cocktail list in the popular bar and make a night of it

Bécasse

204 Clarence Street, Sydney
Tel 9283 3440   Map 1

Modern European

Score 17/20

CHEF OF THE YEAR

The *Guide's* 2007 Restaurant of the Year has lost none of its je ne sais quoi. Led by co-owner Georgia North, passionate and proficient waiters appear bent on delivering a seamless dining experience in a sophisticated environment. A split-level room embracing warm chocolate tones and crisp white tablecloths sparkles under stunning crystal-studded ring lights. Submit to the whim of chef Justin North's sublime spin on French cuisine. A gentle prompt from your fork spills the golden yolk of a smoked duck egg into a puddle of pea mousseline, while jamon iberico brioche crumbs add crunch. A silky king prawn raviolo nestles on a slice of pork belly partnered by a plump seared scallop. Macleay Valley baby rabbit is a striking exploration of braised bunny: roast rack, pastilla of confit shoulder and schnitzel of loin, marked with a streak of pureed courgette. A dazzling vanilla bean brulee brightened by summer berries balances over a glass filled with rose petals. Exquisite.

Hours Lunch Mon–Fri noon–2.30pm;
Dinner Mon–Sat 6–10.30pm

Bill E $22–$36 **M** $38–$49 **D** $19–$22;
2-course lunch $50 pp, 3 courses $70 pp

Cards AE DC V MC

Wine It's almost a novella: a surprisingly affordable mix of mainly Australasian and French varietals; 15 by the glass

Chefs Justin North & James Metcalfe

Owners Georgia & Justin North

Seats 80

Vegetarian Degustation menu available

www.becasse.com.au

And...spoil yourself and try the 10-course degustation for $130

bel mondo

Gloucester Walk, The Rocks
Tel 9241 3700   Map 1

Mediterranean

Score 13/20

High in the loft above the ancient Argyle
Stores, a window table will allow you a peek
at the Opera House sails in this massive
warehouse-like dining room. Its antique
exposed beams, muted organza curtains,
rustic floors and carnival-light effects create
a nightclub milieu. New chef Andy Ball is
still settling in, but expect him to continue
the Mediterranean tradition set by his
predecessors. This included crisp, tempura-
battered zucchini flowers stuffed with rich
taleggio risotto and bolstered by the addition
of a piquant roasted tomato sauce in a
perfect balance of textures. Grilled sardines
with crunchy chickpeas and bitter radicchio
may feature few sardines but, balanced by
the mellow sweetness of roasted onions,
it's an exhilarating dish. Ravioli with goat's
cheese, spinach and sage suffered from
an excess of nut-brown butter, but snappy
service ensures the nourishing Tuscan beef
pie with pancetta and ultra-smooth potato
puree arrives piping hot, the golden pastry lid
lifted to liberate hearty aromas. House-made
gelato comes in a chorus of flavours, topped
with lacy wafers.

Hours Lunch Fri noon–3pm;
Dinner Mon–Sat from 6pm

Bill E $18–$24 **M** $29–$39 **D** $15; 2-course
lunch $35 pp; 10% surcharge on public holidays

Cards AE DC V MC Eftpos

Wine Majority Australian and surprisingly only
2 Italian; 12 by the glass

Chef Andy Ball

Owner Mealand Holdings

Seats 150; private room; wheelchair access

www.belmondo.com.au

And...enjoy a passeggiata through The Rocks
pre- or post-dining

Bellevue Hotel Dining Room

159 Hargrave Street, Paddington
Tel 9363 2293   Map 4b

Contemporary

Score 14/20

Paddington has plenty of pubs for drinking.
This is one for eating. Sure, there's the beer
on tap, big screen and TAB, but in the dining
room you're in another world – a light, bright
space with a skylight, semi-open kitchen,
bentwood chairs and damask-covered tables.
With a French influence you expect from
veteran pub-food maestro Damien Pignolet,
the traditional staples are hard to resist,
though you may have to nibble for a while
on the good sourdough during a busy service,
and it can get noisy. Cauliflower gratin souffle
has lovely texture and a hint of nutmeg.
Buttery, silky mash supports chunky, peppery
sausages with a caramelised onion gravy,
and fine, crisp real pommes frites nestle
beside thin pieces of beautifully cooked steak
with a classic Diane sauce. Textbook panna
cotta balances the creaminess of buttermilk
and acid of blood orange, offset with fresh
mango. So what if the prices outstrip your
average pub? So does the food.

Hours Lunch Mon–Fri noon–2.30pm, Sat–Sun
12.30–3pm; Dinner Mon–Sat 6.30–10pm

Bill E $16–$22 **M** $19.50–$34.50 **D** $14

Cards AE DC V MC Eftpos

Wine Well-constructed list, good range of
Australian and imported wines; 15 by the glass

Chefs Damien Pignolet & Garth Bearman

Owners Damien Pignolet & Ron White

Seats 110; private rooms

Child friendly Kids' portions

www.bellevuehotel.com.au

And...this is value for money with quality
ingredients in generous portions

Bentley Restaurant & Bar

320 Crown Street, Surry Hills
Tel 9332 2344   Map 2

Contemporary

♨♨ 🍷
Score 16/20

What once was a notorious old boozer is now one of the city's most innovative restaurants – with a heart-stopping wine list. In a snappy red, black and timber-toned space, chef Savage flirts with the techniques du jour – foams, jellies, emulsions – and asks you to take a leap of faith: kingfish marinated in squid ink with perfumed fruit and coconut? Why not. Roasted duck breast with smoked leek, black fungi and kohlrabi? Absolutely. Sometimes good ingredients seemed overwhelmed by ideas, sometimes there was too much sweetness on the plate (as in a lamb rump with coffee bread sauce and roasted fig), and sometimes dishes failed to convince. A poached snapper entree, for example, with red pepper jelly and cauliflower puree, is lovely to look at but was ultimately disappointing, the disparate elements remaining aloof. But there are moments of intense flavour and visual artistry, and Savage's playfulness is infectious. And there's that wine list: a Rioja rosé anyone?

Hours Tues–Sat noon–11pm

Bill E $18–$22 **M** $28–$36 **D** $16–$18; 8-course tasting menu $95; 8-course lunch $50

Cards AE DC MC V Eftpos

Wine Nick Hildebrandt's thrilling list roams the world; 25 by the glass

Chef Brent Savage

Owners Brent Savage & Nick Hildebrandt

Seats 60; outdoor seating

Vegetarian Good choices; 8-course menu

www.thebentley.com.au

And...pull up a stool in the bar for super tapas

Beppi's

21 Yurong Street, East Sydney
Tel 9360 4558   Map 2

Italian (Northern)

🍷
Score 12/20

There is a definite buzz in the Poleses' dining room on a Friday night. Regulars and newcomers book the famous cellar room to celebrate special occasions, just as they have for more than 50 years, enjoying old-school Italian fare among the hand-marked wine racks. It's the atmosphere and sense of history that still bring a long line of often notable fans. The food feels familiar, sometimes dated, but service retains some of Beppi's legendary polish and charm. A marinated field mushroom is impressive when presented to the table fresh, and satisfying when baked in herbs, but figs wrapped in prosciutto were prepared with a heavy hand, a thick gorgonzola sauce overpowering the fruit. Osso buco with polenta is good, comforting Italian, but a main of angel hair pasta with crab was overly salty. An ultra-classic zabaglione al Marsala for dessert shows there is a lot to love about this creamy Italian favourite. And a lot to love about Beppi's, too.

Hours Lunch Mon–Fri noon–3pm; Dinner Mon–Sat 6–11pm; bookings essential

Bill E $19–$29 **M** $39–$42 **D** $16–$19

Cards AE DC V MC JCB

Wine Extensive collection of Australian classics with little Italian content; 11 by the glass

Chef Beppi Polese

Owners Beppi, Norma & Marc Polese

Seats 120; private rooms

Child friendly Smaller portions

www.beppis.com.au

And...at 82, Signor Beppi himself may serve you lunch

Berowra Waters Inn ★

Via public wharf, Berowra Waters
Tel 9456 1027   Map 6

French/Contemporary

👑👑🍷

Score 17/20

BEST NEW RESTAURANT

The Masters of the Universe are back, skidding into this riverside icon in seaplanes as though the 1980s never ended. Lesser mortals park opposite and wait for the tinny across the olive-green water. Either way it's an easy trip into an out-of-the-way adventure. Yes, this is where Gay and Tony Bilson and Janni Kyritsis once worked their magic. Now it's Dietmar Sawyere and his polished team, wending over blackbutt floors behind glass-louvred windows. The food is special, too; a minimum four-course, smallish-plate choice, with added amuses, pre-mains, pre-desserts and petits fours. Whipped vichyssoise hiding teensy caviar beads is spectacular with oyster beignets on buttery leek ribbons. Tiny, brined quail with grapes and earthy snails rejoices in textural contrast; likewise just-set ocean trout with a crunchy mud-crab cigar. Desserts verge nicely on the not-so-sugary: a cone of cassata-like semifreddo with raspberries; a fat fig encasing fine hazelnut ice-cream, a sponge-light goat's cheese cake alongside. Berowra is back as a very special spot.

Hours Lunch Fri–Sun noon–3pm; Dinner Thurs–Sat 7–10pm; bookings essential
Bill 4/5/6 courses, $125 pp/$135 pp/$150 pp
Cards AE DC V MC
Wine Lovely, eclectic list; 16–20 by the glass
Chef/owner Dietmar Sawyere
Seats 60; private room; outdoor seating
Child friendly Highchairs; kids' dishes; toys; books
Vegetarian Numerous dishes
www.berowrawatersinn.com
And...an hour from town when the F3's behaving

Big Mama's

51 Moncur St, Woollahra
Tel 9328 7629   Map 4b

Italian

Score 13/20

Unlike its swisher neighbours, this old double shopfront isn't much to look at and it can get noisy and crowded inside. But like its facade, the food at Big Mama's is down-home and honest – pasta, risotto, rabbit and scaloppine. Regulars head straight to the daily specials where the interesting stuff happens. Italian buffalo mozzarella, soft and oozing milky juices, is served on finely sliced local prosciutto. In pappardelle con brasato di manzo (braised beef), the robustly flavoured, meaty sauce does justice to the fresh egg pasta. Stinco d'agnello (lamb shank), cooked in red wine, falls off the bone yet retains plenty of oomph. A rather retro side plate of broccoli and potatoes may seem superfluous but who's complaining, as long as there's still space for the wonderful desserts: panna cotta with pears, zabaglione, tiramisu or a rich chocolate torta. A special of beautifully poached fresh figs arrives with creamy–tangy mascarpone. This is comfort food, Italian-style.

Hours Dinner Tues–Sun 6–10pm
Bill E $17–$22 **M** $27–$35 **D** $10–$12; 10% surcharge on public holidays
Cards AE V MC Eftpos
Wine A small list well suited to the cuisine, with a few good Italians; 8 by the glass
Chef Carlo Lombardo
Owner Michael Currenti
Seats 120; private room; outdoor seating
Child friendly Kids' menu; highchairs
Vegetarian Plenty of vegetarian choices
And...a good fallback when the line's too long at nearby Bistro Moncur

the best of
Harvey Norman
COOKING

Bijolias

Shop 5/540 Sydney Road, Seaforth
Tel 9949 3641   Map 7

Contemporary Indian

Score 13/20

This tiny, unassuming restaurant punches well above its weight, delivering solidly good South Asian standards with touches of lightness and inventiveness in both presentation and ingredients. It makes for a pleasantly surprising dining experience, and it's exciting to find among the entrees dhokla, a Gujarati street dish of semolina and chickpea flour flavoured with ginger, mustard seed and coriander, and steamed to a light sponginess. Papri chutney chat here is a fun take on a Mumbai street standard – piled in a mini Himalayan peak, boiled chickpeas are dressed with a well-balanced mix of tamarind and yoghurt sauces. A clever use of tamarind and grilled coconut gives khatte baingan (pan-fried sliced eggplant) a satisfying sharpness. In palak macchi, the nutmeg and lime gravy hover intriguingly between sharp and menthol, lifting what can be a run-of-the-mill dish of fish fillets with spinach. A not-too-sweet mango kulfi is further proof that there's plenty of life yet in Indian standards.

Hours Dinner Mon–Sat from 5pm

Bill E $7.50–$14.50 **M** $10.50–$19.90
D $4.50–$7.50; 2-course dinner $29.50

Cards AE DC V MC Eftpos

Wine Small list, but a good range of beers to compensate; 8 by the glass; BYO wine only (corkage $2 pp)

Chef Ajay Mathur

Owners Ajay & Neeta Mathur

Seats 32; wheelchair access

Child friendly Highchair

Vegetarian A good range; 3 entrees and 7 mains

www.bijolias.com.au

And...service is warm, genuine and generous

Billy Kwong

3/355 Crown Street, Surry Hills
Tel 9332 3300   Map 3b

Modern Chinese

Score 14.5/20

It's difficult to have anything but respect and admiration for the ethically minded and culinarily gifted Kylie Kwong. Her tiny Chinese eating house – now carbon neutral and committed to using organic, biodynamic and Fair Trade produce – is busier than ever. Patrons line up before opening time to ensure they score an uncomfortable three-legged stool or, at least, their name on the waiting list for later that night. Diners conversing at top volume and the sounds of a cranking kitchen add up to one big din, but a Beijing-style salad of black cloud ear mushrooms and cucumber is a delightfully refreshing and piquant distraction. And while floor staff may miss a few things in the rush, Tasmanian scallop wontons with Sichuan pepper and hot chilli oil are spot-on. Specials might include line-caught snapper, steamed with ginger and shallots and as delicately good as it gets. A seasonal fruit platter with squares of organic dark chocolate takes simplicity and flavour through to the end.

Hours Dinner Mon–Thurs 6–10pm, Fri–Sat 6–11pm, Sun 6–9pm; no bookings except 1 table for 6–8 people

Bill E $12–$29 **M** $20–$49 **D** $14; banquet $89 pp; $3 pp surcharge on weekends; 10% surcharge on public holidays

Cards AE V MC

Wine Brief Australasian list; 7 by the glass; BYO (corkage $10 per bottle)

Chefs Mathew Lindsay & Kylie Kwong

Owner Kylie Kwong

Seats 50

Vegetarian Plenty on offer

www.kyliekwong.org

And...signed copies of Kylie's cookbooks to buy

Bilson's

Radisson Plaza Hotel, 27 O'Connell Street, Sydney
Tel 8214 0496   Map 1

Contemporary French

♕ ♕ ♕ ♉
Score 18/20

Tony Bilson has remained at or near the pinnacle of Sydney fine dining for three decades by pushing the boundaries of French cuisine without fudging its technique. Things may occasionally waver on the floor and on the plate – the desserts must be Sydney's most expensive – but the experience rarely dips far below the expectations of the Bilson moniker. More often, it meets or exceeds them in dishes like scallops with a bitter chocolate tuile and foie gras mousse, Bangalow pork belly with braised cheek, confit partridge leg and savoy cabbage tortellini, or in the charm and professionalism of sommelier Andrew Cullen (formerly of London's Ivy). The room is comfortable and conservative and, befitting its big-end-of-town locale, probably sees more mergers and acquisitions than marriage proposals. Certainly, the kitchen's stocks rise high at the close of proceedings with a muscovado mousse paired with semi-confit celery (yes, really) and green tea ice-cream, and a cherry deconstruction of jelly, mousse and foam that sends us home sweetly satisfied.

Hours Lunch Friday noon–3pm; Dinner Tues–Sat 6–10pm

Bill E $35 **M** $50 **D** $35

Cards AE DC V MC

Wine Depth, quality and diversity, new and old world; 17 by the glass; BYO (corkage $25 pp)

Chefs Tony Bilson & Manu Feildel

Owner Tony Bilson

Seats 80; private room; wheelchair access

Child friendly Highchair; kids' portions

www.bilsons.com.au

And...the art collection is the chef's own, and set menus represent very good value

Bin24 Wine Bar & Wood Fire

The Bakehouse Quarter, 3–24 George Street, North Strathfield
Tel 9764 5084   Map 6

Contemporary

Score 12/20

The converted Arnott's biscuit factory warehouse is now an all-day diner of exposed brick, piping and heavy beams that skilfully blends heritage and contemporary design. At one end are the wine bar's colourful lounges; at the other, the open kitchen looks across the bare tables and white leather chairs and banquettes to a large outdoor dining area. The menu focuses on regional produce in fun fast food: modern-styled wood-fired pizza, burgers, dips and share plates, grills and cheeses. The service is upbeat. Finger-lickin' Bangalow pork baby back ribs are smeared with a sticky, smoky and sweet barbecue sauce on coleslaw. Crumbed golden rods of slightly gooey buffalo mozzarella are lifted by tomato salsa, but Sichuan-peppered calamari on rocket was a little flabby, while an otherwise credible mixed grill of chicken breast, eye fillet and chorizo was let down by pesto mash. Still, your inner child delights in the wickedly excessive banana fudge split and its surfeit of butterscotch sauce.

Hours Daily 11.30am–10pm; bookings essential

Bill E $9–$18 **M** $15–$31 **D** $13; 10% surcharge on public holidays

Cards AE DC V MC

Wine Short, interesting boutique range; 14 by the glass

Chefs Michael Strautman & Jo Ratnayake

Owners Rod Coligado & Robin Tedder

Seats 180; wheelchair access; outdoor seating

Child friendly Highchairs

www.bin24.com.au

And...takeaway pizza, too

Bird Cow Fish

Shops 4 & 5, 500 Crown Street, Surry Hills
Tel 9380 4090   Map 3b

Contemporary

Score 15/20

During the day, there's a smart lunch menu with sophisticated counter snacks (and equally good weekend breakfasts). At night, the mood is more refined in this elegant space, accentuated by dark floorboards with timber chairs and tables. Ultra-efficient service ensures everything runs like clockwork while the kitchen, visible in the back, steadily hums. Alex Herbert's menu displays an original take on traditional dishes. Zucchini flowers are light and crisp but unexpected depth oozes from a salty, creamy cod brandade. Slow-cooked confit of chicken is kept moist by a clever seal of duck fat, while a salad of beetroot, Spanish onion, apple and witlof is an inspired collision of tastes. Char-grilled lamb is perfectly cooked although the caponata of eggplant, green olives and capers dampened the accompanying basil and parsley. Dessert triumphs with the lush tiramisu roulade soaked in marsala, a modern interpretation of a 1970s jam roll. A food-lovers' destination any time of the day.

Hours Breakfast Sat–Sun 8am–3pm; Lunch daily noon–3pm; Dinner Mon–Sat 6–10pm; no dinner bookings

Bill E $18.50 **M** $25–$40 **D** $12.50; 10% surcharge on Sundays

Cards AE V MC Eftpos

Wine Comprehensive Australian boutique list; 20 by the glass; BYO Mon–Thurs (corkage $10 per bottle)

Chef Alex Herbert

Owners Alex Herbert & Howard Gardner

Seats 85; wheelchair access; outdoor seating

Child friendly Highchairs; toys; crayons; kids' portions

www.birdcowfish.com.au

And... Herbert's famous hanger steak

Bistro CBD

Level 1, 52 King Street (cnr York Street), Sydney
Tel 8297 7010   Map 1

Mediterranean

Score 15/20

The lunchtime scene at Bistro CBD is predictable. Light floods through arched windows as smart staff dart around the white room seeing to a full house of suits and city shoppers. Many a deal has been sealed at this consistently good bistro, just a spiral staircase away from an equally popular bar below. New chef Simun Dragicevich has maintained high standards with a simple, impressive menu and good quality produce. Lighter entrees include a colourful ox heart tomato and buffalo mozzarella salad with red witlof, asparagus and basil salsa verde. Ocean trout sashimi also pleases, with fresh flavours and the tangy twist of lime. Mains are heartier, such as oven-roasted spatchcock with fantastic glazed carrots, bread pudding and tarragon jus. A large pickled pork chop is also good comfort food, served with braised red cabbage, sweet stewed apple and the crunch of hazelnuts. Rich chocolate petits fours may cause swooning and are best enjoyed with a nice cup of tea.

Hours Lunch Mon–Fri noon–3pm; Dinner Mon–Fri 6–10pm

Bill E $22 **M** $33–$39 **D** $14

Cards AE DC V MC

Wine Mostly Australian with a few French and NZ drops; 14 by the glass

Chef Simun Dragicevich

Owner Merivale Group

Seats 90; wheelchair access

www.merivale.com

And...nights are a slower paced affair

Bistro-Fax

Cnr Pitt, Hunter & O'Connell streets, Sydney
Tel 8214 0400   Map 1

Contemporary

Score 14/20

In the bullnose of this stunning heritage-listed building is the Radisson's contemporary dining room. A window table offers a view of the city's passing bustle from the spacious, tiered room. Service is skilled and attentive. A short, appealing menu matches wine recommendations by the glass. Summer salad specials are popular with the lunch crowd, while dinner encourages you to linger longer. An entree of saltimbocca quail breast is fragrant with sage, teamed with crisp polenta and grilled figs. Gently seared Queensland scallops are served with an uplifting citrus, mint and fennel salad. Mains are impressive, with tender lamb loin spiced with ras el hanout (a blend of Moroccan spices) complemented by semi-dried tomato couscous and asparagus. Kingfish is crisp-skinned and succulent, topped with tapenade and resting on asparagus, baby leeks and sauce vierge. While roasted peach cassata with raspberry puree wasn't a highlight, there's plenty to savour at this smart city bistro.

Hours Breakfast Mon–Fri 6.30–10.30am, Sat–Sun 7–11am; Lunch daily noon–3pm; Dinner daily 6–10pm

Bill E $17.50–$25 **M** $24–$37.50 **D** $15

Cards AE DC V MC Eftpos

Wine Considered and interesting, mostly local list; 26 by the glass; BYO (corkage $8 per bottle)

Chef Jeremy Clark

Owner Radisson Plaza Hotel Sydney

Seats 100; wheelchair access

Child friendly Kids' menu; highchairs

www.radisson.com/sydneyau_plaza

And...a quiet and efficient alternative for pre-Opera House diners

Bistro Moncur

The Woollahra Hotel, 116 Queen Street, Woollahra
Tel 9327 9713   Map 4b

French

Score 15/20

"Bistro! Bistro!" ("Quick! Quick!") bellowed the Russian Cossacks in the restaurants of Paris after they vanquished Napoleon's troops, launching a fast and assured style of eating. Bistro Moncur epitomises this timeless dining archetype: elegant, polished wood surfaces, a well-oiled kitchen and brisk waiters. Not much changes here, and regulars bless the place for it, although its relentless popularity can lead to service that's more about processing than nurturing you. Classic bistro fare, such as the signature sirloin steak smothered in Cafe de Paris butter, the crab omelette and the provencale fish soup are impeccable. There are also more ambitious dishes and daily specials. Pork rillettes were on the mild side and a little too cold. Roast quail is busy with rabbit ravioli, rabbit jus, pureed spinach and vegetables. Dessert is a triumphant caramel-glazed apple tart, glorious, melting and big enough for two. There are no bookings, so those who know get in early to secure a table; you should, too.

Hours Lunch Tues–Sun noon–3pm; Dinner Mon–Sat 6–10.30pm, Sun 6–9pm; no bookings

Bill E $17–$31 **M** $29–$39.90 **D** $16.50–$18

Cards AE DC V MC Eftpos

Wine An elegant, thoughtful list, mainly Australian with French highlights; 25 by the glass

Chefs Damien Pignolet & Scott Mason

Owners Damien Pignolet & Ron White

Seats 108; outdoor seating

Child friendly Kids' dishes; crayons

www.bistromoncur.com.au

And...dining solo has never been so comfortable

Bistro Moore

Olympic Hotel, 308 Moore Park Road, Paddington
Tel 9361 6315   Map 4b

Contemporary

Score 13/20

At first glance, you'd think little has changed at Bistro Moore. The footy fans still wet their whistles in the main bar, the dark-timber dining room still sports its vintage posters and the menu flaunts all the fashionable labels of most bistros around town: think Kurobuta pork and Hiramasa kingfish. But dig further and you'll notice there's a touch of wizardry going on backstage. A tomato water foam floats on a tangle of noodles with crab, and a goat's curd sorbet teeters on a beetroot tart. Kiwi Ben Sitton, who was understudy to Darrell Felstead at the Three Weeds, is the latest chef trying to get the fans to see this pub bistro as more than sausage sizzles and beer, and mostly he's doing a good job. While some things faltered, such as soggy pastry in a raspberry millefeuille, main courses shine. Pork loin swims in a gorgeous black bean broth, and dhufish with green olives and knobbly gnocchi is top-notch. Service can also waver but overall Bistro Moore is kicking goals.

Hours Dinner Tues–Sat 6–10pm
Bill E $17–$20 **M** $28–$31 **D** $13
Cards AE DC V MC Eftpos
Wine Fairly pedestrian line-up of local labels; 8 by the glass
Chef Ben Sitton
Owner Olympic Hotel Operations
Seats 80; private room
Child friendly Bar menu features fish & chips and chicken schnitzel; can do small servings for kids
www.olympichotel.com.au
And...accommodation upstairs

Bistro Ortolan

134 Marion Street, Leichhardt
Tel 9568 4610   Map 5b

French

Score 16/20

Whether you're tucked into the burgundy-embossed dining room or perched on the white-painted balcony above, this unlikely Leichhardt terrace is a fine-diner's dream. Unlikely only amid the casual clatter of its location, Ortolan assumes a quest for perfection in a determinedly contemporary French vein. From the faintest line of flavoured sea salt to the tiniest sugar-snap pea pod, each dish is a delicate composition of intensely clean flavours and whimsically pretty colours. Granita slush in a shot glass of transparent tomato essence comes alive with bursts of baby herbs. An almost too rosy quail crepinette floats in a darkly meaty consomme, finished with fat snail curls in miniature choux balls, oozing herbed custard as you bite. Line-caught barra with sweetly pink marron, teensy summer vegetables and a cream-laced yabby bisque matches texture with detail, as does an assiette of lamb with slippery, oversized king brown mushrooms. A meltingly warm tart of wafer-sliced peach, dotted with peach-ringed raspberries, is meticulous and marvellous. So is the carefully personal service.

Hours Dinner Tues–Sat 6–10pm
Bill E $16–$26 **M** $28–$36 **D** $16–$18; 10% surcharge on public holidays
Cards AE DC V MC
Wine Tiny, thoughtful French and local list; 12 by the glass; BYO Tues–Thurs (corkage $8 per bottle)
Chef Paul McGrath
Owners Paul & Jenny McGrath
Seats 60; private room; wheelchair access; outdoor seating
www.bistroortolan.com.au
And...the cheese course ($26) is authentically French, too

Bistro Paris

Shop 9, 81–91 Military Road (cnr Ben Boyd Road), Neutral Bay
Tel 9953 5669   Map 5a

French
Score 14.5/20

If the curved courtyard wall painted like the Parisian skyline doesn't place you in that city, the warm welcome and snippets of French conversation soon do. In the intimate interior, the many specials are promptly explained. Some items may read as too adventurous but the food, while drawing inspiration from Italy, shows real skill thanks to a young chef from Lyon. So, stylistically plated kingfish carpaccio works well with celeriac remoulade, flying fish roe, tiny beetroot dice and horseradish sauce. Herb-crusted tuna is pan-seared rare, cleverly served with a textural vitello tonnato-style sauce and perfect baby leeks, asparagus and carrots. A duck special features rosy slices of breast, splashes of parsnip puree, spaetzle and an amazing, hash-brown-like square of soft shredded duck confit. A dessert of pineapple confit in saffron sugar syrup shows lovely balance with a lemongrass sorbet and coriander. The coffee is as good as the service, leaving you certain to return.

Hours Lunch Wed–Fri noon–2.30pm; Dinner Tues–Sat 6–10.30pm; bookings essential
Bill E $15–$25 **M** $24–$32 **D** $12–$14
Cards AE DC V MC Eftpos
Wine Appealing, appropriate, well-priced Australians, some interesting French and a cellar list; 15 by the glass; BYO (corkage $7 per bottle)
Chef Clement Chauvin
Owner Diane Scarr
Seats 66; wheelchair access; outdoor seating
www.bistroparis.com.au
And...there's a bistro lunch for $20, including main course and coffee, or $27 for main, dessert and coffee

Bistrode

478 Bourke Street, Surry Hills
Tel 9380 7333   Map 3b

European
Score 15/20

The decor is unpretentious and the food pure and rustic at this converted butcher's shop, now an exemplary local bistro. White tile-covered walls and a select team of waiters welcome diners into gustatory bliss, created by husband-and-wife team Jeremy and Jane Strode. An entree of deep-fried school prawns served with garlic mayonnaise is a sizeable crowd pleaser. The more-ish, clean flavour of a pig's head terrine is punctuated by crunchy pig's ear. The smallish menu changes daily, but Jeremy's tender wagyu corned beef is a much-acclaimed staple. Chargrilled, seasonal corn on the cob is a winning side dish with succulent Bangalow pork neck and sweet cabbage. While a seven-hour leg of lamb is tender and subtly flavoured, prosciutto-wrapped ocean trout was heavy on the salt. Jane's no-frills desserts satisfy anyone seeking both ends of the richness spectrum. Honey tart and peanut butter ice-cream is deliciously rich, while blackberry jelly and custard is pure comfort food. The cheese selection is equally divine.

Hours Lunch Fri noon–2pm; Dinner Mon–Sat 6–10pm
Bill E $12–$19 **M** $26–$34 **D** $3–$16
Cards V MC
Wine Medium-sized list of reasonably priced French and Australian wines; 10 by the glass
Chefs/owners Jane & Jeremy Strode
Seats 40; outdoor seating
Child friendly Highchair
www.bistrode.com
And...take home Jane's delectable condiments

Blackwater

1/8 Water Street, Sans Souci
Tel 9529 4893   Map 8

Italian

Score 13/20

So the Georges River outlook could lose the public baths and cop shop in between. But with its snappy, dark woods and floor-to-ceiling glass, Blackwater rises above the odds. For a long, long lunch or smoochy dinner, it's about mostly spot-on Italian cooking from smartly navy-capped chefs, wheeling about behind a backlit, crazed onyx kitchen counter. Their breaded cervella (lamb brains) on chickpea mash is splashed with nicely nutty, burnt butter, tiny capers and baby sage leaves. Warmed wholemeal bread and decent olive oil kick things along just fine. But beautifully al dente spaghetti in a buttery vongole sauce suffered from a scarcity of shellfish and juices. A just-as-buttery whole sole cooked acqua pazza (crazy water) style was missing the gentle tomato stain of the Amalfi Coast classic. Capretto (baby goat) in a not-too-rich, not-too-light braise on crushed potatoes is gorgeously fall-apart. After an espresso-drenched tiramisu, a punchy macchiato shows that the consistently competent waiters have their stuff sorted.

Hours Lunch Wed–Fri & Sun noon–2.30pm; Dinner Tues–Sat 6–9.30pm; bookings essential
Bill E $17.80–$19.80 **M** $23.80–$38.80 **D** $14.80; 10% surcharge on public holidays
Cards AE V MC
Wine Good local and Italian list, 14 by the glass; BYO Sun–Thurs only (corkage $3.50 pp)
Chef Riccardo Roberti
Owners Riccardo Roberti & Natasha Battikha
Seats 100; wheelchair access
Child friendly Highchair
www.blackwaterrestaurant.com.au
And...group bookings (10 plus) are $64 for two courses, including bread, veg and corkage

Blancmange

1 Station Street (cnr West Street), Petersham
Tel 9568 4644   Map 8

European

Score 14.5/20

It's hard to believe this cosy cream and blue coloured bistro is around the corner from truck-worn Parramatta Road. The huge window overlooking verdant Petersham Park, the stucco walls and modern paintings, and the plush carpet have a lot to do with it. The room is matched by classic European food. A short menu reveals a pot of jellied rabbit, bacon and prune terrine that is runny and chunky with British pub flavours, and a stolid, twice-cooked cheese souffle that is soothingly cheesy. Tangy house-made sourdough comes in handy for these. Mains unfold with gorgeously plump, juicy quail on a colourful brunoise of vegetables with a delicate herb broth and basil dumplings. Pork belly comes under a lid of crackling, long tendrils of soft flesh marrying happily with white baked beans and less happily, perhaps, with a starchy brandade. Comfort yourself with a handsome pistachio and apricot syrup cake or a creamy chocolate mousse like Mum used to make.

Hours Brunch Sat–Sun 10am–3pm; Dinner Tues–Sat from 6.30pm
Bill E $15–$20 **M** $25–$35 **D** $12; 3 courses $48 (excluding daily specials)
Cards V MC
Wine An affordable list with a global perspective; 12 by the glass; BYO Tues–Thurs (corkage $3.50 pp)
Chefs Gail Sellin & Caroline Read
Owners Gail Sellin & Ian Meggitt
Seats 50; private room; wheelchair access
Child friendly Highchairs; crayons; toys; bespoke meals
www.restaurantblancmange.com.au
And...love the antique and nanna-style crockery in the cabinet

Blue Eye Dragon

Shop 2, 42 Harris Street, Pyrmont
Tel 9518 9955   Map 5b

Taiwanese

Score 14/20

This is Chinese without clatter and clamour, served at a proper pace amid warm, subdued, non-gaudy decor by friendly, helpful waiters. Napkins are starched and the menu is easily understood. Spicy dishes don't have you grabbing for your (regularly replenished) water glass. And the flavours are harmonious and varied. No wonder it's so popular. Pale, supple and satisfying slices of drunken chicken are moist with sauce. Chubby, thin-skinned prawn dumplings cosset a contrasting crunch of vegetables. Agreeably chewy beef shin has a pungent, salty dipping sauce. Chinese turnip omelette is simply satisfying. Tofu stuffed with minced pork and prawns is a fine example of this dish, the saucing delicate and perfectly complementary. A rather prosaic chicken stir-fry with vegetables revealed a twitch of pepper in its "chilli curry". Sticky rice cakes with ginger syrup and oolong tea provide a soothing end to a delightful, relaxed evening.

Hours Lunch Tues–Fri noon–2.30pm; Dinner Tues–Sat 6–9.30pm; bookings essential

Bill E $8–$21 **M** $20–$36 **D** $8–$14

Cards AE V MC Eftpos

Wine BYO (corkage $4 pp)

Chef Jade Chen

Owner Muriel Chen

Seats 60

Child friendly Highchairs; pencils and crayons

www.blueeyedragon.com.au

And...you'll even find street parking and a bottle shop next door

The Boathouse on Blackwattle Bay

End of Ferry Road, Glebe
Tel 9518 9011   Map 5b

Seafood

Score 15.5/20

Paris has the Eiffel Tower, Cairo the pyramids, and the Boathouse has Sydney rock oysters. The daily menu offers at least half a dozen kinds, including the sumptuous, creamy Label Rouge, grown exclusively for this iconic waterfront setting by oyster guru Steve Feletti. Order a mixed plate and revel in the differing flavours. This elegant, glass-encased boatshed offers plenty more reasons to visit, from the legendary truffle-scented snapper pie with smoked tomatoes and mash, dissected at the table, to Brasserie Bread sourdough and sommelier Donna Freeman's wisely sophisticated offerings. Chef Perry Hill's confidently bold flavours let the seafood (and yippee, lesser-seen fish!) strut its stuff, including smoky grilled bonito sweetened with Spanish sherry, emboldened by jamon and creamy pine nuts. Steamed mulloway drifts in a delicate tomato consomme with sweet shards of spanner crab and lotus root for texture. And if the Pedro Ximenez ice-cream with chocolate mousse and coffee granita doesn't set your pulse racing, move to Melbourne.

Hours Lunch Tues–Sun noon–2.30pm; Dinner Tues–Thurs, Sun 6.30–10pm, Fri–Sat 6–10pm (open daily in December)

Bill E $27–$30 **M** $34–$45 **D** $17–$18

Cards AE DC V MC

Wine Superb and affordable international list with good half-bottle options; 15 by the glass

Chef Perry Hill

Owners Tony Papas & Robert Smallbone

Seats 97; wheelchair access

Child friendly A few kids' dishes

www.boathouse.net.au

And...the foyer mural is spectacular

Bodega ★

216 Commonwealth Street, Surry Hills
Tel 9212 7766   Map 3b

Spanish/South American

Score 14.5/20

FAVOURITE TAPAS

You have to love a place where one of the chefs has a rockabilly quiff, tattooed arms and a mint-condition 1970 Valiant parked out the back. Like its staff, Bodega has plenty of attitude. From the striking Spanish matador mural on one wall and the upbeat Franz Ferdinand soundtrack to the exceptional Spanish and South American food, Bodega is a leader among a new generation of Sydney tapas bars. It can be difficult to secure a seat in this cosy shopfront – and the popular Argentinian spiced beef empanadas sell out early on busy nights – but the maitre d' gently soothes frustrated punters. "Fish on toast" is a rustic mix of sashimi, ceviche and dried fish served on crunchy toast with onions and olive oil. A slither of wagyu tongue is paired with a scallop and an apple-dominant coleslaw for an excellent balance of textures and flavour. Chocolate mousse with orange sorbet gets a rock'n'roll twist with cubes of bourbon jelly.

Hours Lunch Thurs–Fri noon–2.30pm; Dinner Mon–Sat 6–10pm; no bookings

Bill Tapas menu $8–$26; **D** $12

Cards AE V MC

Wine An interesting selection of Spanish and South American wines; 8 by the glass

Chefs Elvis Abrahanowicz & Ben Milgate

Owners Joe Valore, Elvis Abrahanowicz & Ben Milgate

Seats 85; wheelchair access; outdoor seating

Vegetarian Plenty of tapas options

www.bodegatapas.com

And...arrive early – we mean 6pm – to be sure of a table

The Book Kitchen

255 Devonshire Street, Surry Hills
Tel 9310 1003   Map 3b

Contemporary

Score 13.5/20

Neighbourhood cafes branching out from their roots into restaurant food and bigger bill territory can trail mediocrity in their wake. Or they can be a real success, like this part-cafe, part-bookshop, part-cosy dinner destination. Once an old Surry Hills garage, the fit-out is minimalist, with a concrete floor, rustic wooden tables, a bookshelf of pre-loved classic cookery books and some new titles for sale, and a neat, partially open kitchen. At breakfast, sleepy-eyed workers munch on muffins or organic scrambled eggs and gulp down The Book Blend coffee. At lunch, it might be fresh buffalo mozzarella with prosciutto and roast tomatoes. Service can be counter-intuitive but eating stays smart. Chef David Campbell doesn't gussy up quality Oz produce: tasty spanner crab souffle with Yamba prawns and bisque is simple and real; he lets a perfect pan-roasted pork cutlet with crackling oink for itself; and an organic banana tarte Tatin is a wow moment.

Hours Breakfast & lunch Wed–Mon 8am–3pm; Dinner Wed–Sat 6.30–10pm

Bill E $12–$20 **M** $16–$35 **D** $12–$15; 10% surcharge on Sundays & public holidays

Cards AE V MC Eftpos

Wine Small but appropriate choice of local and NZ boutique wines; 14 by the glass; BYO (corkage $5 pp)

Chefs David Campbell & Oliver Roberts

Owners David & Nicole Campbell

Seats 60; wheelchair access; outdoor seating

Child friendly Highchairs

www.thebookkitchen.com.au

And...for parking, consider the side streets off Bourke Street

Botanic Gardens Restaurant

Royal Botanic Gardens, Palm Grove Centre,
Mrs Macquarie's Road, Sydney
Tel 9241 2419   Map 2

Contemporary

Score 13.5/20

Sydney's CBD doesn't get more serene than
in the Royal Botanic Gardens, and there are
few more pleasant ways to view them than
from the comfort of the Botanic Gardens
Restaurant. Its white and cream coloured
interior is bright and breezy, with an open
balcony and high ceiling. Diners enjoy
long lunches, gazing at the greenery and
hundreds of fruit bats dangling from nearby
trees. The succinct menu keeps things simple,
with light, fresh-flavoured entrees including
kingfish carpaccio with capers and olive oil
dressing. A leek and fetta tart with salsa
verde works well with a drizzle of sticky-
sweet balsamic reduction. Mains might be a
trio of large ravioli, stuffed with sweet potato
and topped with buttery rosemary and sage
sauce and pine nuts aplenty, or lamb with
a generous serve of mashed potato and
caponata. A dense passionfruit roulade with
berry compote is a highlight for dessert, but
thankfully not enough to tempt the bats
from their trees.

Hours Breakfast Sat–Sun 9.30–11.30am;
Lunch daily noon–3pm

Bill E $16–$20 **M** $26–$35 **D** $16;
10% surcharge on Sundays & public holidays

Cards AE DC V MC

Wine Good local selection with a few French
drops; 10 by the glass

Chef Millan Vasovic

Owner Trippas White Catering

Seats 130; private rooms; wheelchair access

Child friendly Highchairs; kids' menu

www.trippaswhite.com.au

And...ask next door about tours of the gardens

Brass Razoo

533 Willoughby Road, Willoughby
Tel 9958 5734   Map 7

Contemporary

Score 14/20

Easily overlooked from the outside, the
narrow corridor inside has been transformed
into a warm, elegant and always busy dining
spot for a loyal local clientele. When the
guys who own the store run the store, the
service is hard to beat, and that's the case
at Razoo, with the double act of Anthony
Fischbeck behind the stoves and the
charming Sharnette Jol in charge of the floor.
A sassy starter of chilli-salt soft-shell crab is
elevated with a bracing soy vinegar dipping
sauce. There is a refreshing crunch in a salad
of fresh green peas, beans and smoky bacon
drizzled with a sultry soft egg dressing.
A tea-smoked Atlantic salmon fillet is
wrapped in prosciutto, slathered in wasabi
butter and nestled on a bed of nutty sesame
seaweed salad. A terrine of mango and
coconut ice-cream is heavenly, scattered
with pearls of pistachio nut praline. Devoted,
efficient staff will ensure that you return to
take your tastebuds on another culinary tour.

Hours Dinner Tues–Sat 6.30–10pm;
bookings essential on weekends

Bill E $17.50 **M** $29 **D** $12–$13

Cards AE V MC

Wine Concise, very reasonably priced list;
10 by the glass; BYO (corkage $8 per bottle)

Chef Anthony Fischbeck

Owners Sharnette Jol & Anthony Fischbeck

Seats 45

And...the menu includes a list of suppliers
so you know what you're eating

Brown Sugar

106 Curlewis Street, Bondi
Tel 9130 1566   Map 9

Contemporary   ♉
                                    Score 14/20

With its Bondi bold and casual decor and
helpful staff, this cafe-by-day, serious-diner-
by-night may be the pick of beachside
bliss. A large blackboard displays a pan-
Mediterranean menu with a healthy respect
for fresh produce. A special of three plump,
glassy, seared scallops looks pretty as a
picture on a plate swirled with creamy
parsnip puree, dots of reduced balsamic
and a scattering of green leaves. Gently al
dente gnocchi are tossed through excellent
tomato and basil sugo, with melting chunks
of smoked mozzarella adding spark. Portions
are generous. So what if the "seared"
ocean trout is almost cooked through and
the accompanying fattoush salad with thick
croutons is more like a panzanella? It's still
delicious. Well-seasoned scotch fillet with
oh-so-smooth mash and braised eschallots
is tenderly rare as requested. Rustic desserts
show the same flair, especially a buttery
galette of grilled peaches with smooth
hazelnut gelato.

Hours Breakfast & lunch Fri–Sun 8.30am–2.30pm;
Dinner Tues–Sat 6.30–10.30pm, Sun 6–9.30pm

Bill E $12–$16 **M** $22–$29 **D** $9–$12; $1 pp
surcharge on Sundays & public holidays

Cards AE V MC Eftpos

Wine Short, interesting list, almost all under $50;
10 by the glass; BYO (corkage $6 per bottle)

Chef Neil Gottheiner

Owners Neil & Lianne Gottheiner

Seats 48; outdoor seating

Child friendly Highchair; toy box

Vegetarian Multiple options

www.brownsugarbondi.com.au

And...the fish pie with leek and truffle oil is
highly recommended

Bundu Khan

121 Auburn Road, Auburn
Tel 9749 1000   Map 6

Pakistani

                                    Score 13/20

Ah, the changing face of Sydney dining!
No longer content with mere Indian, we
have expanded our horizons to embrace
further South Asian vistas, including modern
Pakistani, thanks to eateries such as this
quarry-tiled, wicker-chaired, mood-lit room.
Cricketing memorabilia adorn one wall as
well-dressed families and groups feast on
smoke-billowing kebab platters, superbly
tandoor-toasted naan and flaky paratha.
Service is attentive and courteous, while
dishes are set on a tableside stand before
being placed in front of you. Often dubbed
the king of curries, haleem is an earthy mush
of flaky beef, lentils and other pulses, while
fresh-sauced karahi dishes arrive in the cute
two-handled flat-bottomed woks that they're
named after. Spicy rice tosses together
apricot strips, sultanas, pulses, black sesame,
cashew slivers, yellow spices and steamed
grains. Pista kulfi (perfumed milk ice-cream
rolled in ground pistachios) is frozen on a
stick like a milky, floral popsicle. It's strictly
halal and no alcohol, but when in Rome…
or in this case, Islamic Auburn, do as the
locals do.

Hours Lunch & dinner Fri–Sun noon–11pm; Dinner
Mon–Thurs 5.30–10.30pm

Bill E $5.50–$16.90 **M** $11.90–$16.90 **D** $4.90

Cards V MC Eftpos

Wine No alcohol; no BYO

Chef Rinku

Owner Kamil Khan

Seats 75

www.bundukhan.com.au

And... Pakistani test cricketers are known
to dine here

Buon Ricordo

108 Boundary Street, Paddington
Tel 9360 6729   Map 2

Italian (Campania)

Score 16.5/20

Armando Percuoco has welcomed back Buon Ricordo alumnus Darren Taylor to the kitchen. Seamless transitions are a hallmark of this Paddington landmark, and neither the service nor the food has skipped a beat. Jacketed waiters still glide through the art-filled dining room as if choreographed, and the silky cream, parmesan and truffled egg of the signature fettuccine al tartufovo is as decadently irresistible as ever. Some things do change: order the salmonata cruda (salmon sliced as thin as a communion host) and savour the fruity tingle of Percuoco's latest innovation – home-pressed olive oil from his Hunter Valley farm. The deeply satisfying flavours of a grilled veal cutlet rolled with spinach and parmesan, seasoned only with lemon juice and oil, capture the simple but technically perfect pleasures of this place. For dessert, a semifreddo studded with crushed torrone on a swirl of raspberry coulis is traditional rather than tremendous. Sommelier Michael Block's intelligent handling of a commendable cellar is the cherry on top.

Hours Lunch Fri–Sat noon–3pm; Dinner Tues–Sat 6–10.30pm; bookings essential
Bill E $29.50–$45 **M** $39.50–$55.50 **D** $18.50
Cards AE DC V MC Eftpos
Wine Formidable Italian-Australasian list with half-bottles available; 13 by the glass
Chefs Armando Percuoco & Darren Taylor
Owners Armando Percuoco & Gemma Cunningham
Seats 100; private room
Vegetarian Separate menu
www.buonricordo.com.au
And...a six-course degustation ($120) of Armando's greatest hits

The Burlington Bar and Dining

6 Burlington Street, Crows Nest
Tel 9439 7888   Map 5a

Modern European

Score 15/20

The Kemps, of Randwick two-hatter Restaurant Balzac, have crossed the harbour for their latest bistro venture. This long terrace's clean and breezy decor is built on classic bistro good looks, with banquettes framing the front room and its bare timber tables, backed up by enthusiastic service. Matthew Kemp blends his English heritage with Mediterranean joy for a delicious, great value menu that's occasionally complex yet elegantly simple. It ranges from Basque-inspired salt cod croquettes with aioli to old-fashioned brawn – sweet, salty and smoky pig's trotter, hock and cheek in a lemony jelly – accompanied by a tangy, creamy remoulade. Skate wing on a potato and rosemary tart with capers and a horseradish and grain mustard vinaigrette is a classy take on fish and chips. Dry-aged angus rib-eye, at 500 grams or a whopping 1 kilogram, and its fine bearnaise, is even better with hand-cut chips, while the sensual bread-and-butter pudding has a creme brulee-style toffee top and cinnamon perfume. Swoon.

Hours Lunch Mon–Fri from noon; Dinner Mon–Sat from 6pm
Bill E $10–$18 **M** $16–$42 **D** $12
Cards AE DC V MC Eftpos
Wine Small, quirky, intelligent global list offered in 250ml, 375ml and full bottle serves; 21 by the glass
Chefs Matthew Kemp & Chad Muir
Owners Matthew Kemp & Lela Radojkovic
Seats 85; private rooms
www.burlingtonbardining.com.au
And...most dishes are offered in both entree and main sizes

Busshari

119 Macleay Street, Potts Point
Tel 9357 4555   Map 2

Japanese

Score 14/20

This is the new age of Sydney Japanese: slick and sexy, casual and cool. After a smiling greeting by manager Ben and the rest of the equally helpful staff, take a comfortable stool in Busshari's moodily bar-lit interior – at one of its high tables or facing the sushi-chef action. Daily specials are explained and dishes served in progression. Wine service may not be the slickest but you'll soon be supping on satisfyingly plump pork gyoza and relaxing into the easy vibe. A rectangle of thick perspex shows off beautifully prepared pristine ocean trout, eel and prawn sushi, and ocean trout, kingfish and tuna sashimi. Gorgeous hand-crafted plates bear grilled oysters, juicily delicate with miso-infused sauce. Wagyu beef packs a punch of flavour, sizzling in a pot with vegetables, astride a claypot filled with hot coals. For late night sushi and sake, or a stylish dessert platter, this is Japanese the way Sydney likes it.

Hours Dinner Mon–Sat 6–11pm;
bookings recommended

Bill E $5–$17 **M** $16–$39 **D** $6.50–$15

Cards AE DC V MC JCB Eftpos

Wine Moderately priced, reasonable list;
10 by the glass; BYO (corkage $7 per bottle);
huge sake range

Chef Nobuyuki Ito

Owner Busshari Restaurant Pty Ltd

Seats 36; wheelchair access

Child friendly Kids' food; highchairs

Vegetarian Salads, tempura, pickles, sushi

And...it's sake heaven with 16 by the glass

buzo

3 Jersey Road, Woollahra
Tel 9328 1600   Map 4b

Italian

Score 14/20

This converted terrace has just the right touch of low-key Italian glamour. Ask for a table upstairs, where the room buzzes with the sounds of a mature, well-heeled local crowd and staff squeeze between tables, offering service that's pleasant if not always prompt. Imaginative antipasti include tender snails curling on a charred crostone that soaks up their garlicky white wine juices. The bright notes of a celery, white anchovy and parsley salad are a zesty counterpoint to the rich pasta dishes that follow, including the signature vincisgrassi (porcini, prosciutto and truffle lasagne) and aromatic bucatini with smoked eel, chilli and garlic. A main of veal with pangrattato is just that – perfectly cooked slices of fillet in rich jus, but they're in need of more balance than the topping of fried breadcrumbs can offer. Black treacle gelato with figs and candied walnuts is a creative addition to the dessert menu, but it's always hard to go past the warm baked chocolate.

Hours Dinner Mon–Sat 6pm–late;
bookings essential

Bill E $18.50–$19.50 **M** $27–$31 **D** $11–$18.50

Cards AE DC V MC

Wine Extensive list of Italian and Australian wines, with a good European selection; 20 by the glass, and a separate list of 16 grappa by the glass

Chefs James Hird & Todd Garratt

Owners James Hird, Todd Garratt & Traci Trinder

Seats 65

www.buzorestaurant.com.au

And...finish with a caffe corretto – espresso with a shot of grappa

Cafe Sopra ★

7 Danks Street, Waterloo
Tel 9699 3174   Map 9
Also at 81 Macleay Street, Potts Point
Tel 9368 6666   Map 2

Italian

Score 14.5/20

FAVOURITE MEDITERRANEAN

With one of Sydney's premier provedores downstairs, chef Andy Bunn gets the freshest zucchini flowers and summer peas for his crinkly mafalda pasta, and the tomatoes and basil for his piquant white anchovy salad come literally off the back of the truck. Skilfully and seemingly effortlessly, he parlays this produce into imaginative, Italian-inspired food that locks in the essential flavours and keeps pretentiousness out. Off the blackboard menu laden with choices, be blown away by a mellow, mighty chicken liver paté with tiny cornichons, capers and eschallots for bite, and sigh over a plate-thin, parmesan-crumbed chicken schnitzel with dressed red cabbage and plump raisins. A tangy buttermilk pudding or a bowl of summer-bright cherries are an elegant finish. Eat early, or late, because you can't book and you won't be seated until all your party is gathered.

Hours Breakfast & lunch Tues–Fri 10am–3pm, Sat 8am–3pm; no bookings
Bill E $8.50–$22 **M** $8.50–$22 **D** $6.50–$12
Cards AE V MC Eftpos
Wine All Italian, including carafe, house bottles and the marvellous riserva (premium) cellar; 14 by the glass; BYO (corkage $5 per bottle)
Chef Andy Bunn
Owner Fratelli Fresh
Seats 80; private room; outdoor seating
Child friendly Highchairs; kid-friendly menu
www.fratellifresh.com.au
And...perch at the long counter and feel molto Italiano

Cafe Sydney

Level 5, Customs House, 31 Alfred Street, Circular Quay
Tel 9251 8683   Map 1

Contemporary

Score 14.5/20

Internally, it's industrial chic – a massive steel glasshouse with recycled blackbutt floors and bathrooms hung with David Moore photographs. Yet all attention is kidnapped by the views of Circular Quay. Exceptional service is attentive and casually persuasive (all those sides soon add up). The seafood focus can be as simple as chilled crustaceans with mayonnaise and lemon, while roasted veal tenderloin with prosciutto, grilled fig, gorgonzola and vincotto are classic flavours that harmonise the sum of their parts. Likewise grilled swordfish with bagna cauda, (a hot bath of anchovy oil), broad and borlotti beans, peas and aioli, cut adroitly by tiny lemon segments. Seared tarragon gnocchi with black truffle, asparagus and pea cream is comfort on a pedestal. Flavours can stray – tandoori-roasted salmon was hard to savour among spiced potatoes and tamarind chutney. All is forgiven with outstanding pistachio and lemon baklava, toffee fig and honey ripple ice-cream.

Hours Mon–Fri noon–11pm; Sat 5–11pm; Sun noon–4pm; bookings essential
Bill E $22–$27 **M** $30–$39 **D** $16
Cards AE DC V MC
Wine Super selection of Australasian, French & Italian, good mark-ups too; 32 by the glass
Chef Matt Bates
Owners Customs House Cafe Pty Ltd
Seats 290; private room; wheelchair access; outdoor seating
Child friendly Kids' menu; highchairs; pencils
Vegetarian Separate vegan menu
www.cafesydney.com
And...a serious cocktail list and Sunday jazz

Cantina Uno

152 Liverpool Street, Darlinghurst
Tel 9361 6442   Map 2

Italian/Mediterranean

Score 13/20

Don't be fooled by the air of simplicity. An elegant professionalism lies at the heart of everything that happens inside this pale-walled eatery with its pizza and pasta focus. While the menu may appear limited (seven entrees and pasta options, six mains, five pizzas) and the decor understated, everything here merits a closer look. Those images on the walls are by significant Australian painters, such as John Olsen, Luke Sciberras and Salvatore Zofrea; the trattoria-style menu is well thought through and skilfully executed, and the service is excellent. House-made rag pasta, marrying cuttlefish, spinach, chilli and parmesan crumbs, has a seductively tender bite. Zucchini flowers stuffed with chicken, spinach and mascarpone are delicately cooked. Boned and crumbed spatchcock is tender and filled with parsley butter and smoked garlic, and there's no faulting the size of the calf's liver on barbecued radicchio with balsamic. Of the house-made desserts, chocolate mousse is achingly good.

Hours Lunch Mon–Fri noon–3pm; Dinner Mon–Sat 6pm–late

Bill E $16–$19 **M** $24–$35 **D** $14

Cards AE V MC Eftpos

Wine Carefully selected Oz–Italian boutique list; 9 by the glass; BYO (corkage $7 per bottle)

Chef Tim Fisher

Owners Tim Fisher & Alex Azzinnaro

Seats 70; private room

Child friendly Pizza always pleases

Vegetarian Several options

And…sit downstairs to enjoy the inner-city buzz on summer evenings

Catalina

Lyne Park, Rose Bay
Tel 9371 0555   Map 9

Contemporary

Score 15.5/20

Beautifully understated elegance and professional service combine in one of the most perfectly positioned restaurants on the planet – harbour view, pottering seaplanes and ferries. An entree of succulent seared scallops, cauliflower puree and shallots arrives with two warm, teardrop-shaped zucchini flowers stuffed with a steamed scallop and chive mousse. A soft, kebab-sized roll of startlingly fresh-tasting poached rock lobster is paired with kipfler potatoes, beans and salmon roe. A main course of hickory-smoked, enviably moist salmon is tied up in a cylindrical parcel that belies its seemingly modest size. A leaf of slightly bitter cavolo nero, parsnip puree and crunchy pancetta manage not to overpower the fish. A classic duck dish is a spread of juicy, gamey roast breast slices with a crisp confit leg on carrot puree, couscous and watercress. As the sun sets, we're seduced into an exquisite coconut pot de creme dessert. Who knew there would be room?

Hours Lunch daily noon–5pm; Dinner Mon–Sat 5–10pm; bookings essential

Bill E $25–$45 **M** $40–$56 **D** $19–$22; 10% surcharge on Sundays & public holidays

Cards AE DC V MC

Wine Huge and varied list – all 26 pages of it – with something for everyone; 20 by the glass

Chef Paul McMahon

Owners Michael, Judy & Paul McMahon

Seats 160; outdoor seating

www.catalinarosebay.com.au

And…go again for suckling pig, slow-cooked for 12 hours, then roasted to order

Catalonia

Shop 2, 31a Fitzroy Street, Kirribilli
Tel 9922 4215   Map 5a

Spanish

Score 13.5/20

Tapas is the new antipasto (and Spanish wine the new Italian). And so to Catalonia. This relaxed venue, which unfurls to embrace the outdoors, is a mix of honey-coloured timbers, courtyard and footpath dining, and a more restaurant-style upstairs area. Service is fun too. Chef Brian Villahermosa (formerly of London's Salt Yard) blends modern flair with tapas classics in almost 30 colourful dishes that play with texture and contrasting flavours – whether in wagyu beef meatballs, curiously matched with cumin-scented caramelised peach, or marjoram-perfumed grilled squid stuffed with rice tangy with preserved lemon and olives, and saffron aioli. Ever-so-lightly battered zucchini flowers are filled with a duet of Valedon blue and goat's cheeses brushed with orange blossom honey sweetness, and, yes, patatas bravas have plenty of chilli zip. Sure, the churros seemed a little dense, but once you dip them in the jaffa-flavoured chocolate chantilly, who notices? With a Spanish rosé at hand, this much fun is such good value.

Hours Lunch Wed–Sun noon–3pm;
Dinner Tues–Sat 6–10pm, Sun 6–9pm

Bill Tapas $10.50–$18.50

Cards V MC Eftpos

Wine Great Spanish & Portuguese choices;
11 by the glass

Chef Brian Villahermosa

Owners Brian Villahermosa & Thomas Hoff

Seats 90; private room; wheelchair access;
outdoor seating

Child friendly Colouring-in books

Vegetarian Numerous tapas

www.catalonia.com.au

And...share 6 or 7 dishes between two

Chequers

Shop 220, Level 2, Mandarin Centre,
65 Albert Avenue, Chatswood
Tel 9904 8388   Map 7

Chinese (Cantonese)

Score 13/20

It might rival Chinatown's big hitters as king of the yum cha dumplings, but for the past 11 years Chequers has punched above its weight when it comes to a la carte dining by night. In one corner of a shopping mall food court, it delivers a warmly low-key approach to Cantonese cuisine. Service is more succinct than sensational in this cosy room stuck in a 1970s-decor time warp, but as the room fills with chattering diners, waiters portion out a classic Peking duck at the table with a practised touch. A second course of duck sang choi bau comes with oyster, XO or chilli sauce. A mountain of king prawns, lathered in a chilli and garlic Sichuan sauce, is surrounded by a ring of steamed broccoli while whitebait and calamari in a light salt-and-pepper batter are far too addictive. Adventurous eaters can set their heart racing with a hotpot of mushrooms, gelatinous duck flippers and large, snail-like whelks.

Hours Lunch Mon–Fri 11am–3pm, Sat–Sun 10am–3pm; Dinner daily 5.30–11pm

Bill E $6.80–$24.80 **M** $18.80–$108
D $3.50–$6.80; $2.50 per adult and $1 per child surcharge on public holidays

Cards AE DC V MC

Wine Limited conservative list; 9 by the glass;
BYO (corkage $5 pp)

Chef Shen Jia Hua

Owner Airfoal Pty Ltd

Seats 290; private rooms; wheelchair access

Child friendly Highchairs

Vegetarian An entire menu section

And...whole crisp-skin suckling pig on weekends

Chinta Ria… Temple Of Love

Level 2, The Roof Terrace, Cockle Bay Wharf, Darling Park, 201 Sussex Street, Sydney
Tel 9264 3211   Map 1

Malaysian

Score 12.5/20

A huge, beaming Buddha adorned with flowers and burning incense sits smack in the middle of this circular eatery, a temple to the public's appetite for quick, South-East Asian, hawker-style fare. Tables radiate away from the statue, while staff zip past with lightning speed. Communication can be fraught as Chinta Ria is one of Cockle Bay's busiest spots (it takes reservations only for lunch; evening diners may have to queue), and the emphasis is on fast-table trade. The atmosphere is as strongly flavoured as the food, with the music and some dish names echoing owner Simon Goh's passion for jazz. Entrees that rock include Ella's Wrap – stuffed, pastry-wrapped prawns, and Parker's Gems – battered balls of minced chicken and potato with a coriander tang, although not everything hit the right note. Chilli prawns proved discordant – the egg-blend sauce was rather overwhelming – but a deep-fried banana dessert is well worth crooning about.

Hours Lunch daily noon–2.30pm; Dinner Mon–Sat 6–11pm, Sun 6–10.30pm; bookings for lunch only

Bill E $7–$9 **M** $13.50–$28 **D** $7.50; 10% surcharge on public holidays

Cards AE DC V MC

Wine Workmanlike Australasian selection; 23 by the glass; BYO (corkage $10 per bottle)

Chef Donny Pang

Owner Simon Goh

Seats 160; wheelchair access; outdoor seating

Child friendly Highchairs; spring rolls; satays

Vegetarian Menu has vegetarian options section

www.chintaria.com

And…beef rendang is a traditionalist's delight

Cibo e Vino

Shop 2, 299 Old Northern Road, Castle Hill
Tel 8002 0912   Map 6

Italian

Score 13.5/20

Red, white and green signage and a catchy name point to predictable suburban Italian. But there's no pizza, pasta and tomato sauce sameness about this friendly, fresh-looking cafe–eatery opposite the monolithic Castle Towers. The vino might be missing (unless you BYO) but the cibo (food) is intelligently market driven, served with a certain rustic charm. Piadina (Romagna-style flatbread) is draped with translucent prosciutto over milky-fresh warm ricotta; feathery, golf ball-sized salt cod fritters come with real-egg garlic mayo; and earthy wedges of roast beetroot pair beautifully with melted brunet, a gently aged goat's cheese. Soft little house gnocchi are faultless, drenched in a sharpish tomato sauce. Only a main of duck, piled with pomegranate, diced chestnut and roasted, skin-on pumpkin, was a touch rough and ready. Thankfully, chewy mini-florentines served with textured chestnut and honey ice-cream, and sugar-dusted crostoli with a pot of fine loose-leaf tea, show care and thought way beyond the average suburban Italian.

Hours Lunch Tues–Sat noon–3pm; Dinner Tues–Sat 6–10pm

Bill E $12–$18 **M** $27–$35 **D** $8–$13

Cards AE V MC Eftpos

Wine BYO only (corkage $6 per bottle); licence pending

Chef Paul Toogood

Owner Wijaya family

Seats 55; wheelchair access; outdoor seating

Child friendly Highchair; crayons; can adapt meals to suit kids

www.ciboevino.com.au

And…a good range of (Italian) vino at the Castle Towers Dan Murphy's

Ciel Rouge

Level 1, 292–294 Victoria Street, Darlinghurst
Tel 9356 3255   Map 2

French

Score 14/20

A chandelier-hung, shabby chic salon is not what you'd expect one flight up on Victoria Street. Cooking this good also surprises, until you learn that chef Damien Wright lists Pier and London's Michelin-starred Pied a Terre on his CV. If the floor has to ask who is having what, that's because the atmosphere is more friendly than formal. Hawkesbury River calamari pairs simply with pickled carrot and coriander salad, the plate brought to life by a bright brushstroke of carrot puree, while a generous mound of chicken liver paté with red onion confit and cornichons reminds that there is good value here, too. That is confirmed by labour-intensive mains, which mostly hover on the right side of $30, such as a roasted boneless pork rack, cauliflower puree and soft apple on a pillow of cabbage and bacon or, for a few dollars more, a perfectly cooked veal cutlet with a herbed crumb coating, accompanied by a cherry tomato and basil salad.

Hours Dinner Tues–Sat 6–10pm
Bill E $11.50–$16 **M** $24–$32.50 **D** $12.50;
2 courses $34 pp, 3 courses $43 pp
Cards AE V MC Eftpos
Wine Well-priced and succinct list; 15 by the glass
Chef Damien Wright
Owners Clive & Sue Delmenico
Seats 50; private rooms
www.cielrouge.com.au
And...open late, but it can get loud

Civic Dining

NEW

Level 1, Civic Hotel, cnr Pitt & Goulburn streets, Sydney
Tel 8080 7040   Map 3a

Modern Mediterranean

Score 15/20

It's a joy to see chef Peter Conistis back, and cooking the distinctive and elegantly modern Greek dishes that made his reputation at Omega and Eleni's. He's also broadened his repertoire with sunshiny flavours from across the Mediterranean and Middle East. A loud, lively yet smart art deco pub that's popular with large groups, the Civic does casual fine dining with tan leather banquettes and dark timber tables. The brilliant scallop moussaka with taramasalata (a Conistis signature) is as welcome as a prodigal son, joined by fabulous newcomers such as Hiramasa kingfish kibbeh nayeh (raw minced fish with sesame seeds) with horseradish-sharpened tzatziki and nigella-seed flatbread. Pomegranate-roasted quail with a sheep's milk fetta, chorizo, mint and watermelon salad is a giddy blend of sweet, salty and sour. Confit duck and sour cherry filo pie with pomegranate sauce and walnut-crunchy skordalia is wonderfully opulent. A glass biscuit cone filled with white chocolate and orange blossom sorbet on an orange and date salad is worthy of Zeus himself.

Hours Lunch Mon–Fri noon–2.30pm; Dinner Tues–Sat 6–10pm
Bill E $19–$25 **M** $32–$35 **D** $14
Cards AE DC V MC
Wine Short, well-priced domestic boutique range with some Mediterranean drops; 12 by the glass
Chef Peter Conistis
Owner Jim Kospetas
Seats 120; private room; outdoor seating
www.civichotel.com.au
And...there's a funky bar right next door

Clareville Kiosk Dining

27 Delecta Avenue, Clareville Beach
Tel 9918 2727   Map 7

Contemporary

Score 14.5/20

A warm, friendly atmosphere draws you into this small, brightly maintained room. From its polished wood floor and fresh flowers to local art on white walls, the pride and dedication of a new owner are obvious. A complimentary sherry glass of warm lobster consomme bodes well for a vibrant, well-balanced, seasonal menu from chef Cameron Johnston (ex Pier). A dinky cube of luscious pork belly with a sprinkle of pomegranate and soft eschalots excites. Beautifully cooked kingfish with a bright carrot puree revels in a dark, deliciously sticky chicken-stock reduction. Pan-fried gnocchi with a julienne of globe artichoke and asparagus sets a new benchmark. Deconstructed dessert is a tasty, textural triumph of pure persimmon puree, a clump of creamy rice pud, tart yoghurt sorbet, caramelised orange, toasted walnuts and brioche crumbs. This is gracious dining with a light touch, as ceiling fans twirl, sea air is soft through the frangipani, and even designated drivers smile.

Hours Lunch Sat–Sun noon–2.30pm; Dinner Wed–Sun 6-9pm

Bill E $19.50–$25.50 **M** $35.50–$40.50 **D** $16.50; 10% surcharge on public holidays

Cards AE DC V MC

Wine An elegant, involving list; 10 by the glass

Chef Cameron Johnston

Owner Padie Starr

Seats 40

Child friendly Kids' menu

www.clarevillekiosk.com.au

And…a car park opposite

Claude's

10 Oxford Street, Woollahra
Tel 9331 2325   Map 4b

Modern French

Score 18/20

Some things never change: the smoked salmon consomme; the souffle a la Suissesse; the chocolate indulgence. There's also the subtle lighting, flourish of Limoges plates and hushed tones and poise of the waiters. But after four years at the helm, Australia's leading female chef has made the menu her own, showing that beneath the calm she's wild at heart. While long-term devotees might crave the old Claude's, others welcome chef Chui Lee Luk's vigour and experimentation, which delivers bolder, more complex and challenging flavour combinations. Most work blissfully well, such as quills of blue-eye with sorrel butter, brittle squid, pickled asparagus and a mulligatawny-style sauce. Others, such as chicken-liver parfait sandwiched between celeriac pancakes, beside poached lobster, lobster jelly and dandelion, seem at odds with the restrained surrounds. Yet the overwhelming sophistication of the meal, the superbly contrasting flavours in duck dumplings and the simple pleasure of perfect spring lamb or an immaculate pineapple souffle dessert cast the Claude's spell time and again.

Hours Dinner Tues–Sat from 7.30pm; bookings essential

Bill 3-course menu $135 pp; tasting menu $165 pp

Cards AE DC V MC

Wine Intriguing, well-priced list, Old and New World offerings, great dessert wines and half bottles; 11 by the glass; BYO ($15 corkage per bottle)

Chef/owner Chui Lee Luk

Seats 45; private room

www.claudes.com.au

And…the minimalist menu can be explained if you're hesitant

Coast

Level 2, The Roof Terrace, Cockle Bay Wharf,
Darling Harbour, Sydney
Tel 9267 6700   Map 1

Italian

Score 14/20

There are few finer places to spend a
sumptuous evening than on the expansive
timber deck here as the sun slips behind
Darling Harbour's monolithic tourist hotels.
Coast's interior, however, is as attractive as
the attentive service in this modern light-filled
pavilion behind huge slanted glass windows.
The menu is crafted with an Italian slant. A
starter of South Australian calamari perched
on ultra-crisp wafers of eggplant is lifted by
a piquant salsa. A main of crisp-skinned,
slow-roasted lamb shoulder is succulent, juicy
and rich, nestled on a bed of tart silverbeet
and enhanced by the intensity of almond and
garlic paste. The brininess of perfectly cooked
line-caught barramundi complements the
earthiness of cavolo nero, while sweet raisins
and slinky pine nuts add Sicilian flair. An
excellent cheese list may tempt you to bypass
the six decadent dolci. A luscious taleggio
from Lombardy is salty, yeasty and creamy,
accompanied by meaty medjool dates.

Hours Lunch Mon–Fri noon–2.30pm;
Dinner Mon–Sat 6–10pm

Bill E $17–$32 **M** $34–$38 **D** $16; 10% surcharge
on public holidays

Cards AE DC V MC

Wine Extensive international list with 13 half
bottles; 15 by the glass

Chef Jonathan Barthelmess

Owners Tim Connell & Michael McCann

Seats 250; private room; outdoor seating

Child friendly Kids' menu; books; coloured pencils

Vegetarian Tasting menu

www.coastrestaurant.com.au

And...the chef's market menu is four shared
courses, home-style, inspired by seasonal produce

The Codfather

83 Percival Street, Stanmore
Tel 9568 3355   Map 8

Seafood

Score 13/20

You won't see any codfish smoking cigars
and cruising the floor with violin cases,
making offers "chew cain't refoose", but
there are guaranteed surreal twists coming
from the kitchen. Chef Javier Carmona
has teamed up with Ross Godfrey from
Newtown's Oscillate Wildly to create
another little crucible of inner-west charm.
A converted corner shop is now a (noisy!)
glass box with minimalist decor and a
funky length-of-the-room mural. Service
is welcoming, informative and efficient, if
somewhat stretched on busy nights. Dishes
swagger from harmonious thrills to over-
ambitious spills, but all are sensationally
cooked. Japanese aesthetic creeps into
caramelised scallops with eggplant, silken
tofu and sweet black sesame crisps.
Alfonsino (red fish) with bouillabaisse
reduction, confit chicken wing, carrot puree
and "kettle chips" is confusing to read yet
deliciously logical in the mouth. Fish curry
is sensationally moist, with pan-fried blue-
eye fillet paddling in a pool of beautifully
balanced spice, accompanied by chutney
and a quirky chickpea mash.

Hours Lunch Sun noon–4pm;
Dinner Tues–Sat 5.30–10pm

Bill E $14–$16 **M** $23–$26 **D** $10

Cards V MC Eftpos

Wine BYO (corkage $3 pp); licence pending

Chef Javier Carmona

Owners Javier Carmona, Chris Sharpe &
Ross Godfrey

Seats 50; private room; outdoor seating

Child friendly Kids' menu; highchairs; colouring in

And...don't rely on the local bottleshop, BYO

The Cook's Larder

Shop 1, 21–23 Old Barrenjoey Road, Avalon
Tel 9973 4370   Map 7

Contemporary

Score 13/20

Let us count the ways they celebrate food here. There are the pantry products and deli items for sale; cooking classes; good coffee and superlative cakes; and a sophisticated lunch and dinner menu. Think fresh, unfussy dishes such as a basil, ricotta, cucumber, olive and cos lettuce salad with tomato vinaigrette; or fiendishly buttery spaghettini with nothing but chilli, garlic and basil. Even better is succulent chargrilled lamb with eggplant, tomato, goat's cheese and mint dressing. On Friday nights, the kitchen trio ups the ante with an ever-changing and adventurous menu that might feature free-range roast pork loin cutlet with grilled peaches, celeriac and star anise-spiced glaze. There's an eclectic edge to the rustic decor – we love the line of antique egg beaters strung up above the tables – which perfectly suits this indoor–outdoor space spilling out into Avalon's swish shopping strip. A rhubarb and coconut cake with rhubarb syrup will have you signing up for cooking classes on the spot.

Hours Breakfast daily 8–11.30am; Lunch daily noon–3pm; dinner Fri only 6.30–9pm; bookings for dinner only

Bill E $16–$18 **M** $17–$22 **D** $5.50–$12; 15% surcharge on public holidays

Cards AE V MC Eftpos

Wine BYO (corkage $2 pp)

Chefs Mick Micklewright, Linda Irvin & Dan Bell

Owners Samantha & Dugal Mackie

Seats 50; wheelchair access; outdoor seating

Child friendly Highchairs; crayons

www.thecookslarder.com.au

And...takeaway dinners and free recipes to inspire you

Cottage Point Inn

2 Anderson Place, Cottage Point
Tel 9456 1011   Map 7

Contemporary

♉

Score 13.5/20

Some turn up in style by seaplane or boat, yet driving through the national park to this quaint little former boatshed and general store at the junction of Cowan Waters and Coal and Candle Creek is equally spectacular. Service can be distracted but there's no doubting the passion and intent of the cheery waiters who deliver chef Kevin Kendall's contemporary array of dishes. Twice-cooked quail is spot-on with a lightly spiced eggplant, coriander and yoghurt salad, while pan-seared Queensland sea scallops share the plate with crisp pancetta, onion jam and a subtle walnut mayonnaise. Oven-roasted wild kingfish rests on a salad of fennel, watercress, ruby grapefruit and artichoke, but a fillet of Northern Rivers veal on a bed of porcini tagliatelle, cornichons and pimento was confused by a braised ox tongue jus. As ripples of water seduce the shoreline, succumb to a large vanilla bean creme brulee with orange and cardamom ice-cream. Like the view, it's made for sharing.

Hours Lunch daily noon–3pm; Dinner Fri–Sat 6.30–9.30pm; bookings recommended

Bill E $19–$28 **M** $39–$42.50 **D** $19–$23.50; $6.50 pp surcharge on weekends & public holidays

Cards AE DC V MC

Wine Broad selection of regional varietals from mainly Australia and NZ; 12 by the glass

Chef Kevin Kendall

Owners Daniel McKinnon & Amanda Cameron

Seats 70; outdoor seating

Child friendly Kids' menu; toys; colouring in

Vegetarian Comprehensive menu

www.cottagepointinn.com.au

And...plan ahead and stay the night in one of two apartments

Courtney's Brasserie

70 Phillip Street, Parramatta
Tel 9635 3288   Map 6

Contemporary

Score 13/20

It's quiet, with a soothing air and warm welcome – just what you expect in this charming 1840s brick cottage. While the room may seem a little dated, it's comfortable, with soft blue walls and dark wood fittings. The well-spaced linen-laid tables extend to an outdoor area on balmy nights. Service is charming and attentive, dishing up excellent home-baked sourdough on arrival. The combinations occasionally seem over the top, yet veteran chef Paul Kuipers pulls it off, to our surprise and delight. Tapas of king prawn three ways – as tempura; in a plump tortellino on gazpacho; and ceviche-style with passionfruit – is daring but works. Sichuan-roasted magret duck breast, sliced rare with salt-and-peppered scallops on sweet–sour orange sauce may not sound like a marriage made in heaven, yet it harmonises handsomely with rich, luscious flavours. Delicate pan-fried whiting fillets rest on a moist crab fritter, lovely with fennel puree and baby peas. Raspberry souffle with pistachio anglaise and a chocolate tuile is a fitting finale.

Hours Lunch Mon–Fri noon–5pm; Dinner Mon–Sat 6–10pm

Bill E $14.90–$28 **M** $29–$36 **D** $15.90

Cards AE DC V MC Eftpos

Wine Thoughtful list of quality brands and some boutiques; 9 by the glass

Chefs Paul Kuipers & Federico Rekowski

Owners Paul & Deanne Kuipers

Seats 77; private room; outdoor seating

Child friendly Kids' menu; highchair on request

Vegetarian Separate menu

www.courtneysbrasserie.com.au

And...take a twilight stroll along the river

Cucina 105

105 Moore Street, Liverpool
Tel 9602 1300   Map 6

Italian

Score 12/20

A black glass facade screens Cucina 105 from Liverpool's CBD, but office lunchers and locals know to ask for a table on the pleasant wooden deck it hides. The breezy decor continues inside, where white, moulded chairs sit on polished concrete, and flatscreen TVs flicker on the walls. Big groups have potential to slow the pace, but service is friendly and regulars are treated like famiglia as they order favourite pizza, pasta and specials from the blackboard. While the pizza lacked the flavour of the wood-fired oven, it made up for it with a topping of juicy, fennel-studded Italian sausage. The Italian-mama-generous mains include vongole in their shells, almost hidden among a turban of fresh pappardelle, while a special of slow-roasted duck, a tad salty, is tender and well-matched with roasted blood plums and garlicky cavolo nero. Dessert staples include tiramisu and gelato, balanced by a worthy espresso to finish.

Hours Lunch Mon–Fri noon–3pm; Dinner Tues–Sat 6–10pm

Bill E $14–$16 **M** $12–$29 **D** $7–$16

Cards AE V MC Eftpos

Wine Mostly Australian list; 9 by the glass; BYO (corkage $3.50 pp)

Chef Dennis Kekatos

Owners Angelo Cucchiaro & Dennis Kekatos

Seats 100; private room; wheelchair access; outdoor seating

Child friendly Kids' menu; highchairs

Vegetarian Various entrees, pizza & pasta

And...stop in for an after-dinner coffee and ricotta cheesecake

Cucina di Lusso

281 Parramatta Road, Glebe
Tel 9660 7555   Map 5b

Italian

Score 13/20

With a large, covered area on the footpath and a smaller indoor dining room, it has the look and feel of a sizeable Glebe coffee shop, but it's actually a cross between an enoteca and a trattoria. All the wine comes from the owners' Mudgee vineyard, and the menu features the simple, unfussy food of Italy. Sicilian olives in olive oil are a welcome greeting. Stuffed zucchini flowers are wonderfully crisp. Baccala mantecato – salt cod minced with olive oil and potatoes – is smooth with a strong sea taste. Whitebait fritters have the required crunch, but a panzanella salad was short on flavour and underdressed. Bistecca alla fiorentina (Florentine-style grilled thick T-bone) is the perfect excuse to try di Lusso's interpretation of a local "super Tuscan" wine. Duck and gorgonzola agnolotti is big on flavour although the sauce was overwhelmingly bigger. If the usual suspects – panna cotta, gelato and zabaglione – don't appeal for dessert, why not explore the selection of fine Italian cheeses?

Hours Lunch Tues–Fri noon–3pm; Dinner Tues–Sat 6–9.30pm

Bill E $10–$18 **M** $23–$37 **D** $12–$14; 4 courses $59, 6 courses $95

Cards AE DC V MC Eftpos

Wine Small list of Italian varietals from Mudgee's di Lusso vineyard; 12 by the glass

Chef Brendan Marshall

Owner Robert Fairall

Seats 210; private room; outdoor seating

Child friendly Smaller portions; highchairs

Vegetarian Six-course tasting menu, other options

www.dilusso.com.au

And...their olive oil and condiments are for sale

Cucina Viscontini

4a The Piazza, 21 Bennelong Road, Homebush Bay
Tel 9739 8888   Map 6

Italian

Score 12/20

A sidewalk cafe, wine shop, foodstore, bakery, deli and trattoria all in one, this place oozes Italian style. Built as part of the Waterfront complex, it has the look and feel of an Italian bar in a resort town. The food is based on simple classics. Breakfast is popular and whether you fancy a snack or something more substantial, there's plenty of choices. The antipasto plate features freshly sliced salami and prosciutto along with home-preserved vegetables. Seafood pasta, with squid, prawns, mussels, vongole and octopus, delights with a clean, clear seafood flavour. Deep-fried calamari is nicely crisp and tender. Pizzas stick to the Neapolitan classics with a soft, fluffy base. An otherwise flavoursome special of porchetta with deep-fried new potatoes dumped on top was too dry and needed sauce, and the balsamic dressing on a rocket salad seemed a tad aggressive. Desserts are based on daily offerings from the pasticceria cabinet and there's always gelato.

Hours Breakfast daily 7.30–11.30am; Lunch daily noon–3.30pm; Dinner Thurs–Sat 5.30–9.30pm

Bill E $12–$16 **M** $18–$30 **D** $3.50–$12

Cards AE V MC Eftpos

Wine Reasonable prices with a basic Italian selection; 4 by the glass

Chefs Fabio Durpetti & Gennaro Barretta

Owners Roberto, Rita, Vanessa & Valerio Viscontini

Seats 100; wheelchair access; outdoor seating

Child friendly Highchairs; pencils; kids' menu

Vegetarian Pasta, salads & panini

www.cucinaviscontini.com.au

And...take home artisan-made Italian pasta from the foodstore section

Cucinetta Ristorante

103 Woolwich Road, Woolwich
Tel 9817 2125   Map 7

Italian

Score 14/20

It's not all about the spectacular Harbour Bridge view at this pan-Italian gem. Cucinetta (little kitchen) is just small enough to give you a cosy, laidback feel, and the right dose of attentiveness makes diners feel special. In warmer months, couples and families enjoy the cool breeze and, all year round, entrees showcase fine seasonal produce. Prosciutto crostini with fig and truffle oozes melted pecorino, gorgonzola and parmigiano, although the truffle flavour is subtle. Pasta dishes are well portioned. The creamy sauce coating Balmain bug tagliolini brims with crustacean flavour, and a zing of chilli takes it up a notch. The selection of mains is equally sublime. Fish of the day (john dory) cooked in tomatoey acqua pazza (crazy water) is magical with red capsicum sweetness, a chilli tingle and a light, sprightly broth. A partly boned spatchcock is meaty and boldly flavoured with glistening jus to match. Finish with the delightfully wobbly creme al latte; its orange and vanilla notes will leave you asking for more.

Hours Lunch Thurs–Fri & Sun noon–3pm; Dinner Tues–Sat 6–10pm; bookings essential

Bill E $18–$27 **M** $35–$39 **D** $16; 10% surcharge on public holidays

Cards AE DC V MC Eftpos

Wine Familiar Australian brands (and Moss Wood back vintages), plus some Italian; 23 by the glass; BYO Tues–Fri (corkage $8 per bottle)

Chef Vincenzo Mazzotta

Owners Vincenzo Mazzotta & Giovanni Finocchiaro

Seats 64; outdoor seating

Child friendly Highchairs; kids' pasta choices

www.cucinetta.com.au

And...the ferry docks nearby, easy parking

da Gianni trattoria

127 Booth Street, Annandale
Tel 9660 6652   Map 5b

Italian

Score 14/20

After a peripatetic year in Sydney kitchens, Giovanni Spinazzola (ex Bistro Moore) has found a fine home for his rustic yet modern Italian cucina. The former Three Clicks West site is a quaint, nook-filled Federation shopfront of booths, brown timbers and crisp white tablecloths that's smarter than the trattoria epithet implies. While his wife Cinzia leads the snappy and snappily-dressed floor team, Giovanni tweaks Italian classics in the kitchen, drawing on his family's southern heritage. Orecchiette Pugliese-style (pasta with lightly mashed broccoli, chilli, anchovy, pancetta and garlic) is bold and gutsy. Venison carpaccio with micro herbs and tangy pomegranate, sharpened by vincotto, is similarly flavour-packed. Fregola (toasted pasta balls) soak up the briny, wine-sharp juices of mussels alla marinara, while rosemary-scented Roman-style roast suckling lamb is angelically soft. The harmony of roasted peach souffle with an amaretto kick and basil sorbet leaves you wishing everyone had a da Gianni nearby.

Hours Lunch Fri noon–3pm; Dinner Mon–Sat 6–10pm; bookings essential

Bill E $16–$19.50 **M** $26–$31 **D** $14–$16

Cards V MC

Wine Small, appealing and affordable, with some Italian; 15 by the glass; BYO Mon–Wed only (corkage $7 per bottle)

Chef Giovanni Spinazzola

Owners Cinzia & Giovanni Spinazzola

Seats 70; private room

Child friendly Kids' menu; books; colouring in

www.dagianni.com.au

And...you can catch a bus there from the city

Danks Street Depot

1/2 Danks Street, Waterloo
Tel 9698 2201   Map 9

Contemporary

Score 14/20

Slow Food true-believer Jared Ingersoll produces a clever balance of tradition and innovation, healthiness and indulgence. A daily-changing menu based on seasonal produce sourced from local producers is a practical application of the worldwide movement's mantra that food should be "good, clean and fair". It's served in the complementary ambience of a medieval long gallery of subdued earthy tones and polished wood by staff of unfailing friendliness. Now if they'd just turn the music down a notch... Chunky ox-heart tomatoes mix with cubes of crisp fried sourdough and silky slivers of roasted capsicum in panzanella salad. A thick, flaky jewfish fillet beaches on a chowder of smoked fish, speck and diced root vegetables. Quail roasted to pull-apart perfection sits contentedly in a puddle of black grape, fennel seed, chilli and vinegar – oh, for a bread trencher instead of a plate! Poached white nectarines sprinkled with pistachio blush seductively in raspberry jus.

Hours Breakfast Mon–Fri 7.30–11am, Sat 8–11am, Sun 9–11am; Lunch daily 11am–3pm; Dinner Thurs–Sat 6–10pm

Bill E $16.50–$18.50 **M** $19.50–$38 **D** $15; breakfast $6–$18.50; 10% surcharge on Sundays & public holidays

Cards AE V MC Eftpos

Wine Some interesting local and foreign wines; 21 by the glass

Chef/owner Jared Ingersoll

Seats 100; wheelchair access; outdoor seating

Child friendly Highchair

www.danksstreetdepot.com.au

And...if the service is a tad slow, relax – this is Slow Food, after all

Darbar

134a Glebe Point Road, Glebe
Tel 9660 5666   Map 5b

Indian

Score 12/20

With its rich sandstone walls, low ceiling and the gentle, wafting perfumes of spice, this subterranean dining room is very inviting. The many familiar greetings suggest it's a favourite haunt for locals. The menu plumps for many of the southern Indian gems you'd expect, and the Mysore masala dosa won't disappoint with a generous serve of spiced potato wrapped inside the crisp, rolled pancake, although the swirling, ornate sauces on the Darbar chat are a tad too sweet. Among the mains, prawn lababdar has a good measure of ginger and fresh tomato and a fine hit of fenugreek with coriander, while that Goan staple, chicken vindaloo, isn't too overwhelming in its punch, allowing the spices to shine through. Side dishes can't be faulted for their size, and vegetarians are very well served by a diverse menu. If the service can seem a little distracted, at least the perfumed kulfi and hot gulab jamun will appease.

Hours Lunch Tues–Sun noon–2.30pm; Dinner daily 5–11pm; bookings essential

Bill E $12.90–$15.90 **M** $15.90–$19.90 **D** $8.90–$14.90; 2 courses $27.90 pp, 3 courses $34.90 pp

Cards AE DC V MC

Wine Standard list; 18 by the glass; BYO wine only (corkage $3 pp)

Chef Narayana Reddy

Owners Anita Bobba & Vinay Yahamanchili

Seats 180; private rooms

Child friendly Kids' banquet

Vegetarian Separate menu

www.darbar.com.au

And...have coffee at one of the many cafes nearby

Dome

First Floor, Arthouse Hotel,
275 Pitt Street, Sydney
Tel 9284 1230   Map 1

Contemporary

Score 13/20

They started hanging art here in 1836,
and still do today. Paintings cover the grey,
half-padded walls which, along with the
black glass kitchen surround, sit somewhat
awkwardly with the splendid stencilled
ceiling and original, imposing dome. Friendly
staff cope graciously as the lounge fills and
spills into the expansive dining room. Drinks
and good bread arrive quickly. Fetta with
warm olives and a twitch of chilli eases
you into a varied menu where a generous
kingfish carpaccio responds well to a bite
of horseradish in the accompanying creme
fraiche. Roast snapper fillets are moist;
cornfed chicken breast, if a little dry, is
redeemed by cannellini beans and a lively
gremolata. The brulee and bavarois brigade
are well represented, a molten Belgian
chocolate pudding oozing seductively.
With comfortable, padded armchairs and
a relaxed atmosphere, Dome is a cheerful
place to unwind before wending your way
up to the Attic bar for a nightcap.

Hours Lunch Mon–Fri noon–3pm;
Dinner Tues–Sat 6–10pm
Bill E $18–$22 **M** $30–$35 **D** $15
Cards AE DC V MC
Wine Straightforward all-Australasian list
at friendly prices; 16 by the glass
Chefs Tim Michels, pasta by Franca Manfredi
Owner Liz Willis-Smith
Seats 120; wheelchair access
www.thearthousehotel.com.au
And…a "Fast" menu is available: $55/$65
for 2 or 3 courses, with a glass of wine

Ecco

Drummoyne Sailing Club,
2 St Georges Crescent, Drummoyne
Tel 9719 9394   Map 8

Italian

Score 13.5/20

Long-time kitchen understudy Yasmine
Othman now has a chance to shine in
this sparkling location following Giovanni
Spinazzola's departure. Othman, a seven-year
veteran of this dress-circle diner, has amped
up the seafood focus to complement Ecco's
glass-walled water views to North Sydney. Her
fritelle di nannata, melting whitebait fritters
paired frankly with a lemon aioli, are a fine
start. Chargrilled and deboned spatchcock,
daubed with chilli and garlic and resting on
speck and kipfler discs, is surprisingly yet
pleasingly fiery, but sometimes listless service
could do with some chilli zip too. Everyone
seems to order the signature grigliata di mare:
a pleasant platter of grilled seafood and
fried squid, with a slender swordfish cutlet
holding standout flavour. To finish, a mango
creme brulee may be low on fruity thrills
but features a classic contrast of textures to
match that classic harbour outlook.

Hours Lunch Tues–Fri & Sun noon–3pm;
Dinner Tues–Sat 6–10pm
Bill E $22–$25 **M** $27–$36 **D** $12–$14
Cards AE DC V MC Eftpos
Wine Very reasonably priced and well-picked list,
including some cheeky Italians; 14 by the glass
Chef Yasmine Othman
Owners Claudio & Carmel Carnevale
Seats 180; private rooms; wheelchair access;
outdoor seating
Child friendly $30 kids' menu
www.ecco.com.au
And…a separate function menu offers two
courses for $65

Efendy

79 Elliott Street (cnr Darling Street), Balmain
Tel 9810 5466 Map 5b

Modern Turkish

Score 13/20

The former Ottoman Empire was way ahead of the tapas bandwagon, calling them mezze. This elegant Victorian home (formerly L'Unico) with its large courtyard for alfresco dining, plus numerous nooks filled with white linen tables, gives a modern makeover to great-value rustic Turkish flavours. For mezze, choose six of 10 daily changing options – perhaps fantastic kadayifi karides: king prawns enshrouded in shredded pastry with bite from a mild Syrian chilli and walnut dip; sweet, dill-flecked and sweet fava (broad) bean puree topped with artichoke hearts; and a mound of cerkez tavugu, a classic Circassian chicken dish in tarator – a sauce of walnuts, bread and sheep's milk yoghurt. It's all delivered with beaming hospitality. Mains include marinated lamb skewers on hummus with pastirma (cured beef) and braised beef cheeks on smoked eggplant mash. Chocolate baklava with Pedro Ximenez-drenched sour cherries and Turkish delight ice-cream mightn't be traditional, but deserves to be a classic.

Hours Breakfast Sat–Sun 9am–3pm; Lunch Fri–Sun noon–5pm; Dinner Tues–Sun 6–11pm

Bill E $16–$21 **M** $27–$34 **D** $12–$14; mezze platter for two $35

Cards AE V MC Eftpos

Wine Approachable, international list; 15 by the glass; BYO Tues–Fri, wine only (corkage $5 pp)

Chef Christien Darvall

Owner Somer Sivrioglu

Seats 130; private rooms; outdoor seating

Child friendly Kids' menu; highchairs

Vegetarian Mezze platter, mains & entrees

www.efendy.com.au

And...cocktails in the subterranean bar

Element Bistro

163 King Street, Sydney
Tel 9231 0013 Map 1

French

Score 14/20

There's no fancy entrance and no expensive fit-out, but the lawyers and bankers who frequent these parts know a good thing when they find it. This cosy bistro, where the timber tables and bentwood chairs sit cheek by jowl, is a fine nook for beaming service and reassuring, old-fashioned comfort food. Chef Matthew Barnett's concise menu revels in excellent produce, at prices to please your inner accountant. Robust rillettes of Macleay Valley white rabbit display excellent texture, while a crisp salmon croquette with a green bean and sweetcorn salad is a solid starter. A thick slice of corned beef sits on carrots and peas in a puddle of mustard cream, offering the joy of food you wish you cooked at home but never do. Rigatoni in basil cream was less exciting. Pursue the comfort-food motif with Eton mess: a jumble of whipped cream, fresh strawberries and crisp meringue. We'd board here if we could.

Hours Lunch Mon–Fri 11.45am–3pm; Dinner Tues–Sat 5.30–9pm

Bill E $15–$19 **M** $21–$29.50 **D** $12

Cards AE V MC Eftpos

Wine Well-priced, concise and friendly list; 10 by the glass; BYO (corkage $7 per bottle)

Chef Matthew Barnett

Owners Matthew Barnett & Phil Biviano

Seats 38; outdoor seating

www.elementbistro.com.au

And...a serious contender for the city's best-value dining

Eleni's at Civic ★ NEW

Ground Floor, Civic Hotel, cnr Pitt & Goulburn streets, Sydney
Tel 8080 7030   Map 3a

Greek

Score 12.5/20

FAVOURITE BARGAIN

While her son, Peter Conistis, is busy upstairs weaving his elaborate Mediterranean magic at Civic Dining, mum Eleni serves simple, traditional Greek dishes for workday lunch in this delightful 1930s art deco pub. It's order at the counter and pay up front. At $15 for a main, it's a bargain – one dish comfort food, although the rustic horiatiki, aka Greek salad, full of chunks of fresh tomato, cucumber, red onion and capsicum, plus fetta and olives – is designed to share. Grab a seat in the saloon bar or the small mocha-coloured dining nook in front of the open kitchen as mama bustles about, smiles and chats, before sending out generous serves. While convenience occasionally triumphs over conviction, the lamb moussaka is rich and appealing. Unfortunately stifatho, a beef and onion stew, arrives with rice, rather than the menu's promised tomato skordalia, but the scent of chicken braised in tomato, cinnamon and wine would make even Athena hungry.

Hours Lunch Mon–Fri noon–3pm; no bookings

Bill M $15 **D** $7.50

Cards AE V MC

Wine Modest, reasonably priced domestic range; 12 by the glass

Chefs Eleni & Peter Conistis

Owner James Kospetas

Seats 60; private room

Child friendly Highchair; kids' meals

www.civichotel.com.au

And...classic baklava for dessert

Emma's On Liberty

59 Liberty Street, Enmore
Tel 9550 3458   Map 8

Lebanese

Score 12.5/20

Enmore Road is rife with multinational eating opportunities and marauding crowds. African, Danish, Turkish or Pakistani anyone? A block away from the action, in a converted corner shop, Emma's does inner-west Lebanese – of the clean, contemporary, attractively presented kind – in a big, long room with wide-open windows in summer and a large communal table in the centre. If it feels a bit squeezy and impersonal, it's because Emma Sofy and her crew know how to feed people, preferably in two sittings, sliding a tight mound of quartered Lebanese bread and za'atar-spiced olive oil onto your neatly laid table as you arrive. There's nothing formulaic about smooth, tahini-rich hummus, a smoky babaghanoush or a plate of gorgeous ladies' fingers, oozing runny, more-ishly spiced mouthfuls of minced lamb. Mini zeppelins of deep-fried kibbe were a little icy inside, but superbly grilled marinated chicken with fluffy white toum (garlic sauce) comes to the rescue, as does a square or two of buttery baklava.

Hours Dinner Tues–Thurs 6–10pm, Fri–Sat 6–10.30pm; bookings essential

Bill Dishes range from $9–$17; 7-course banquet $37 pp

Cards Cash only

Wine BYO (corkage $2.50 pp)

Chefs/owners Anthony & Emma Sofy

Seats 60

Vegetarian Half the menu

And...expect to eat early or a little late, given the two-sittings system

Emmilou Lounge & Tapas Bar

413 Bourke Street, Surry Hills
Tel 9360 6991   Map 2

European (Spanish)

Score 12.5/20

The old bordello-red Moog site has been reborn as a bar and late-night tapas haunt. Chef Chris Cranswick-Smith (his winemaker dad Graham is responsible for the Benson Rise white cabernet) spent time at Aria and est. It shows in the careful and impressive presentation, yet a preponderance of pork in many dishes, and ambitious combinations, detracted from the overall impact. Among the tapas, king salmon sashimi with pickled shimeji mushrooms and salmon roe tastes as pretty as it looks; patatas bravas are reworked as confit potato beside an escabeche of prawns and jamon. But duck liver mousse was superfluous to pan-seared squid with crisp jamon. Twice-cooked lamb neck with sweetbreads, cut by lemon, is more assured, and a generous serve of gorgonzola dolce latte on croutons with truffled honey is a wickedly rich ending.

Hours Lunch Fri–Sat from noon (open all day); Dinner Mon–Sat 5pm–1am

Bill Tapas $6–$32; **D** $15

Cards AE V MC Eftpos

Wine Interesting, broad international list; 10 by the glass

Chef Chris Cranswick-Smith

Owners Chris & Graham Cranswick-Smith

Seats 50; outdoor seating

www.emmilou.com.au

And...cocktail courses for wannabe mixologists

est.

Level 1, 252 George Street, Sydney
Tel 9240 3010   Map 1

Contemporary

Score 18/20

The tentacles (or should that be vines?) of the Hemmes family's Merivale empire now extend to its latest pleasure-dome, Ivy. But jeepers, creepers, Ivy will have to work hard to eclipse est.'s star – a magnificent, heritage-ceiled space above the generously proportioned downstairs bar. Peter Doyle is among Sydney's most accomplished, confident and sophisticated chefs, only too evident here in the well-balanced mix of surf and turf, with some interesting Asian and Gallic flourishes. A pencil-thin fillet of Angus minute steak with watercress salad and chips is a succulent triumph, and the perfect lunch for the fund-manager crowd. Immaculately steamed snapper fillet on sand crab, cucumber and shimeji mushrooms is a marvel of flavour in a ginger, shallot and mirin-sweetened broth. Occasional service delays fail to mar a world-class experience. Wine service and selection hit great heights, as does a Valrhona chocolate fondant with peanut parfait and raspberry sorbet. And a crema-topped espresso comes with a gleaming row of delicate petits fours.

Hours Lunch Mon–Fri noon–2.30pm; Dinner Mon–Sat 6–10pm; bookings essential

Bill E $33–$39 **M** $44–$49 **D** $24; Degustation lunch/dinner $110/$150 pp; 5-course chef's menu $130 pp

Cards AE DC V MC

Wine Exceptional and extensive list; 29 by the glass

Chef Peter Doyle

Owner Merivale Group

Seats 90; private room; wheelchair access

Vegetarian Full vegetarian menu

www.merivale.com

And...new lunchtime tasting menu (tables only)

Euro Lounge

Shop 21, The Piazza, Castle Towers,
Castle Street, Castle Hill
Tel 8850 7077   Map 6

European

Score 12/20

To the side of a huge mall, on a busy road surrounded by food chain outlets, sits a refuge from all the action outside. Young, enthusiastic waiters, a tasteful wood-panelled interior, elegant leather chairs and white-linen-covered tables further soften the mood. The menu casts a wide net of options, including a happily retro entree of oysters Kilpatrick, liberally lashed with bacon and Worcestershire sauce. Mains include a large selection of above-average pizzas, from simple napoletana to modern combinations such as smoked salmon and brie, with the wood-fired oven ensuring a soft dough and crisp crust. A main of tender pork fillet and kumera mash brings together old friends, but the accompanying caramelised chestnuts and apples didn't gel as well. The perfect combo is moist sticky date pudding and butterscotch sauce, with fig and almond ice-cream melting around it.

Hours High tea daily 10am–4pm; Lunch daily 11.30am–3.30pm; Dinner daily 5pm–late

Bill E $12–$23 **M** $19–$35 **D** $9–$15; 2-course lunch $22.50 pp; 7-course degustation $82.50 pp; 10% surcharge on public holidays

Cards AE DC V MC Eftpos

Wine Solid Australian list; 23 by the glass

Chef Alexander Hau

Owners Peter & Karlene Dimbrowsky

Seats 160; private rooms; wheelchair access; outdoor seating

Child friendly Fantastic kids' meals for $9.90; highchairs

www.eurolounge.com.au

And...enclosed outdoor dining section

Fare Nosh

117 Smith Street, Summer Hill
Tel 9716 6300   Map 8

Contemporary

Score 13/20

Let's hear it for a neighbourhood stayer where it's easy to park, you can BYO if you please and you're greeted like a friend. The room is long and narrow with dark-stained floorboards and matching sturdy tables, and appealing art on the walls. Bread is house-baked in crisp yet soft-centred baby loaves, and favourites stay on the menu, such as the ever-popular seafood antipasto. Others feature as specials – nicely handled john dory fillets with rocket pesto, for example, encased in crisp filo pastry and finished with hollandaise. An entree of plump scallops, marinated in mirin, then pan-seared to perfection, served with Japanese seaweed and wasabi mayonnaise, is hauntingly beautiful. Meat dishes were less distinguished, such as a deboned quail with a nondescript stuffing, strewn on kumera slices with a strongly orange and somewhat thick Grand Marnier "jus". But a fluffy cheesecake souffle with ice-cream and mixed berries will win you back.

Hours Dinner Tues–Sat 6–10pm

Bill E $18.50–$19.50 **M** $24–$32.50 **D** $12–$24

Cards AE V MC

Wine Concise well-priced interesting list with a few French offerings; 5 by the glass; BYO (corkage $3 pp)

Chef/owner Peter Meijer

Seats 34; wheelchair access

And...the Piglet's plate, a dessert extravaganza, remains by popular demand

Fiorenzoni

Shop 1, 809 Pacific Highway, Chatswood
Tel 9419 6411   Map 7

Italian (Central)

Score 13.5/20

Plain black and white decor sets the scene for the simple flavours of this Italian local. The menu may be a touch confusing for Italophiles, with antipasti called entrees and primi piatti (usually first courses of pasta and risotto) offered as main-sized servings. But once you crack the code, the kitchen's excellent fresh produce sings for itself. Chargrilled squid is tender yet crisp and smoky on the edges, tossed through a jumble of salad with a good hit of chilli. Bresaola (cured beef) is fanned in wafer-thin slices with shavings of good pecorino and slivers of pears. House-made gnocchi with gorgonzola and walnuts have good texture, and four milk-fed Flinders Island lamb cutlets are superbly succulent; the accompanying "cake" of smooth polenta topped with a very smoky slice of provolone. Service is cheerful, if occasionally forgetful. A shared dessert platter combines highs and lows. Opt for the good panna cotta, mini creme brulee and an excellent white chocolate and macadamia semifreddo.

Hours Lunch Mon–Fri noon–2.30pm; Dinner Mon–Sat 6–9.30pm

Bill E $14.90–$19.50 **M** $25.90–$34.90 **D** $14.90

Cards AE DC V MC Eftpos

Wine Short, well-priced list, with only a few Italians; 8 by the glass; BYO tables of 6 or under only (corkage $8 per bottle)

Chefs Mario Nogarotto, Anita Nogarotto & Andrea Rossi

Owner Mario Nogarotto

Seats 50; wheelchair access; outdoor seating

www.fiorenzoni.com.au

And...try the Italian cheeses

Fish Face

132 Darlinghurst Road, Darlinghurst
Tel 9332 4803   Map 2

Seafood

Score 15/20

Packed to its high-stool tables and window benches by customers who will queue for the freshest, most carefully handled seafood around, Fish Face is a study in contrasts. The food on the plate is the essence of calm and simplicity while the energy of this tiny restaurant is nothing short of frenetic. Front-of-house, on the other hand, is as smooth as ever, with appropriate wine advice and enthusiasm. The appetite is sharpened by silky butternut pumpkin soup, spiked with chilli, ginger and coriander root with a prawn on top. Start a seasonal special of Arctic char from the thinner end, as it will continue to cook at the other – the crisp-skinned fish is moist to the last bite, balanced by a touch of acidity and sweet, crushed peas. Prawns are perfectly steamed in their shell to capture their delicate flavour, and salads are clean and uncluttered. Passionfruit souffle is an ethereal masterpiece, finished with passionfruit sauce and ice-cream.

Hours Dinner Mon–Sat 6–10pm, Sun 6–9pm

Bill E $16.50–$19.50 **M** $28.50–$34.50 **D** $15; 5% surcharge on Sundays & public holidays

Cards AE V MC

Wine Concise, well-considered list with some well-priced gems; 19 by the glass

Chefs Stephen Hodges, Zachary Sykes, Aidan Wood, Michiaki Miyazaki & Prihandini Hassan

Owner Stephen Hodges

Seats 34; outdoor seating

www.fishface.com.au

And...try for one of three outside tables or sit at the sushi bar

Fisherman's Wharf

NEW

1st Floor, Sydney Fish Market,
Bank Street, Pyrmont
Tel 9660 9888   Map 5b

Chinese

Score 12.5/20

You'd expect the seafood to be fresh at this huge, plush, understated Cantonese diner above the Fish Markets. And fresh it is: straight from the futuristic, glowing turquoise seafood tanks. Crabs, molluscs, a wide range of fish and even eels can be wickedly deep-fried in a light tempura batter with chilli and pepper. Just make sure you know how much you're paying beforehand or it could be a shock. Large TVs screening sport can distract from working waterside views to the Anzac Bridge, while the chatty and good-natured service needs the occasional prod if you're keen for adventure. The expansive (130 dishes) menu's exotica includes an earthy, aniseed-flavoured hot pot of braised whelk, dried sea cucumber and duck feet. Drunken prawns (drowned in rice wine before being poached at the table) are divine, but a cornflour-thick sauce dulled pippies stir-fried Chiu Chow-style. Our fortune cookies say we'll return.

Hours Lunch Mon–Fri 11am–3pm, Sat–Sun 10am–3pm; Dinner daily 6–11pm

Bill E $5.50–$17.80 **M** $16.80–$98 **D** $6–$9.50; $3 pp surcharge on public holidays ($1 for children)

Cards AE V MC Eftpos

Wine Reasonable, commercial range of popular brands; 6 by the glass; BYO (corkage $4 pp)

Chef Allen Lai

Owner Jim Luu

Seats 380; private rooms; wheelchair access; outdoor seating

Vegetarian banquet

And...two entrances – via Pyrmont Bridge Road or through the Fish Market

Fix St James

111 Elizabeth Street, Sydney
Tel 9232 2767   Map 1

Mediterranean

Score 14/20

This smart diner, just up from DJs and opposite Hyde Park, is a welcome haven in a gastronomically starved end of town. Suited corporate types drop in for dinner between deals, mixing with city-dwelling couples and hungry shoppers drawn by Fix's reliable and flexible menu. Dishes are ordered in three sizes, so you can savour a small taste of the richly satisfying duck ragu on hand-cut pappardelle then follow it with a pared-down slice of Berkshire pork belly, beautifully cooked and presented on a bed of smashed Jerusalem artichoke. Likewise, you needn't miss seasonal highlights such as a classic trio of plump figs, serrano ham and buffalo mozzarella. And you can have your cake, too: a darkly decadent tiramisu was heavy on chocolate and coffee but not on the stomach. Owner/sommelier Stuart Knox, formerly of Bibendum in London and Forty One, offers intelligent wine matches for each dish, and diners are welcome to design their own degustation menu.

Hours Lunch Mon noon–3pm, Tues–Fri noon–5pm; Dinner Tues–Wed 5–9pm, Thurs–Sat 5–10pm

Bill E $10–$28 **M** $22–$36 **D** $8–$14; 4 piccolo plates $49 pp

Cards AE DC V MC Eftpos

Wine A savvy, well-priced selection of Australasian and European labels; 30 by the glass

Chef Kristin McGuirk

Owner Stuart Knox

Seats 80; outdoor seating

Vegetarian Several options

www.fixstjames.com.au

And...the front half morphs into a lively bar in the evenings, offering bar snacks and tapas

aniel from Pony Lounge and Dining

The Rocks

A STORY AROUND EVERY CORNER

40 RESTAURANTS, 11 PUBS, 12 BARS EAT HAPPILY EVER AFTER

Experience the culinary creations of some of Sydney's best chefs in the winding streets of The Rocks. With fine food, fine wine, fine company and eight Chef's Hats, there's something to entice every palate in The Rocks.

THEROCKS.COM

bour Foreshore Authority

Flavour of India

120–128 New South Head Road, Edgecliff
Tel 9326 2659   Map 4a

Indian
                                        Score 13/20

There is something a little Raj dining hall about this chandeliered, wood-ceilinged, split-level dining space and its entrance sculpture of whitened figures in solar topees and Bombay bloomers. But the food takes a big step forward into the contemporary South Asian milieu, tweaking here, creating there. It's not always fully realised – okra nuggets are nutty with raw peanuts but could have done with a tad more okra. On the other hand, shredded crab with chilli, lime and spices served in tissue-paper-thin potato skin comes together well. Pumpkin curry is a welcome addition to the usual range of vegetables, here in a dhal, tomato and ginger gravy and with an unexpected smokiness that nicely balances the sweetness. A green fish curry is more traditional, with firm chunks of white fish complemented by a coconut and coriander gravy. A dessert of mango kulfi returns the meal to the modern with a frill of fresh mango and strawberry syrups.

Hours Lunch Fri noon–3pm; Dinner daily 6–11pm

Bill E $8.50–$15.50 **M** $14.50–$24 **D** 9.50–$10.50

Cards AE DC V MC

Wine A limited range but complementary to the cuisine; 9 by the glass; BYO (corkage $5 per bottle)

Chef Hayat Mahamood

Owner Lola Crossingham

Seats 100

Child friendly Highchairs; pencils

Vegetarian A good creative range

www.flavourofindiaedgecliff.com.au

And...service is warmly welcoming and unobtrusive

Flavours of Peking

Shop 7, 100 Edinburgh Road, Castlecrag
Tel 9958 3288   Map 7

Chinese (Northern)
                                        Score 14/20

Going Chinese used to mean Cantonese. Then came the 1990s and a new wave of Chinese immigrants, bringing the food of Beijing and Shanghai. And so we learned about pot-stickers and wheat-flour dumplings, shredded "Peking" beef and shallot pancakes. Between large Chinese groups and non-Chinese couples and families, most nights this large, plain room at the back of a shopping mall is as full-to-bursting as the house specialty, north Chinese dumplings. The "Peking pastries" menu lists a variety of forms – from crisp-bottomed fried to pale, sticky, utterly meaty, steamed versions. Most Chinese groups order Peking duck, a two-course excursion into moist meat, lacquered skin, tissue-fine pancakes and great house hoisin, followed by a noodle or sang choy bow second course. An equally theatrical alternative is aromatic Sichuan-style half duck, gently five-spiced, and forked off the bone at your table. Hold out for a fruit platter at the end, unless you love fortune cookies, and be glad going Chinese has become so interesting.

Hours Lunch daily noon–3pm; Dinner Sun–Thurs 5.30–10pm, Fri–Sat 5.30–11.30pm; bookings essential

Bill E $7.80–$16.80 **M** $17.80–$50.80 **D** $6.50–$11.80; $2.50 pp surcharge on public holidays

Cards AE DC V MC

Wine Reasonable choice; 2 by the glass; BYO (corkage $2.50 pp)

Chef/owner Zhi Feng Chen

Seats 190; private room

Child friendly Absolutely, families galore; highchairs

Vegetarian Many dishes

And...park in the centre's carpark directly below

Flying Fish

Jones Bay Wharf, 19–21 Pirrama Road, Pyrmont
Tel 9518 6677   Map 5b

Seafood

Score 15.5/20

Is this Sydney's sexiest dining room? Few others match the good looks of this converted wharf's heavy beams and earthy timbers, its inner harbour views, moody waterside bar and soft lighting which sparkles like the Milky Way. Enjoy mostly polished service as you watch the action at the raw bar, where the loveliest oysters are opened to order. Peter Kuruvita's vibrant, exotic flavours, include a bold pairing of seared yellowfin tuna with roast pork and crackling, lifted by ruby grapefruit. His heritage comes through in the lush Sri Lankan king prawn curry with basmati rice, eggplant brinjal and green mango pickle, while lovers of terrestrial protein are remembered with mushroom-crusted wagyu sirloin with cepes gnocchi and garlic puree. And if the warm chocolate ganache with Pedro Ximenez ice-cream, prunes and roasted hazelnuts doesn't get your heart beating faster, best check for a pulse.

Hours Lunch Tues–Fri noon–2.30pm, Sun noon–3.30pm; Dinner Tues–Sat 6–10.30pm, Sun 6–9.30pm; bookings essential

Bill E $30–$36 **M** $44–$49 **D** $12–$32; 8% surcharge on public holidays

Cards AE DC V MC

Wine Impressive global range of benchmark wines; 16 by the glass

Chefs Peter Kuruvita & Jodie Wallace

Owners Peter Kuruvita & Con Dedes

Seats 199; private rooms; wheelchair access; outdoor seating (for bar food & dessert)

Child friendly Colouring-in; highchairs; kids' menu

Vegetarian Vegan degustation menu

www.flyingfish.com.au

And...raw bar menu for nibbles in the bar

Fook Yuen

Level 1, 7 Help Street, Chatswood
Tel 9413 2688   Map 7

Chinese

Score 12/20

Perched on a corner overlooking the forlorn remodelling of Chatswood town centre, this family favourite continues to pull in the yum cha crowds for lunch, and extended family and friends for dinner – retaining its reputation for simple, honed seafood specials. The decor is cookie-cutter Cantonese (perhaps a little tired), brought shudderingly into the 21st century with enormous plasma screens scrolling the day's specials. The Fookie is all about seafood: hotpots of mud crab with cellophane noodles, lobster and pippies stir-fried or steamed, prawns or squid in a classic salt-and-pepper batter, or barramundi, morwong and parrot fish brought flapping to the table and returned somewhat more sedate, steamed with ginger and shallot. There are some decent landlubber dishes, too, including crisp-of-skin and moist-of-flesh Peking duck and Shandong chicken. Service, and an over-abundance of deep-fried and battered fare, can disappoint the unsuspecting gweilo. But if unsure about what to order from the enormous menu, look around and copy the locals.

Hours Lunch Mon–Fri 10.30am–3pm, Sat–Sun 10am–3pm; Dinner daily 6–11pm

Bill E $14–$18 **M** $18–$38 **D** $5.80–$6.80; $2.50 pp surcharge on public holidays

Cards AE DC V MC

Wine Reasonably priced, predictable list including some Chinese rice wines; 2 by the glass

Chef Kai Chiu Leung

Owner ALLFX Pty Ltd

Seats 320; private rooms

Child friendly Highchairs

Vegetarian Good variety of dishes

And...very busy, so double-check your booking

Forbes & Burton

252 Forbes Street (cnr Burton Street),
Darlinghurst
Tel 9356 8788   Map 2

Contemporary

Score 13.5/20

By day, the massive sandstone-walled rooms
are packed with breakfast queues and the
school mothers' crowd at pavement tables.
By night though, cafe casual re-emerges as
bistro basic dining, with a plain, single-sheet
menu and paper-topped tables. Happily, other
trappings are more festive – flickering candle
lamps throwing light on ruby red ceiling
beams. Competent waiters bring entrees of
brandade soup – cream-laden salt cod bisque
boosted by gloriously sea-sweet, crunchy
oyster beignets. A "terrine" of chilled leek
with hazelnut and exotic mushrooms was less
enticing, as were thick white-cooked poussin
slices served with nuggety truffle dumplings.
Barramundi is beautiful in a gently flavoured
shellfish "essence" (more like a broth),
deshelled black mussels tucked underneath.
Buttermilk panna cotta is a faintly tangy foil
for a firm but juicy poached pear. It's not
the fine diner of yesteryear, although prices
remain lofty, but as a reliable local by day or
night, F&B continues to deliver.

Hours Breakfast & lunch Mon–Fri 7am–2.30pm,
Sat 8am–2.30pm, Sun 9am–3pm; Dinner Tues–Sat
6.30–10pm

Bill E $17–$19 **M** $28–$33 **D** $15;
10% surcharge on Sundays & public holidays

Cards AE DC V MC Eftpos

Wine A neat little list with some enticing
Australian and international labels; 13 by the glass

Chef Dave Pegrum

Owner Brendan Mahony

Seats 68; wheelchair access; outdoor seating

Child friendly Toy box by day

And...F&B's fabulous breakfasts are legendary

Forty One

Level 42, Chifley Tower, 2 Chifley Square,
Sydney
Tel 9221 2500   Map 1

French

Score 16/20

Dietmar Sawyere has taken diners to dizzying
heights for a long time, and we don't just
mean the location. A quaint oriental garden
designed by Japanese landscaper Ken Lamb
leads into a 42nd-floor room decorated with
myrtlewood panelling and deep blue Thai
silk. Eastern views of the Botanic Gardens
and harbour leave you breathless. Enthusiastic
waiters are occasionally raw and don't quite
match the precision and passion embodied in
the master chef's menu – a DIY degustation,
choosing between four dishes in each of four,
five or six courses, depending on your bank
balance and stomach. Citrus-cured ocean
trout with spiced avocado works well enough
but succulent balsamic grilled figs with buffalo
mozzarella are spot-on. Squab (pigeon) breast
is absolutely gorgeous – moist, rich and
perfectly balanced with truffled arancini and
spinach puree – and a crown roast of wild
hare is as stunning in its aesthetics as it is on
the palate. A delicate lemon tart with basil
sorbet rounds off a pleasant evening.

Hours Lunch Tues–Fri noon–2.30pm; Dinner
Mon–Sat from 6pm; bookings essential

Bill Lunch 2 courses $65 pp, 3 courses $80,
4 courses $90; Dinner 4 courses $130 pp,
5 courses $140, 6 courses $150

Cards AE DC V MC

Wine Global marques in this list guaranteed
to please any wine lover; 10 by the glass

Chefs Dietmar Sawyere & Rainer Korobacz

Owner Dietmar Sawyere

Seats 120; private rooms; wheelchair access

Vegetarian Excellent options in each section

www.forty-one.com.au

And...a loo with a view

Four In Hand Dining Room

105 Sutherland Street (cnr Elizabeth Street), Paddington
Tel 9362 1999   Map 4b

French

Score 15/20

The giant squid's eye of a massive Luke Sciberras watercolour dominates the interior of this small, smart-looking bistro, while a pig's ear – crisped and served with confit neck, calvados apples and hazelnut vinaigrette – gets most of the attention on the menu. It's a beguiling entree, befitting a restaurant that raised the bar for Sydney pub dining and now hums along under Colin Fassnidge (whose CV mentions Raymond Blanc and Gordon Ramsay). Seasonality and good produce drive another entree of wagyu carpaccio with fig and zucchini flowers, while seafood reigns supreme in mains that pair perfectly cooked marlin with oxtail-stuffed baby squid; and jewfish with white anchovies, green olive puree and more of those zucchini flowers. The usually busy floor – it's loud – keeps things moving along at a good pace. Before you know it, you're faced with a dilemma: the excellent cheese board or a spectacular, herb-flecked panna cotta with strawberries and basil granita. Go on, have both.

Hours Lunch Tues–Sun noon–2.30pm; Dinner daily 6.30–10pm; bookings essential

Bill E $22 **M** $32 **D** $16; 5-course menu $70 pp, 8 courses $90 pp

Cards AE DC V MC

Wine Wide-ranging list free of usual suspects; 22 by the glass; BYO (corkage $15 per bottle)

Chef Colin Fassnidge

Owners Joe Saleh & Paul Bard

Seats 50; private rooms

Child friendly Highchair; kids' menu; book for prams

www.fourinhand.com.au

And...a lovely private dining room upstairs

Foveaux Restaurant + Bar

65–67 Foveaux Street, Surry Hills
Tel 9211 0664   Map 3b

Modern European

Score 15/20

The narrow dining room is all vintage sandstone, restrained lighting and subdued chatter but there's nothing last century about chef Darrell Felstead's cooking. With savoury ice-creams and curried fruit salad on the menu, it's one of few Sydney venues to grapple fearlessly with contemporary cooking techniques and styles. It's probably not for the culinary faint-hearted but diners willing to brave "nachos" – sour-cream ice-cream, heritage tomato and turtle bean salsa, avocado puree and a corn dip – the rewards are considerable. Ceviche of kingfish, crab ice-cream and a baby herb salad is much more palate pleasing, as is blue-eye with smoked eggplant puree, kumato (Black Russian tomato) and zucchini vierge, red capsicum paint and black olive jelly. Then there's a divinely rich coffee-braised beef brisket with "milk air", cauliflower and sauteed baby squid. For more fabulously fun food partners, try icy chocolate rocks with peanut mousse, raspberry jelly and a salted peanut biscuit. Pushing boundaries is Foveaux's raison d'etre. And we're thrilled.

Hours Lunch Fri noon–3pm; Dinner Tues–Sat 6pm–late; bookings essential

Bill E $22 **M** $34 **D** $15; 5-course menu $70 pp

Cards AE DC V MC Eftpos

Wine A stellar list to reflect the exciting menu; 14 by the glass

Chef/owner Darrell Felstead

Seats 46; wheelchair access

www.foveaux.com.au

And...cocktails in the basement bar are a must

Fratelli Paradiso

12–16 Challis Avenue, Potts Point
Tel 9357 1744   Map 2

Italian   ☿

Score 13.5/20

At this casual but oh-so-cool eatery, "ciao bella" is far more likely to be accompanied by an air-kiss than an old-school Italian cheek-pinch. Good quality, modern Italian fare is the order of the day (and most nights, except, surprisingly, Saturday). One-word descriptions are writ large on the blackboard – risotto, carpaccio, lasagne and more – with elaborations delivered by sometimes harried staff. Lightly battered calamari (a perennial favourite) is tender, with a perfect twist of lemon. Tangy tuna carpaccio also impresses; dotted with tiny, diced tomato, it'll be gone in a flash. A rustic pork ragu adds lovely texture and flavour to soft pillows of gnocchi, while dessert may include apple strucolo (strudel) studded with pine nuts and juicy sultanas. It's a nice finale, accompanied by a fine espresso of course, and a good excuse for keeping the next lot of dedicated Fratelli fans waiting for their table. For an encore, or alternative, dine in or take away from the adjoining pasticceria.

Hours Mon–Fri 7am–11pm, Sat–Sun 7am–5pm; no bookings

Bill E $19–$23 **M** $23–$30 **D** $12–$14; 10% surcharge on public holidays

Cards AE DC V MC

Wine Great, appealing Italians, plus some locals; 14 by the glass

Chefs Teofilo Nobrega & Toshiyuki Nakayasu

Owners Enrico & Giovanni Paradiso & Marco Ambrosino

Seats 64; private room; wheelchair access; outdoor seating

And...browse at the great bookshops nearby

Fu Manchu

249 Victoria Street, Darlinghurst
Tel 9360 9424   Map 2

Chinese (South-East Asian)

Score 12.5/20

Malaysian-born Annie Lee is back in charge, and, thankfully, this skinny, inner-city haunt, slick with sparse metal surfaces and hard red lacquer stools, is back on track. Service is beyond obliging – waiters treat you as a long-lost friend, genuinely concerned about your enjoyment and eager to make recommendations. They are right about the duck wraps – a fun DIY entree of warm mandarin pancakes to fill with juicy fowl and plum sauce. Opulent steamed gow gees, popping with flavour, are a fine starter, too. Chilli salt-and-pepper pumpkin and eggplant is juicy and crisp. A special of fresh bean curd, baby scallops and Chinese mushrooms is soft and gently flavoured. Ocean trout with soy, ginger and shallots sits in a light, fragrant broth for a richer take on steamed white fish. Fu Manchu is a health nut's dream, offering brown rice as an accompaniment and non-meat chow mein. You'll leave smiling, and not just from the cheery farewell and complimentary Chinese milk sweets.

Hours Lunch Mon–Fri noon–3pm; Dinner daily 5.30–10.30pm; bookings essential

Bill E $5–$18 **M** $8–$20 **D** $5; 10% surcharge on public holidays

Cards AE V MC Eftpos

Wine 4 organic wines plus Asian beers; 2 by the glass; BYO wine only (corkage $2 pp)

Chefs Tony Huang & Annie Lee

Owner Annie Lee

Seats 40; private room; outdoor seating

Child friendly Kids' menu

Vegetarian Excellent and unusual options

www.fumanchu.com.au

And...10% takeaway discount if you bring your own containers

Cooking, like life itself, depends on water as a key ingredient.

"I passionately source every product to serve the best food; FIJI Water is an essential part of a unique dining experience."

Serge Dansereau –
THE BATHERS' PAVILION

In the great kitchens of the world, it all begins with water. In this case, FIJI Water, because top executive chefs are using it as one of their starting ingredients. From an unspoiled ecosystem and a naturally protected aquifer, it has a smooth taste that is unparalleled. And as any chef will tell you, great dishes start with the best ingredients.

NATURAL ARTESIAN WATER

Galileo

The Observatory Hotel, 89–113 Kent Street,
Millers Point
Tel 9256 2215   Map 1

French/Japanese

Unscored

Heavy mahogany chairs, crystal chandeliers,
brocade curtains, and restrained service
exude old-world charm at this boutique hotel
restaurant. But after five years of wowing
diners, chef Haru Inukai has hung up his
toque. The good news is that his successor,
young gun Masahiko Yomoda, looks set
to maintain the French–Japanese tradition,
having worked with Haru-san at Tony Bilson's
ephemeral Ampersand, as well as sharing his
colleague's Robuchon training. Masahiko-
san heads to this elegant and opulent
dining room from his own Michelin-starred
restaurant in Tokyo. With a bit of luck, the
amuse bouche might be similar to chef
Haru's signature egg cocotte with an airy
ginger foam. We also hope he creates other
new dishes to match the venison terrine with
a subtly sweet red wine jelly and ethereal
cream sauce, and pan-seared john dory
paired aptly with light vongole jus, but for
now, we must leave Galileo unscored.

Hours Breakfast Mon–Fri 6.30–10.30am,
Sat–Sun 6.30–11am; Dinner daily 6.30–10.30pm

Bill 2-course menu $78 pp, 3 courses $98 pp;
7-course degustation $120 pp, 9 courses $165 pp

Cards AE DC V MC Eftpos

Wine Substantial list of global wines; 22 by the
glass (150ml and 70ml sizes available)

Chef Masahiko Yomoda

Owner Orient-Express Hotels, Trains & Cruises

Seats 65; private rooms; wheelchair access

Child friendly Kids' menu; highchairs

Vegetarian Options on a la carte menu;
vegetarian degustation available

www.observatoryhotel.com.au

And...live music in the Globe Bar Fri–Sat

Garfish

1/39 East Esplanade, Manly
Tel 9977 0707   Map 7
Also at 2/21 Broughton Street, Kirribilli
Tel 9922 4322   Map 5a
Also at 6/29 Holtermann Street, Crows Nest
Tel 9966 0445   Map 5a

Seafood

Score 13/20

Flickering bamboo torches lend a touch
of *Survivor*-like excitement to this buzzy
wood-and-glass eatery. Full-length windows
open to Manly Wharf across the road,
as the briny sea breeze drifts in. Garfish
is crowded as everyone chows down on
seafood of all descriptions. The pick-your-
own blackboard features the day's fresh
catch, cooked as you choose and teamed
with one of several salads. The main menu
includes an aromatic kingfish curry, zingy
salt-and-pepper squid, creamy snapper pie
and good old beer-battered fish and chips.
Spanner crab tagliolini staggers under an
enthusiastic weight of garlic and chilli, but
oven-roasted ocean trout is firm and sweet,
a lovely contrast to nutty chickpea salad.
Steak and spatchcock options, along with a
lush flourless chocolate cake and gallantly
cheerful, accommodating staff, ensure that
even the grumpiest carnivore leaves happy.

Hours Breakfast daily 7.30–11am; Lunch daily
noon–3pm; Dinner daily 5.30–10pm

Bill E $16–$20 **M** $24–$32 **D** $10–$12;
5% surcharge on Sundays, 10% on public holidays

Cards AE DC V MC

Wine Good antipodean list at reasonable prices;
20 by the glass; BYO (corkage $3.30 pp)

Chefs Stewart Wallace & Michael Nash

Owners Mark Dickey & Mark Scanlan

Seats 140; private room; wheelchair access

Child friendly Kids' menu; booster seats;
drawing placemats

www.garfish.com.au

And...a nice range of pre-dinner cocktails

glass brasserie

Level 2, Hilton Sydney, 488 George Street, Sydney
Tel 9265 6068   Map 1

French Brasserie

Score 14.5/20

Start with a drink beneath the adjoining bar's soaring jarrah wine towers with views of the Queen Victoria Building through floor-to-ceiling glass windows. It's a very Sydney outlook, and Luke Mangan's local take on the French brasserie sits comfortably within the surroundings, whether in sashimi of scallops made pretty with sprinklings of confit potato, avruga roe and nasturtium petals; artisan charcuterie; or chicken-liver paté teamed with fennel and raisin toast. Mains are either from the sea or off the grill, and when the menu keeps it as simple, it mostly succeeds. Macleay Valley rabbit features the rack, double loin and a flavoursome confit leg. A 500-gram T-bone of Nolan 110-day grain-fed Charolais – a French breed, natch – is cooked as ordered, but otherwise-efficient floor staff may have trouble locating mustard when asked. Still, this is a stylish and comfortable space that invites lingering. The kitchen's stocks rise again thanks to a classic raspberry soufflé with raspberry ice-cream and chocolate sauce.

Hours Lunch Mon–Fri noon–3pm; Dinner daily 6pm–late; bookings recommended

Bill E $17.50–$24.50 **M** $29.50–$39.50 **D** $15.50–$19.50; 10% surcharge on Sundays & public holidays

Cards AE DC V MC

Wine A wide-ranging list of new- and old-world marques; 30 by the glass

Chefs Luke Mangan & Joe Pavlovich

Owners Luke Mangan & Hilton Hotels

Seats 200; private rooms; wheelchair access

Child friendly Kids' menu; highchairs; colouring in

www.glassbrasserie.com.au

And...don't be surprised if Luke Mangan pops by

Glebe Point Diner

407 Glebe Point Road, Glebe
Tel 9660 2646   Map 5b

Contemporary

Score 15/20

The bistro/brasserie of yesteryear has been reborn as the diner. And whatever the epithet, we love eating like this. Right down the bay end of Glebe, GPD is the sum of careful casualness, fashionable functionality and cleverly comforting food, pulling customers in droves and handling it just fine. From folded printouts to great big blackboard menus, heaps of local wines and well-cooked, three-food-groups-on-a-plate meals, this is a happy place to hang. School prawns with real aioli are as saltily irresistible as a bowl of fries, while a ripe green fig, sweetly shaved fennel and nutty parmesan salad is balanced just so. Quivering-fresh barra with vongole and peas, or crackling-edged piglet with savoy cabbage and lentils are gloriously complete. And as for the amazing honey-rosemary panna cotta and real berry ice-cream and jelly... From the focused but friendly crew in the open kitchen corner to the easy, alert service, we really do love eating like this.

Hours Lunch Fri–Sun noon–3pm; Dinner Wed–Sat 6–9pm; bookings essential

Bill E $16–$18 **M** $24–$30 **D** $10–$14

Cards V MC

Wine Great, low-mark-up list, lots of NSW; 14 by the glass or half-bottle; BYO (corkage $15 per bottle)

Chef Alex Kearns

Owners Charles Plumridge & Steven Tracy

Seats 45; wheelchair access; outdoor seating

Child friendly Crayons

And...given the evening throng, lunch is a fine time to visit

Golden Century

393–399 Sussex Street, Sydney
Tel 9212 3901   Map 3a

Chinese (Cantonese)   ♉
                                Score 14.5/20

It has the most live fish tanks, the longest lines of hungry diners and the highest decibel level in Chinatown. Golden Century has long wowed lovers of pure Cantonese food. The main menu has been simplified, daily specials are clearly translated and the wine list has grown enormously. The food is better then ever but the service is still Cantonese brisk. Silky smooth baby spinach is served in superior broth, tasting of real chicken. Tender pork hock with pepper is a full blast of pure flavour. Sea cucumber braised with king mushrooms shows the contrast in tastes for which the Cantonese are famous. Steamed coral trout is perfect. The waiters may not plate the fish but it's easy to grab firm flakes falling from the bone. There's even a dish of baked Chinese biscuits to finish. Order wisely here and you will eat like an emperor. Our advice? Go in a group and balance your choices, including some specials and something from the tanks.

Hours Daily noon–4am

Bill E $6–$12 **M** $16–$32 **D** $2.50–$6;
10% surcharge on public holidays

Cards AE DC V MC Eftpos

Wine Large list; lots of rare wines and vintages, including a full page of prestige French, plus 4 pages of Chinese rice wines and spirits; 12 by the glass; BYO (corkage $5 pp)

Chef Lee Ho

Owners Eric Wong & Kevin Kam

Seats 600; private rooms

Child friendly Highchairs; booster seats

Vegetarian Big choice with a large separate menu

www.goldencentury.com.au

And...lunch is quieter, without yum cha crowds

Grand National

161 Underwood Street, Paddington
Tel 9363 4557   Map 4b

Contemporary   ♔ ♉
                                Score 15/20

Charming Paddo pub on the outside, inside this is a favourite food destination, thanks to the culinary skills of Ian Oakes. Add warm, accomplished service and it's easy to see why regulars lap it up. The room is casual sophistication at its best – white walls and dark furniture, crisp linen, a sparkling open kitchen and much contented chatter. The menu matches the mood: finely crafted favourites with an interesting spin. A cream of sweetcorn amuse bouche precedes a superb entree of marlin carpaccio, semi-dried tomato and baby basil. Tender, sliced Aylesbury duck on charcutiere (brown) sauce is flavour-filled and cleverly textured with celeriac remoulade. Although our Bangalow pork cutlet was a little dry, it's well-matched with chorizo, braised fennel and mustard dressing, plus a side of crisp green beans, fetta and lemon vinaigrette. To finish, lemon parfait has just the right bite, while the popular Eton mess is a classy, tidy tumble of strawberries, mascarpone and meringue.

Hours Lunch Fri–Sun noon–3pm; Dinner Tues–Sat 6–10.30pm, Sun 6–9pm; bookings essential

Bill E $16–$19 **M** $26–$34 **D** $14–$16

Cards AE DC V MC

Wine Impressive list of well-chosen local and European labels; 10 by the glass

Chef Ian Oakes

Owner Alexander Avramides

Seats 80

Child friendly Highchairs; kids' menu; crayons

And...invest in a taxi or plenty of patience; parking is difficult

Grappa

Shop 1, 267–277 Norton Street, Leichhardt
Tel 9560 6090   Map 5b

Italian

Score 13/20

This vast dining room has the monopoly at the northern end of Leichhardt's restaurant-heavy Norton Street. But a large room makes for a large noise – families and groups love it – so don't come expecting an opportunity for an intimate tete a tete. Not that Grappa can't be romantic. We lean in close to share a generous, flavour-driven entree of grilled wild pine mushrooms tumbling over a pile of gremolata, asparagus and reggiano. But we stick staunchly to our own sides of the table when the mains arrive. Veal risotto with porcini, pancetta and spinach is a standout we're not sharing. This matters not since a salacious smearing of mascarpone over the base of a pizza topped with San Daniele prosciutto, mozzarella, cherry tomatoes and rocket creates an original and memorable dish. We are reunited by dessert, grabbing two spoons to share creamy-rich homemade gelato.

Hours Lunch Tues–Fri & Sun noon–3pm; Dinner Tues–Sun 6–10pm

Bill E $16.50–$30 **M** $17–$39 **D** $10.50–$19

Cards AE DC V MC Eftpos

Wine Healthy selection of Italian reds and whites; 14 by the glass; BYO (corkage $4.50 pp)

Chefs Leo Mancini, Oscar Atriano & Wade Revell

Owners Charlie & Antonio Colosi

Seats 118; wheelchair access; outdoor seating

Child friendly Kids' menu; highchairs

Vegetarian Good options across the menu

www.grappa.com.au

And...a free underground car park is linked by a handy lift

Green Gourmet

538 Pacific Highway, St Leonards
Tel 9439 6533   Map 5a

Asian Vegan

Score 12/20

Basic, blond-wood furniture, a thriving potted bamboo garden and a servery counter give this mock-meat vegan restaurant a casual feel. Peking-not-duck is a hit – super-thin pancakes smeared with a smoky hoisin sauce topped with duck-tasting soy protein that even has the crunch of skin. Slivers of carrot replace the more usual green onions in this Taoist version, where members of the onion family are non grata. Crunchy-outside/ yielding-inside deep-fried bean curd skin with a not-too-cloying sweet-and-sour sauce also hits the spot. Monk's choice vegetable hotpot is hearty and filling, rich with greens, mushrooms and red dates, and salt-and-pepper tofu is hot and crisp with a great, just-set interior. Tofu "ice-cream" lacked the smoothness of its dairy counterpart, but a bright green sago pudding has the familiar sweet, creamy smoothness of good sago gula melaka (Malaysian pudding with palm sugar syrup). Waitstaff are attentive, if not always able to answer questions about the menu.

Hours Lunch Tues–Sat 11.30am–2.30pm; Dinner Tues–Thurs, Sun 5.30–9.30pm, Fri–Sat 5.30–10pm

Bill E $3.30–$12.80 **M** $12.80–$18.80 **D** $5.50–$8.80

Cards V MC

Wine No alcohol allowed but a great tea list

Chef Mr Ho

Owners Peter & Doris Wong

Seats 70; private room

Child friendly Highchairs

Vegetarian Vegan

And...banquet menus start at $19.80 per person and include a wheat-free option

Guillaume at Bennelong

Sydney Opera House, Bennelong Point, Sydney
Tel 9241 1999   Map 1

Contemporary/French

♔ ♔ ♡

Score 17/20

Enjoying the city's finest views, an iconic setting and a reputation for decadent French fine dining, chef Guillaume Brahimi could rest on his laurels, especially with a new Melbourne venture. But the mark of his talent is an ability to continue Bennelong's evolution; balancing modern appeal with traditional French opulence. Of course, the super-smooth Paris mash remains, alongside more recent classics such as a scampi turban – a precisely arranged headdress of pasta enclosing three perfectly poached crustaceans on a light caviar cream sauce. Brahimi's cooking has always boasted a passionate depth of flavour and superb craftsmanship, but it's pleasing to see greater balance and restraint return, even if we still cut loose over duck foie gras with a spectacular sauternes jelly. White River veal rib is paired with sweetbread croutons; Berkshire pork cutlet with crisp crackling celebrates fine produce. When the clarity of apple sorbet explodes in the mouth beside a vanilla creme brulee, it lifts tradition to new heights, while the service, despite the demands of theatre crowds, is a fine servant of two masters.

Hours Lunch Thurs–Fri noon–3pm; Dinner Mon–Sat 5.30pm–late; bookings essential

Bill E $30–$45 **M** $38 **D** $25–$35; 10% surcharge on public holidays

Cards AE DC V MC

Wine A superb Australian list of Australian wines, plus benchmark French drops; 19 by the glass

Chefs Guillaume Brahimi & Jose Silva

Owner Guillaume Brahimi

Seats 110; private rooms; wheelchair access

www.guillaumeatbennelong.com.au

And…the rolling cheese trolley is a French treat

harbourkitchen&bar

Park Hyatt Sydney, 7 Hickson Road, The Rocks
Tel 9256 1661   Map 1

Mediterranean

♡

Score 13.5/20

This magical waterfront setting certainly gives more fancied (and expensive) rivals competition. The Park Hyatt's revamped restaurant is an elegantly modern space of pale granite, gleaming blackbutt and glass walls that entices the sea air and a sparkling harbour panorama. Such spectacular surrounds invite high expectations, and chef Alessandro Pavoni's signature tuna tartare lives up to them: a small tower of succulent fresh fish paired with truffled dwarf peaches and intensely yolky, soft-boiled quail eggs. Unfortunately, service can oscillate between attentive and neglectful – at these prices, no one should have to pour their wine all meal, or be left stranded waiting to be seated. Thankfully, the food makes amends, including a creamily heady al dente risotto studded with glossy black marron halves, zucchini flowers and white tomato. A light tomato and olive crust on a tender plank of saltwater char is refreshingly balanced by a bright salad of radish, grapefruit and fennel. With retractable glass walls, this is a lovely spot to sit and gaze.

Hours Breakfast daily 6.30–10.30am; Lunch daily noon–2.30pm; Dinner Sun–Thurs 6–10pm, Fri–Sat 6–10.30pm

Bill E $18–$25 **M** $30–$46 **D** $15–$19; 2-course lunch $59 pp, 3 courses $69 pp; 10% surcharge on Sundays & public holidays

Cards AE DC V MC

Wine 17-page oenological omnibus; 17 by the glass

Chef Alessandro Pavoni

Owner Park Hyatt Sydney

Seats 150; private rooms; wheelchair access

Child friendly Kids' menu; highchairs; colouring in

Vegetarian Separate menus

www.harbourkitchen.com.au

And…ask about the valet parking deal

Southern Cross UNIVERSITY
A new way to think

THE HOTEL SCHOOL SYDNEY

A DEGREE A JOB A FUTURE

The Hotel School Sydney is a unique partnership between Southern Cross University and Mulpha Australia's hotel portfolio including InterContinental Sydney, Hayman Great Barrier Reef, Sanctuary Cove, Hyatt at Sanctuary Cove, Hilton Melbourne and Bimbadgen Estate Wines.

Our aim is to prepare well-rounded graduates for employment in hotel and tourism management positions in Australia and internationally. Candidates are selected on the basis of academic performance, achievements and an interview.

YEAR 1   Diploma - six months study and six months paid internship at one of our partner hotels

YEAR 2   Associate Degree

YEAR 3   Bachelor of Business

FEE-HELP SCHEME AVAILABLE

For further information please contact The Hotel School Sydney
117 Macquarie Street Sydney NSW Australia 2000
Phone 02 9240 1280 Fax 02 9240 1338 e-mail hotel@scu.edu.au
www.hotelschool.scu.edu.au

Hugo's Bar Pizza

33 Bayswater Road, Kings Cross
Tel 9332 1227   Map 2

Modern Italian

Score 13/20

The insanely long queues may be gone, but
the place is still buzzing with the it crowd.
The no-bookings policy doesn't deter people
from rocking up in big groups to take over
the marbled, enticingly lit bar before plonking
down on plush seats. Glamazons sip cocktails
while nibbling on the tasting plate entree
of well-spiced meatballs, crisp calamari,
unctuous garlic prawns, and serrano ham
with fig. Men in suits are happily silenced
by the wood-fired pizza, before heading up
to the adjacent Hugo's Lounge for serious
partying. The crust is thin but pliant, the
toppings new-wave yet appealing. Eggplant
pizza with smoked mozzarella and basil
goes down nicely, as does pork belly with
radicchio. Gnocchi with flaked snapper
is a standout, along with tagliatelle alla
carbonara with slow-cooked confit egg.
Mango and zabaglione pizza with airy vanilla
gelato is a fun dessert to wrap up – unless,
of course, another round of cocktails is next.

Hours Dinner Mon–Wed 6pm–midnight, Thurs–
Sat 6pm–1am, Sun 3pm–midnight; bookings
for more than 8 people only

Bill E $18–$24 **M** $25–$28 **D** $10–$14;
10% surcharge on Sundays & public holidays

Cards AE DC V MC

Wine Solid list of Italian and local wines;
15 by the glass

Chefs Peter Evans & Leandro Panza

Owners Peter & David Evans and David Corsi

Seats 75; outdoor seating

Vegetarian Various pizzas and pastas

www.hugos.com.au

And...outside seating for people-watching
later in the night

Icebergs Dining Room and Bar

1 Notts Avenue, Bondi Beach
Tel 9365 9000   Map 9

Italian

Score 17/20

Sure, you can come here for the view. But
who would overlook Robert Marchetti's
joyous cooking, with dishes that soar
through delicate whispers to triumphant,
full-blooded roars? From a beguiling fresh
fig salad to salt-crusted baby lamb and
500 grams of crusted poetry-in-pink from
the steak menu, these are instant Sydney
benchmarks. Flavours meld gloriously in a
tangle of sweet, deftly seasoned crabmeat in
a puddle of soft polenta so fine it's almost a
puree. Truffled Tuscan dwarf peaches impart
earthen, tangy tones to a silken, glistening
patty of chopped tuna tartare. Desserts
excite: a buffalo milk panna cotta doused
with warm milk chocolate sauce is sublime
in texture. The atmosphere is unpretentious
yet sexy, portions are generous and service
is friendly and highly professional. The long,
narrow room of soothing aqua tones gives
everyone a view from the comfortable wicker
armchairs. Once you're sated, one of the
world's greatest ocean panoramas makes
a fine digestif.

Hours Lunch Tues–Sun from noon; Dinner
Tues–Sun from 6.30pm; bookings essential

Bill E $22–$28 **M** $36–$54 **D** $16–$20;
10% surcharge on Sundays & public holidays

Cards AE DC V MC Eftpos

Wine New and old world with the variety, brio
and gusto of the food; 22 by the glass

Chefs Robert Marchetti, Ben Horne &
Damien McCleery

Owners Robert Marchetti, Maurice Terzini,
Kimme Shaw & Tony Zaccagnini

Seats 105; wheelchair access

www.idrb.com

And...parking can be iffy; try valet parking, $30

il baretto

496 Bourke Street, Surry Hills
Tel 9361 6163   Map 3b

Italian

Score 12/20

Like moths to a light, at six o'clock, inner-city types flutter in, trying to snare a table at this much-loved local. If late, the faithful wait at the workers' pub across the road for a beer on tap and buy their BYO. This long, thin space stretches out the back to more intimate butcher's-paper-topped tables and metal chairs. And it's popular because the small and largely unchanged menu gets the simple things right. A selection of pasta includes spaghetti with juicy mushrooms enhanced by parsley, plus salty pancetta for a punchy counter balance. Beef carpaccio tasted a little tired, but parmesan and rocket on top adds a much-needed kick. It's hard to find good risotto, but not here. The rice retains a good consistency in a simple dish with pesto, parsley and slivers of chicken for added interest. Share a light, fluffy tiramisu, order a neat macchiato and everything's fine at this little bar.

Hours Lunch Tues–Sat noon–3pm; Dinner Mon–Sat 6–10pm; no dinner bookings

Bill E $6–$15 **M** $13–$25 **D** $3–$7

Cards None

Wine BYO (corkage $2 pp)

Chefs Tim Standing & Dirk Bischoff

Owners Gabriella Fedeli & Domenico Santopadre

Seats 40; outdoor seating

And…you can book for lunch

Il Perugino

171 Avenue Road, Mosman
Tel 9969 9756   Map 7

Italian

Score 14/20

This much-loved Mosman trattoria has dished up authentic Italian fare for more than two decades. The menu, recited in Italian, then explained in English, is still an integral part of the theatre and guarantees to have you drooling in anticipation. It's all buzz in the bright, compact room with engaging, attentive service and tables cheek by jowl. Quality produce is highlighted in the popular antipasto platter and a heavenly pile of fresh figs, buffalo mozzarella and prosciutto with a splash of virgin olive oil. There's plenty of seafood and pasta. Pappardelle teams superbly with fresh tomatoes, Italian pork sausage, sage and leek. To the delight of offal fans, pan-fried calf's liver, flavoured with leek and thyme, rests on robust port wine sauce. Slow-roasted pork belly, fragrant with lemon, garlic and rosemary, is topped with crisp crackling and deftly matched with baked red capsicum filled with spinach, ricotta, walnuts and mushrooms. Tiramisu to finish is too tempting to resist.

Hours Lunch Wed–Fri noon–2.30pm; Dinner Mon–Sat 6–10pm; bookings essential

Bill E $18.50–$19.50 **M** $27–$30 **D** $12

Cards V MC

Wine BYO (no corkage)

Chefs Melinda Hagan & Lesley Mencio

Owners Mencio-Hagan family

Seats 60; private rooms

And…take a bottle of your best: the food deserves it

il piave

639 Darling Street, Rozelle
Tel 9810 6204   Map 5b

Italian

Score 14.5/20

A chain of small and bigger rooms behind
a modern glass-framed shopfront, cherry-
stained floors and a fairy-lit, covered
courtyard enclose one of Sydney's most
notable Italian eateries. Only the less-than-
scenic open kitchen between the narrow
front and spacious back sections detracts
from the Martin siblings' ease at the stove
and on the floor. There's lots you'll want to
order: clever, seasonal antipasti, airily-soft
gnocchi (tossed with cream, asparagus,
broad beans and wilted spinach) or slippery,
silky ravioli discs filled with shredded duck
and ladled with sweetish veal jus. Gutsy
secondi can be a masterpiece in contrasts,
such as grilled quail on buttered fregola
(a giant toasted couscous) with zucchini
and cherry tomatoes, while a pot roast of
rosemary-scented lamb, bones and all, has
all the Sunday lunch comfort of northern
Italian home cooking. A shell of crackly
meringue around ricotta cream, lemon
curd and sorbet is tinged with the herbal
bitterness of lemon Campari syrup: the
pavlova reborn, with Italian ingenuity.

Hours Dinner Tues–Sat 6–10pm;
bookings essential

Bill E $18.90–$21.90 **M** $26.90–$34.90
D $13.90–$14.90

Cards AE V MC Eftpos

Wine Good Australian and Italian bottles; 8 by the
glass; BYO Tues–Thurs only (corkage $8 per bottle)

Chefs Vanessa Martin & Amber Diog

Owners Robert & Vanessa Martin

Seats 65; outdoor seating

Vegetarian Special vegetarian menu option

And...noise levels can be high but your bill won't
be, not for this quality at least

Il Punto

387 Hume Highway, Liverpool
Tel 9822 2005   Map 6

Italian

Score 13/20

Ensconced at Il Punto (the point) it's hard to
believe you're on arguably Sydney's busiest
stretch of bitumen. Affable waiters whisk
you into a comfortable, smart environment
of brown and beige as wonderful aromas
emanate from the pizza oven in the corner.
While the pizzaiolo tosses balls of dough
to order, chef Joe (Giuseppe) De Francesco
proves he's the man for the pans. While
portions are a little over-generous, his food
is simple and the combinations are superb.
A twice-cooked pork belly is rich, crisp-
skinned flesh nestled on a bed of rocket,
walnuts and mustard fruits. Fresh pappardelle
embraces slow-braised meatballs in a tomato
sauce that would make nonna proud.
Organic chicken served in a rotolo (rolled
and baked) rests on baby spinach lubricated
by warm pine nut butter. A splendid piece
of dry-aged beef rib-eye is decorated with
kipfler potato, although the olive tapenade
was administered a little heavy-handedly.
To end? Tiramisu, of course.

Hours Lunch Thurs–Fri noon–3pm; Dinner
Tues–Sun 6–10.30pm

Bill E $14–$18 **M** $15–$34 **D** $10.50–$12; pizza
$15–$24; 10% surcharge on public holidays

Cards AE DC V MC Eftpos

Wine Simple and very affordable; 6 by the glass;
BYO (corkage $3 pp)

Chef Giuseppe De Francesco

Owners Giuseppe & Alison De Francesco

Seats 76

Child friendly Kids' menu; highchairs;
pencils & paper

And...takeaway and home-delivery pizza
and pasta

Infusion@333

Mezzanine Level, 333 George Street, Sydney
Tel 9290 3333   Map 1

Modern Asian

Score 14/20

Swap pool cues for chopsticks upstairs in this contemporary city bar. Striking red laminated pillars stand tall along this oblong corner room, bound by full-length windows. Prawn crisps and crisp service await at tables covered in butcher's paper so city whizzes can divvy up the bill. On a well-balanced menu of Asian influences, juicy kingfish is wrapped in nori on a bed of julienned cucumber, splashed with a restrained rock sugar dressing sparked by minced ginger. Red curry of duck with Thai baby eggplants, lychees, baby tomatoes and corn is substantial, the sauce rich and manageably hot. Crisp battered king prawns crown a pad thai thicket of noodles and bean sprouts. Desserts are sensibly limited to a cheese platter (you do have to get back to work after all) and palate-cleansing sorbets, including an intriguing, intense pepper berry version served with fresh fruit. It all adds up to one of the CBD's sounder lunchtime investments.

Hours Lunch Mon–Fri noon–3pm

Bill E $21 **M** $28–$44 **D** $14–$16

Cards AE DC V MC Eftpos

Wine Interesting, varied, well-chosen list, mainly Australasian; 13 by the glass

Chef Darrien Potaka

Owner John Ryan

Seats 90; wheelchair access

Child friendly Kids' menu; paper, pencils and stamps

Vegetarian Several menu options; do ask.

www.bar333.com.au

And...will open evenings for groups of 20 or more

Intermezzo Ristorante

Ground Floor, GPO, 1 Martin Place, Sydney
Tel 9229 7788   Map 1

Italian (Neapolitan)   ♥

Score 13/20

What a thrill it is to sit in such a historic Sydney setting at double-clothed tables, served by smart waiters in crisp white jackets. Then there's the stunning seven-metre wine tower of mostly Italian drops, from the Alps to the toe, and the hum of salarymen doing deals on white and dark-chocolate banquettes. The glorious 1870s GPO building and its soaring atrium is a fine backdrop for chef Mario Percuoco's Neapolitan-style fare. Those in the know favour sea scallops on the shell, dressed with tomato and shreds of ginger, or linguine crowned with scampi, tomato and chilli. Other regulars are backing the veal that comes as golden-crumbed torpedoes rolled around smoked mozzarella and pancetta. A tuna steak was less successful, arriving overcooked, with an accompanying lemon and garlic sauce and tomato salad doing little to help. Dolci can be as simple as semifreddo or as decadent as a double chocolate tart.

Hours Lunch Mon–Fri noon–3pm; Dinner Mon–Sat 6–10pm

Bill E $19–$22 **M** $29–$41 **D** $16.50

Cards AE DC V MC Eftpos

Wine 200-plus, mostly Italian, split into regions, some local offerings; 20 by the glass

Chef Mario Percuoco

Owner Peter Petroulas

Seats 80; wheelchair access; outdoor seating

Child friendly Highchairs; can adapt dishes to suit

www.gposydney.com

And...choose from one of three dining areas, including alfresco on Martin Place

Jaspers

54 Alexandra Street, Hunters Hill
Tel 9879 3200   Map 7

Contemporary

Score 14/20

In recent years they've changed the guard at this heritage stalwart more often than at Buckingham Palace. But with its pretty sandstone walls, clever lighting, double-damasked tables and caramel-and-chocolate interiors, Jaspers maintains a refined consistency. The new team includes former Luke Mangan disciple Martin Stacey, who has returned the menu to the contemporary Australian camp, with a touch of Gallic gloss – and buttery richness – here and there. While service struggles at times to match the fine-diner focus, there's lots to love about an entree of deboned, "drunken" quail and brussels sprouts with a smooth chestnut and bread sauce; and luxurious, twice-cooked Kurobuta confit pork belly on cauliflower puree and scented with star anise. Pan-fried ocean trout with sweetcorn in a plate-lickingly good blue swimmer crab sauce is a glorious combination. A mouthful of the generously sized, rich chocolate tart with clotted cream ice-cream is a reminder of why locals love Jaspers, and have done so for three decades.

Hours Lunch Tues–Fri noon–3pm; Dinner Mon–Sat 6–10pm

Bill E $20–$24 **M** $28–$38 **D** $16–$20; 10% surcharge on Sundays & public holidays

Cards AE DC V MC

Wine A thoughtful, broad selection, 16 by the glass; BYO (corkage $7 pp)

Chef Martin Stacey

Owner Erudite Trust Pty Ltd

Seats 75; private rooms

Child friendly Kids' menu; highchairs

www.jaspersrestaurant.com.au

And...special wine dinners, and Christmas in July

Jimbaran

129 Avoca Street, Randwick
Tel 9398 8555   Map 9

Indonesian

Score 12/20

The heady mix of incense and spice is the first thing you notice. Then there are the damask-style cloths with matching chair covers – a kind of Kath-and-Kim-do-Bali look. But whatever the pitch, it's working because Jimbaran is heaving, right through to the courtyard with its fairy lights and banquet-sized tables. The BYO policy also helps, along with a menu under $30. Anyone preferring the zing of Thai or more refined Cantonese food might be disappointed, but if you're seduced by Bali and beyond, this is nirvana. Beef pancakes are flaky and subtly spiced, and teeny satay sticks (chicken or lamb) arrive over a mini charcoal grill. Whole snapper is big, coming four ways, including deep-fried and wearing a sambal-like paste. Fatty lamb cutlets swimming in a rendang curry were a let-down, while kangkung (water spinach), hot off the pan and laced with belachan, ticks all the boxes. Order cendol, the gooey green noodle dessert, as the perfect chilli foil.

Hours Lunch Sun 11am–3pm; Dinner Tues–Sun 6–9pm; bookings essential

Bill E $6–$8 **M** $8–$29 **D** $4–$8; 10% surcharge on public holidays

Cards V MC Eftpos

Wine BYO (corkage $1.50 pp)

Chef Alina Lucia Lucas

Owners Christanto Lie & Alina Lucia Lucas

Seats 90; outdoor seating

Child friendly Booster seats

Vegetarian Lots of dishes on offer: stir-fries, curries and vegetable dishes

www.jimbaran.com.au

And...the courtyard is great for balmy banquets, but only until 10pm

jimmy liks

186–188 Victoria Street, Potts Point
Tel 8354 1400   Map 2

South-East Asian

Score 14/20

Who is Jimmy Lik and how does he keep the east's fabulous nobodies coming back for more? To be sure, it's something to do with the super cool bar and hey-look-me-over communal dining space. But we hope it's also because the ingratiating palm sugar hit has left the menu and there's more integrity in the dishes than we remember. Start your night with a kick-arse mojito and briny fresh oysters dressed with nam jim, while your name reaches the top of the list for a place at the long communal dining table. The tasting plate is great value. Highlights include poached chicken and crab salad, sticky-licky caramelised pork hock with a sour tamarind sauce, and very lovely braised beef with a mint and lime dressing. There's a balance in the dishes that feels quite authentic, and we should be thankful for it. Wine partnering is made easy by a thoughtful wine list. Waitstaff are young, friendly and well-informed.

Hours Dinner daily 6–11pm; bookings for 6–7pm only

Bill E $3.80–$19 **M** $22–$33 **D** $14–$16; 9-course banquet menu $55 pp; 10% surcharge on Sundays & public holidays

Cards AE V MC Eftpos

Wine Smart, compatible Australasian list; 23 by the glass

Chef Ali Carter

Owner Joe Elcham

Seats 100; outdoor seating

www.jimmyliks.com

And...on busy nights, get your name on the list when you arrive

Jonah's

69 Bynya Road, Whale Beach
Tel 9974 5599   Map 7

Contemporary

Score 15/20

The special-occasion restaurant of the northern beaches rises to its reputation. There are oysters, listed by provenance and species, shucked on the spot and served with spectacular simplicity on a deep green glass platter. There's the wide-open ocean beyond and below. Add a superb cheese course – four Australians, four imported – plus chef George Francisco's utterly ingenious desserts, such as a millefeuille of creme brulee slices zinged with caramelised pineapple, and you've picked the winners. An entree tian of smoky beetroot, ocean trout, sweetish eel and tiny capers is followed by undeniably creative main courses, some more spot-on than others. Cocoa nibs in a blue-eye crusting added little to paprika-spiked peperonata and saffron sauce, and a buttery-beautiful lobster tail was at odds, somewhat, with melting veal cheeks in red wine. But with friendly service, excellent wines and an outlook that morphs by the minute as the sun sets, your meal will more than match your special occasion.

Hours Breakfast daily 8–9.30am; Lunch daily noon–3 pm; Dinner daily 6.30–9pm (Wed–Sun only April–Oct); bookings essential

Bill E $27–$31 **M** $38–$51 **D** $16–$18; 10% surcharge on Sundays & public holidays

Cards AE DC V MC Eftpos

Wine Great list, mostly Australian, plenty from NSW and interesting aged whites; 21 by the glass

Chef George Francisco

Owner Jonah's Restaurant Pty Ltd

Seats 100; private room; wheelchair access; outdoor seating

Child friendly Kids' menu; highchairs; drawing

www.jonahs.com.au

And...have an aperitif on the terrace

Jugemu & Shimbashi

NEW

246 Military Road, Neutral Bay
Tel 9904 3011   Map 5a

Japanese

Score 13.5/20

It's all about the noodles. Or not, since this is two restaurants in one: a teppanyaki bar, plus a soba noodle house, with two names, two entrances and two decors – red and yellow. Chef Masahiko Tojo hand-makes fresh buckwheat noodles daily in the front window of Shimbashi: perhaps long cool green tea noodles to dip in a warm, sweet and smoky dashi broth; or slippery white noodles to accompany sliced duck breast and grilled shallots in a sweetly perfumed duck and dried mackerel broth. They're the work of a true artisan. On the Jegumu side, it might be divine sashimi, beautiful gyoza (wagyu beef, Kurobuta pork and veg dumplings) with ponzu sauce, deep-fried miso-marinated snapper or the house specialty, okonomiyaki: savoury pancakes like a bubble-and-squeak omelette. With so much to choose from in this best of both worlds, plus deferential service keen to ensure contentment, this is refined, traditional Japanese cooking at prices that will keep you coming back.

Hours Lunch Tues–Sat noon–2pm; Dinner Tues–Sat 6–9.30pm, Sun 6–9pm; bookings essential

Bill E $5–$16 **M** $12–$35 **D** $5–$10

Cards AE DC V MC Eftpos

Wine Minimal and boutique, plus good sake and shochu list; 7 by the glass

Chefs Masahiko Tojo & Koji Sano

Owner VWC International Pty Ltd

Seats 86; private room; wheelchair access

Child friendly Highchairs

And…a sushi and tempura bar is planned for upstairs

Kam Fook

Level 6, Westfield Shopping Centre, Bondi Junction
Tel 9386 9889   Map 9
Also at Level 6, Westfield Shopping Centre, Chatswood
Tel 9413 9388   Map 7

Chinese (Cantonese)

Score 13/20

Chinese in upscale shopping centres? Kam Fook has cornered the market. While the Chatswood branch still struggles, the glitzier, more atmospheric Bondi Junction venue makes diners feel welcome. So too do cleverly placed carved screens and chocolate tones, which scale down the huge room. It can get frantic – and waits can be long for yum cha – but dinner is more civilised, complete with a comprehensive wine list and duck-shaped decanters. Take the hint and try their excellent Peking duck, carved at the table, or opt for the sweet succulence of lamb pancakes. Hotpots are another favourite, though a pork and eggplant version could have done with more pep and pungency. A spicy seafood soup owes more to Thailand than China, wafting aromas of lemongrass and chilli, but we're back to the main game with the rest of the seafood, the house specialty. Let the tank-fresh fish shine with simple ginger and shallot.

Hours Lunch daily 10am–3pm; Dinner Mon–Sat 5.30–10.30pm, Sun 5–10pm

Bill E $6–$16 **M** $20–$38 **D** $7–$12

Cards AE V MC Eftpos

Wine A huge list, from the affordable to the eye-wateringly expensive; 16 by the glass

Chefs John Leung (Bondi) & Ping Lam (Chatswood)

Owner Rosetta Lee

Seats 230 (Bondi), 600 (Chatswood); wheelchair access

Child friendly Highchairs

Vegetarian Extensive choices

www.kamfook.com.au

And…after 5pm, there's free Westfield parking

Kazbah on Darling

379 Darling Street, Balmain
Tel 9555 7067   Map 5b

Middle Eastern
Score 13.5/20

Don't be fooled by the tagine-heavy decor; there's a lot here worth exploring. The mezze plate is a meal in itself: grilled octopus in a stingingly garlicked skordalia; smoky babaghanoush that's not over-pureed; soft-shell crabs crusted with chermoula; fried cauliflower with yoghurt sauce; and quail glazed with pomegranate juice are among many other perfectly produced nibbles. But pace yourself. Generous slices of juicy pan-fried duck nuzzle up against dukka-crusted felafel and honey-preserved quince, topped with thin sweet potato chips. A thick chunk of grilled fish rests on chermoula beans and a mash of purple congo potatoes, drizzled with preserved lemon gremolata. The flavours are intense, complex and alluring. A standout fattoush is the ideal accompaniment at the Balmain end of Morocco. Unfailingly courteous, informed service (we love their trick of pouring water from great heights, mint-tea style) and welcoming, warm surrounds encourage you to take the meal slowly.

Hours Breakfast Sat–Sun 9am–3pm; Lunch Sat–Sun noon–3pm; Dinner Wed–Sat from 6.30pm; bookings essential

Bill E $9–$16 **M** $33–$36 **D** $14–$18; 2 courses & glass of wine $40 pp (Wed–Thurs only)

Cards AE DC V MC

Wine Excellent list for a local casual dining restaurant; 14 by the glass; BYO (corkage $3.50 pp)

Chefs Zahi Azzi & Francis Bingham

Owners Zahi & Penny Azzi

Seats 85; wheelchair access; outdoor seating

Child friendly Kids' meals; crayons

Vegetarian Several mezze options

www.kazbah.com.au

And...try mafroukeh: nuts, biscuit and pashmak

Kensington Peking

172 Anzac Parade, Kensington
Tel 9313 7100   Map 9

Chinese (Peking)
Score 12/20

They come not for the decor but for the duck and dumplings. And come they do, hordes of families and friends hungry for northern Chinese dishes delivered by friendly waiters eager to steer indecisive diners in the (usually) right direction. Crisp duck is shredded at the table and served with hoisin, cucumber, spring onions and sometimes too-floury pancakes. Go all out for Peking duck that returns for its second act with noodles or as sang choi bau ($1 extra, per head, for the latter). Steamed chicken or prawn and snow pea dumplings are a delight, but Sichuan chicken lacked the anticipated chilli hit. Winners at nearby Royal Randwick might like to splash out on tank-caught mud crab, ocean perch, lobsters or steamed prawns. For the rest of us punters, classics such as fried rice and deep-fried ice-cream are a safe bet. So too is a wait for a table, so do book.

Hours Lunch Thurs–Tues 11am–3pm; Dinner Mon–Tues & Thurs 5–10.30pm, Fri–Sun 5–10.30pm

Bill E $5.80–$12.80 **M** $10.80–$42.80 **D** $6.80–$16; $2 pp surcharge on public holidays

Cards V MC Eftpos

Wine BYO (corkage $2 pp)

Chef/owner Peter Lo

Seats 160; private rooms

Child friendly Highchairs; booster seats

Vegetarian Non-meat options available; wide range of Asian greens

And...there's more seating and private rooms upstairs

Kuali

1st Floor, Lane Cove Arcade,
115 Longueville Road, Lane Cove
Tel 9418 6878   Map 7

Malaysian

Score 13/20

Kuali's obscure location makes it tricky to find. Once through the mall and the fluorescent arcade and up the utilitarian stairs, however, you'll find the mood is relaxing and unpretentious. The whirr of brass fans overhead, colourful Malay murals and friendly informative staff make it a family favourite. Plump WA scallops steamed for a nanosecond are perfect crowned with ginger and shallots in a mild soy sauce. Curry puffs, however, were dry and ho-hum. From the list of hawkers' favourites, poached Hainanese chicken rice is not to be missed – meltingly tender and served with a particularly good treacle-like kecap manis (dark sweet soy) and citrussy house-made chilli sauce. The regulars are only here for the huge platters of crab with Poh's secret curry sauce. Durian ice-cream would benefit from more of the pungent fruit but comforting sago gula melaka pudding with its pool of palm sugar syrup and coconut cream is an absolute delight.

Hours Dinner Tues–Sun 5.30–10pm
Bill E $4.50–$11 **M** $12–$27 **D** $6.50–$9.50;
10% surcharge on public holidays
Cards AE V MC Eftpos
Wine Small, basic list; 6 by the glass;
BYO (corkage $2.50 pp)
Chef/owner John Poh
Seats 120
Child friendly Highchairs; coloured pencils to draw on the paper table cloths
Vegetarian Separate menu
www.kuali.com.au
And...hot, flaky roti chanai is extremely more-ish with rich curry sauce

La Brasserie

Shop 28, 118–126 Crown Street,
Darlinghurst
Tel 9358 1222   Map 2

French

Score 13/20

From the rattan chairs outside to mirrors serving as specials boards, La Brasserie aims for an upfront Parisian vibe. Cosy lighting, dark banquettes and heavy red drapes all work to create a convivial feel. The waiters are authentically French, with charming Gallic accents going some way to make up for often inattentive and occasionally forgetful service. Garlicky snails come with crusty baguette slices, while each spoonful of an intensely flavoured French onion soup brings melted gruyere stretching from a golden crouton. Some offal and meat dishes, such as the duck-liver cognac sauce with duck confit, may seem unrelentingly rich, but a perfectly cooked 250-gram sirloin steak, crowned with Cafe de Paris butter, is a crowd pleaser. So is a veritable mountain of crisp, airy fries on the side – and you'll probably finish every last one. Marmalade-flavoured citrus confit and pine nut tart crumbles too easily but its scattering of toffee-like dark nougat with toasted nuts is a crunchy delight.

Hours Lunch Mon–Fri noon–3pm;
Dinner daily 6–10pm
Bill E $13–$19 **M** $25–$31 **D** $13–$16;
10% surcharge on public holidays
Cards AE V MC Eftpos
Wine User-friendly mix of French and Australasian;
19 by the glass
Chef David Bransgrove
Owners Philippe Valet, Andrew Salouros
& Lionel Asseraf
Seats 110; private room; outdoor seating
Child friendly Highchair
www.labrasserie.com.au
And...set menus in the elegant private room

La Grande Bouffe

758 Darling Street, Rozelle
Tel 9818 4333   Map 5b

French
Score 13.5/20

The chefs seem to turn over annually, but the important things remain the same at this corner cafe and bistro. Tea lights glimmer through the long windows, and even a pair of elderly grandes dames look as though they're straight out of Paris Central Casting, sitting at a dark wooden table against the dramatic red-and-black wallpaper backdrop. The dinner menu, too, has a French accent as pronounced as those of the solicitous waiters. Complimentary escargots are quickly followed by golden seared scallops on leek fondue, speckled with faintly smoky Avruga caviar. More dainty than traditional, duck and pork rillettes comes as a crisped disc, stacked with fresh fig slices and surrounded by overly liberal swirls of balsamic reduction. A main of moist yellowfin tuna melds beautifully with earthy lentils and carrot puree, and no matter what the creme brulee du jour (maybe rhubarb or passionfruit), its topping is so perfectly glassy you could skate across it.

Hours Breakfast daily 7.30am–noon; Lunch daily noon–2.30pm; Dinner Tues–Sat 6.30–9.30pm

Bill E $18.50 **M** $29 **D** $10–$18; 10% surcharge on public holidays

Cards AE DC V MC Eftpos

Wine Decently priced, mostly French selection with some Australasian choices; 13 by the glass; BYO Tues–Thurs only (corkage $10 per bottle)

Chef Robert Hodgson

Owners David & Meredith Poirier

Seats 50; wheelchair access; outdoor seating

Child friendly Highchairs

www.lagrandebouffe.com.au

And...it's a cafe by day – French brekkie options include omelettes and a duck egg croque madame

La Grillade

118 Alexander Street (cnr Albany Street), Crows Nest
Tel 9439 3707   Map 5a

French/Steakhouse   ♀
Score 13/20

For 30 years, this corner house has turned out food as reliable as the heavy wooden beams criss-crossing its rustic dining rooms. Northsiders, many now streaked with grey, flock in for straight-up French favourites, from garlic snails to twice-cooked pea and ham souffle with a gruyere crust, lashed with velvety sauce. There are occasional attempts to branch out, but chilli and lime prawns aren't natural allies of salt cod croquettes. The name means the grill and it's the steak we come for: five options, listed by breed, provenance and feed regimen and served with bearnaise, green peppercorn or red wine sauce. A sirloin, however, didn't have quite enough star quality, although crisp chips and garlicky beans are a fine back-up. Beef bourguignon is another sturdy take on a classic. Service hums along beautifully in the busy rooms. Finish with another old favourite: the Grand Marnier or mango souffle, as high and wobbly as a French chef's toque, and even better with vanilla ice-cream.

Hours Lunch Mon–Fri noon–3pm; Dinner Mon–Sat 6–10.30pm; bookings essential

Bill E $16–$28 **M** $29.50–$45 **D** $16–$18.50

Cards AE DC V MC

Wine Great list, with interesting inclusions from around the world; 17 by the glass

Chef Jason McDonald

Owner AIH Group

Seats 140; private rooms; outdoor seating

Child friendly Kids' menu

www.lagrillade.com.au

And...come early for a pre-dinner drink at the bar

Find your perfect dinner partner.

	GOLDEN ALE	PILSENER	I.P.A.	AMBER ALE	PORTER
SEAFOOD	CRAB CAKES, FRESH PRAWNS, LIGHT WHITE SEAFOOD WITH CITRUS DRESSING, WHITE BAIT	BATTERED FISH, MUSSELS			OYSTERS
HIGHLY SPICED	LAKSA, NACHOS	THAI FOOD, SALT & PEPPER SQUID, CHILLI PRAWNS, SPICY PIZZA	SPICY INDIAN CURRIES, VINDALOO		
MEAT DISHES		VEAL	VENISON, DUCK	RACK OF LAMB, LAMB SHANKS, GAME MEATS, GLAZED MEATS	PORTERHOUSE STEAK, GOULASH, ROAST BEEF
CHEESE	GRUYERE	PECORINO	STILTON	CHEDDAR	SMOKED

La Locanda

65B Macpherson Street, Bronte
Tel 9389 3666   Map 9

Italian

Score 13.5/20

Bi-fold windows open to the street at twilight and, from the window seat, a touch of Italy unfurls. As darkness falls and candles are lit, a murmuring trattoria ambience emerges. An elegant miniature chocolate box in olive green shades, La Locanda is a delicately narrow neighbourhood treat that's pure adult Italian. That means few surprises on the classically inclined blackboard menu – four antipasti, four pasta, main and dessert listings – but each is well balanced, confidently cooked and smoothly served. Vitello tonnato is true to the template – sliced veal with a sharp, smooth, slightly over-salted tuna mayonnaise. Stuffed squid (a daily favourite) works nicely with a dab of tomato sugo, as does a twist of slippery pappardelle with a rich duck ragu. Right through to a sleekly creamy semifreddo dessert, it's simple, seasonal and unselfconsciously authentic in a "whatever's fresh today" kind of way. And if it's full most nights, that's because the locals love it. As do their friends.

Hours Dinner Tues–Sun 6–10pm
Bill E $15–$17 **M** $22–$27 **D** $13–$15
Cards V MC Eftpos
Wine Nice Italianate selection, 9 by the glass; BYO Tues–Thurs & Sun only (corkage $3 pp)
Chef Andrea Vagge
Owners Andrea Vagge & Fiona Bloomer
Seats 50; outdoor seating
Child friendly Highchair; kids' pasta
And...booking is definitely advised

La Perla

255 Victoria Road, Gladesville
Tel 9816 1161   Map 7

Italian (Southern)/Seafood

Score 13/20

On an unexciting strip of Victoria Road, this truly is a shining pearl, with its bright lights and full tables. Inside the ocean-coloured room, the noise and laughter of diners and swift waiters delivering vast plates grab the attention. Don't fill up on the bread, regularly deposited at the table, because portions are huge. An entree plate of mussels stuffed with prawn, breadcrumbs and capers is so copiously sized we're glad we are splitting it. A main-size serving of homemade ravioli stuffed with lobster and ricotta arrives as three bulging pieces finished with a generous sauce. Misto di mare – a huge platter filled with juicy prawns, mussels, clams, crab and calamari all swimming in a steaming broth of tomato and garlic – could feed a party of six. Oh, hang it, more bread, please. Somehow we manage to squeeze in creme brulee made with white chocolate and this time we wish we had one each.

Hours Lunch Tues–Fri noon–3pm; Dinner Tues–Sun 6–10pm
Bill E $16–$24 **M** $23–$45 **D** $9–$14
Cards AE DC V MC Eftpos
Wine Pleasing list of inexpensive Italian and locals; 10 by the glass; BYO (corkage $4 pp)
Chef Dominic Bertuccio
Owner Giorgio Colosi
Seats 130; private room; wheelchair access
www.laperla.com.au
And...look out for the numerous fish-of-the-day options

La Sala

Ground Floor, 23 Foster Street, Surry Hills
Tel 9281 3352   Map 3a

Italian

Score 13.5/20

The vibe is noticeably less spirited since founding frontman Andrea Mellas and chef Darren Simpson left the building, but this warehouse restaurant still delivers some fine food in dramatic surrounds. The sexy, Soho-style space, with its duplex kitchen and a dining area decked in rich chocolate tones, industrial timbers and concrete, attracts a loved-up and cashed-up crowd for chef Ruben Martinez's heart-warming Italian fare. His blood-red bresaola comes cleverly matched with red cabbage, raisins, pine nuts and gorgonzola dolce. Standard issue calamari fritti were a tad overdone and chewy, but all is forgiven after a mouthful of tagliatelle (made in the upstairs show-kitchen amid the cheese wheels and olive oil tins), tossed simply but sensationally with a little nutmeg, chives, parmesan and Martinez's homemade truffle butter. The tiramisu is equally artless and just as rewarding – a dark, intense hit of espresso-soaked biscuit and sabayon, with some stewed rhubarb on the side just to heighten the pleasure.

Hours Lunch Thurs–Fri noon–3pm; Dinner Tues–Sat 6pm–late; bookings essential

Bill E $17–$21 **M** $25–$36 **D** $15–$16.50

Cards AE DC V MC Eftpos

Wine Tight list of extravagantly priced local and Italian varietals; 18 by the glass

Chef Ruben Martinez

Owner AIH Group

Seats 120; private room; wheelchair access

Vegetarian Full vegetarian menu

www.lasala.com.au

And...a communal table downstairs for group dinners

La Tratt

Fairfield RSL, 14 Anzac Avenue, Fairfield
Tel 9727 5000   Map 6

Italian

Score 12.5/20

Rich, earthy colours, clever lighting, modern fittings and charming service … this is not your average club dining room. Then there's the short menu – an enticing read for any Italophile, listing classic dishes and the books that have inspired them (from Italy's kitchen bible, *The Silver Spoon*, to several by Melbourne's Guy Grossi). Good bruschetta is a promising start and pizza napoletana impresses with minimal topping and Italian mozzarella di bufala, though the thin crust lacked crunch. Fettucine carbonara gets full marks for the absence of cream, and calamari fritti, though a touch soggy, are lifted beautifully by a lightly zesty lemon aioli. Still-glassy White Bay scallops look and taste great with a crunchy almond and herb crust and scattering of micro cress, while a generous portion of tender White River veal scallops is perfect under a porcini ragu. House-made gelato comes in a range of authentic flavours, the vanilla bean served with espresso and nocello (a nut liqueur) in a classic affogato.

Hours Dinner Wed–Sat from 6pm

Bill E $14.90–$17.50 **M** $29.50–$33.50
D $11.50–$15.90

Cards AE DC V MC Eftpos

Wine Short, well-priced list of Australians plus a few Italians, plus a cellarmaster's selection; 8 by the glass

Chefs Robert Green & Jason Joannou

Owner Fairfield RSL Memorial Club

Seats 60; wheelchair access

Child friendly Kids' menu; highchairs; pencils

Vegetarian Variety of vegetarian options

www.fairfieldrsl.com.au

And...at the cosy bar, there's wine by the glass, arancini, olive grissini and panzarotti

L'étoile

211 Glenmore Road, Paddington
Tel 9332 1577   Map 4b

French
                              Score 13/20

Paddo's firmament boasts a new star. The
long, elegant Victorian terrace (formerly Local)
is moodily candlelit, with honey-coloured
timbers, paper-on-cloth tables, a funky bar
serving great bar nibbles and a covered rear
sandstone courtyard to savour balmy nights.
French-born Frederic Booms (ex Brisbane's Pier
Nine) mines French brasserie classics – garlic
snails anyone? – while mixing authenticity
with contemporary flair. Service shows equal
panache and warmth in a package that's the
next best thing to a plane for Paris. Moreton
Bay bug and gruyere souffle is pleasingly
lush, a veal tartare sharpened by a green
peppercorn mustard. But bouillabaisse lacked
the depth and personality we'd hoped
for, while Glenloth chicken breast with
boulangere potatoes tasted like one cliche
too many, thanks to the superfluous brandy-
flambeed lobster. It matters little when an
oldie but very goodie – chocolate profiteroles
with vanilla ice-cream – reminds you it was
the French who invented savoir faire.

Hours Lunch Wed–Sun noon–3pm; Dinner
daily 6pm–late; bookings essential

Bill E $14–$22 **M** $28–$35 **D** $14–$16;
10% surcharge on public holidays

Cards AE DC V MC

Wine Small, appealing range of premium French,
and Australasian wines; 12 by the glass

Chef Frederic Booms

Owners Yannick and Michele Besnard
& Frederic Booms

Seats 110; outdoor seating

www.letoilerestaurant.com.au

And...crepes, brioche and croque monsieur
et madame for weekend breakfast

Le Bukhara

Level 1, 55 Bay Street (cnr Cross Street),
Double Bay
Tel 9363 5510   Map 4a

Mauritian/Indian
                              Score 13/20

An upstairs position buys extra real estate for
this Double Bay stalwart of nearly 20 years,
meaning there's plenty of space between
the white-clothed tables. The menu is a
win–win situation, whether you choose the
above-average take on Indian classics or the
Mauritian creole dishes that are specialties
of chef Vijay Baboo. Combine entrees of
plump samosas and tandoori lamb cutlets
with cumin-and-garlic-marinated scrolls of
squid Mauritian style. Mains are served in
striking asymmetrical white bowls, but their
uneven sides pose a sauce-tsunami risk –
and you won't want to waste a drop of the
spiced gravy surrounding tender goat on the
bone or mailapuri fish, fragrant with curry
leaves. The promised five whole spices in the
Mauritian duck weren't prominent in its rich,
tomatoey sauce, but green beans thoran
(a Kerala specialty) is a winner, sauteed with
mustard seeds and shredded coconut. Ditto
chai masala ice-cream.

Hours Dinner Sun–Thurs 5.30–10.30pm,
Fri–Sat 5.30–11pm

Bill E $7.90–$11.90 **M** $12.90–$21.90 **D** $6.90–
$8.90; degustation menu $50 or $75 with wine

Cards AE DC V MC Eftpos

Wine Small but reasonable Australian list;
13 by the glass; BYO (corkage $3 pp)

Chef Vijay Baboo

Owners Vijay Baboo, Jean Noel Seetaloo
& Heman Pullut

Seats 100; private room

Child friendly Highchairs

Vegetarian Full vegetarian menu and other
choices

www.bukhararestaurant.com.au

And...ask about the next Mauritian feast night

Le Pelican

411 Bourke Street, Darlinghurst
Tel 9380 2622   Map 2

French/Basque

Score 14/20

It's easy to love this little haven in the hurly-burly that is the Taylor Square-end of Bourke Street. Adorned with menus from some legendary French and Basque restaurants, its sandstone and whitewashed walls, bentwood chairs, starched white tablecloths and timber floors create a bistro atmosphere free of formality. Service is enthusiastic if occasionally haphazard. The menu changes weekly but zucchini flowers filled with brandade (salt cod) are a delight, all the more so for being served fresh rather than deep-fried. Lightly seared scallops are accompanied by a stack of sliced button mushrooms and thinly sliced chorizo in a nod to classic Basque tapas. Chef/owner Jean-Francois Salet's rich culinary education comes into its own with duck two ways – slivers of pink, roasted breast meat and rich, luscious confit. Ocean trout fillet sits on a pastry base with roasted teardrop tomatoes. And while the solid texture of a blueberry tart disappointed, good value champagne by the glass is a fine dessert on its own.

Hours Lunch Wed–Fri noon–3pm; Dinner Tues–Sun 6–10pm; bookings essential

Bill E $16–$18 **M** $26–$33 **D** $13–$14; 2-course lunch $40 pp

Cards AE V MC Eftpos

Wine A small, joyous, eclectic global list with a few French offerings; 14 by the glass; BYO (corkage $10 per bottle)

Chef/owner Jean-Francois Salet

Seats 48; private room; outdoor seating

Child friendly Kids' menu

And...request a backroom table to peek at the kitchen action

Libertine

1 Kellett Street, Kings Cross
Tel 9368 7507   Map 2

French/Vietnamese

Score 12.5/20

With its neon pink street awning, Libertine could almost be mistaken for one of the neighbouring strip clubs. Add to that an interior that resembles an opulent French boudoir – bold red walls, chandeliers, silk cushions – opening out to a small, private courtyard. No wonder this place buzzes on weekends as groups gear up for a night on the town. Waiters keep pace with brisk, if not entirely polished, service. The kitchen draws more readily on Vietnam but chicken liver paté with cornichons shows its French roots. Barely seared kingfish with a sweet-and-sour cucumber salsa is neither too sweet nor too sour, but Vietnamese roast duck with fragrant herbs and ginger sauce was let down by overcooked pancakes. Ocean trout in a claypot is perfectly moist and nicely balanced with Asian greens, shallots and chilli, and a beef brisket hotpot is surprisingly tender. There's just a trio of desserts, but kaffir lime brulee is a neat cross-cultural twist.

Hours Dinner Mon–Sat 6pm–late

Bill E $6–$20 **M** $18–$29 **D** $9–$12

Cards AE V MC

Wine Local and European labels and a good selection of half-bottles; 14 by the glass

Chef Joel Manton

Owners Andrew Baturo & Jamie Webb

Seats 95; private rooms; outdoor seating

www.libertine.net.au

And...an interesting selection of Asian-influenced salads such as green papaya and spicy green apple

LA GRANDE ANNÉE 1999

The Light Brigade

2a Oxford Street (cnr Jersey Road), Woollahra
Tel 9331 2930   Map 4b

French

Score 15/20

After pleasing the Bistro CBD lunch crowd, chef James Privett has charged across town, adding his polished pizzazz to this elegant art deco pub. While the din from weekend drinkers can jar with the crisp, classic bistro good looks, maitre d' Gavin Day and his attentive team ensure smooth service. Most pub menus trot, but Privett's refined flavours gallop thanks to sound technique, impressive presentation and a touch of whimsy. Thus a succulent trio of rolled quail breasts, one crowned with rillettes of the leg, stand beside a pretty nicoise salad. King prawns snuggle against a fennel and pistachio salad with the surprise of an appealing curry sorbet on a crisp filament of fish skin. Roast lamb cutlets with spinach-wrapped braised shank, baby carrots and potato cake blends class with comfort. Whether you opt for the passionfruit pav or the self-saucing choc pud, dining here is an impressive ride.

Hours Lunch Fri–Sun noon–3pm; Dinner Tues–Sat 6–10pm

Bill E $17–$21 **M** $30–$38 **D** $14;
10% surcharge on Sundays

Cards AE DC V MC

Wine Spectacular global list with benchmark and boutique domestics; 30 by the glass

Chef James Privett

Owner Haritos Hotels

Seats 80

Child friendly Kids' menu; coloured pencils

Vegetarian At least one entree and one main

www.lightbrigade.com.au

And...fun and flavoursome bar menu when you're watching the footy

The Lincoln

36 Bayswater Road, Kings Cross
Tel 9331 2311   Map 2

European

Score 14/20

Walk into a private club where the maitre d' ushers you to your usual table in a dimly lit corner. Settle into a plush cream leather banquette and order a perfect Manhattan. This is the sophisticated fantasy of The Lincoln, amid the madness of Bayswater Road. Smooth yet amiable waiters know their French-accented menu, with deft touches of Spain, Italy and even Asia. Duck confit salad with a tangy mustard dressing delights, while a pretty and delicate crab and shallot salad with rice pancake rolls seemed a little weak by comparison. Greeting customers at the next table, the chef recommends seared scallops with eggplant caviar and tomato confit, and he should – it's a daring example of the shellfish standing up to strong accompaniments. Equally smart is a rich, luscious and satisfying pastry-wrapped rabbit and spinach croustade. A perfect passionfruit souffle with white chocolate sauce is worth the wait. We'll have the usual table again tomorrow night, thank you.

Hours Dinner Wed–Sun 6pm–midnight; bookings essential

Bill E $19–$24 **M** $29–$44 **D** $15–$16;
tasting plates $8–$16

Cards AE V MC Eftpos

Wine Well thought out, with quality champagnes and boutique Australians; 20 by the glass

Chef Richard Duff

Owner Bay36 Pty Ltd

Seats 40; private room; wheelchair access

www.thelincoln.com.au

And...party on in the front bar, The Deck, with its spectacular cocktail list

Longrain

85 Commonwealth Street, Surry Hills
Tel 9280 2888   Map 3a

Thai

Score 15/20

The funky fashionista set knows the drill, piling in at an early hour. No dinner bookings and squeezy communal tables don't deter. It's straight to the dark, good-looking bar where a resident DJ adds energy to the cool, contemporary space. A cocktail or two with a morsel from the bar menu ease the wait and tease the appetite until your turn at the dining table comes around. With the integration of more balanced, savoury notes into his electric Thai repertoire, inspired co-owner/chef Martin Boetz turns a simple dish of stir-fried wagyu beef with chilli jam, asparagus and basil into a flavour-packed triumph. Crisp soft-shell crab topped with shredded betel leaves is superb, although it struggled a little in an intense pineapple curry. Boetz's legendary eggnet encloses a crisp pile of pork, prawns, peanuts and bean sprouts, and sparkles with freshness. Service is slick and personable given the frenetic pace. Fresh lychee and mango salad with mixed sorbet is a heavenly finish.

Hours Lunch Mon–Fri noon–2.30pm; Dinner daily 6–11pm; no dinner bookings
Bill Dishes range from $23.50–$49.50; 10% surcharge on Sundays & public holidays
Cards AE DC V MC
Wine Wise and stylish, well selected to match the food; 16 by the glass plus a stunning cocktail list
Chef Martin Boetz
Owners Sam Christie, John Sample & Martin Boetz
Seats 100; private room; wheelchair access
Child friendly Highchairs; colouring pencils
Vegetarian Separate menu of four good options
www.longrain.com
And...bookings available for lunch

Lotus

22 Challis Avenue, Potts Point
Tel 9326 9000   Map 2

Contemporary

Score 14/20

An almost suburban outpost of the Merivale empire, Lotus is the neighbourhood eatery we all want, sexily sultry as only a Potts Point resident can be. Dimmer than dim lighting may deter some (the light on your phone is handy to illuminate the menu) but if it's ambience you're after, Lotus oozes it. Youthful head chef Daniel Hong works from a global palette, but his clearest strengths are in the Asian zone. Slightly too lukewarm chargrilled cuttlefish with spicy chorizo fingers revels in a ripe romesco sauce, but preserved lemon notes were muted in wakame-topped kingfish sashimi. Tandoori-esque spatchcock with minty cucumber and piri piri is finger-licking territory, however, and Vietnamese herbs, lime and roasted rice give a neat new lift to beef carpaccio. Steamed blue-eye with black fungi sits in a gorgeously gingery broth. A choc-fudge sundae with raspberries, honeycomb and peanuts plays cleverly with salt and sugar. It's the bomb, say the uber-cool casual waiter boys. And it sure is.

Hours Lunch Fri–Sat noon–3pm; Dinner Tues–Sat 6pm–late; bookings essential
Bill E $18–$23 **M** $32–$35 **D** $12–$15
Cards AE DC V MC
Wine A great list of interesting locals and good imports, 17 by the glass
Chef Daniel Hong
Owner Merivale Group
Seats 55; outdoor seats
www.merivale.com
And...the baby back bar has plump ottomans and lush cocktails

Lucio's

47 Windsor Street, Paddington
Tel 9380 5996   Map 4b

Italian (Northern)

Score 16/20

Great service is a fine art. A quarter-century on at this Paddo institution, Sydney's most casually professional service is kept in check by host Lucio Galletto's precise attention to detail and beneficent omnipresence. Some come for the chaotic puzzle of Australian paintings strewn across the walls, while well-heeled locals worship the simple formula of a warm welcome and precision on the plate. There's nothing rustic or robust about the menu: the signature fine green noodles with blue swimmer crab remains unblemished by time and – like its sibling salad of prosciutto, figs, slices of green apple, witlof and buffalo mozzarella – speaks of purity of ingredients touched by the lightest of hands. Fish of the day could be a just-firm blue-eye fillet on fregola (toasted pasta balls), dotted with baby squid and served with lemon-infused butter. Desserts are sensational – including a tasting plate of ice-cream terrine with pistachio praline, soft meringue rolled around almonds and white chocolate with raspberry jelly.

Hours Lunch Mon–Sat 12.30–3pm; Dinner Mon–Sat 6.30–11pm

Bill E $29–$32 **M** $39–$44 **D** $17.50; 2 courses $62.50 pp, 3 courses $95, 6 courses $115

Cards AE DC V MC Eftpos

Wine Classy list of Italian and Australians, with some good value options; 18 by the glass

Chef Logan Campbell

Owners Lucio & Sally Galletto

Seats 75; private rooms

Vegetarian Separate 8-dish menu

www.lucios.com.au

And…a book of recipes from Lucio's home town is out in October

Machiavelli

123 Clarence Street, Sydney
Tel 9299 3748   Map 1

Italian

Score 13/20

Governments may change (occasionally anyway) – and the princes of business, too – but Machiavelli ain't going nowhere. Neither is the loyal lunch tribe, who cram into this legendary below-stairs restaurant for food that isn't changing any time soon. A scene-setting central table groans under the weight of antipasto plates, meat slicers and bowls of fresh produce while salami hang overhead. Traditional Italian? Definitely. Old-fashioned? Yes, but in the best possible sense. Straight from another era come steak diane and prosciutto with melon as well as waist-coated waiters, delivering dishes with flair, firing gueridon pans and plating up at the table. A special of prosciutto-wrapped figs topped with gorgonzola is classic comfort food with no shortage of flavour. A copious main course-sized mound of linguine gamberi is perfectly al dente and generously dotted with prawns, while veal saltimbocca is moist and more-ish. And of course you'll make room for another old favourite, vanilla bean creme brulee.

Hours Lunch Mon–Fri noon–2.30pm; Dinner Mon–Fri 6–9.30pm; bookings essential

Bill E $16–$42 **M** $16–$55 **D** $14–$18

Cards AE DC V MC

Wine Extensive list of Italian and Australian wines; 38 by the glass

Chef Laurent Cambon

Owners Giovanna Toppi & Caterina Tarchi

Seats 230

Vegetarian Plenty of non-meat and fish options

www.machiavelli.com.au

And…spot the business and political bigwigs and watch them table-hop

YOU ARE HERE

to taste it all

Cafés

Baia San Marco	9283 3434
Blackbird Café	9283 7385
CMC	9283 3393
Lindt Chocolat Café	9267 8064
Nick's 103	9267 4404

Restaurants

Chinta Ria	9264 3211
Coast	9267 6700
I'm Angus Steakhouse	9264 5822
Nick's Seafood Restaurant	9264 1212

Bars

Home Bar	9266 0600
Pontoon Bar	9267 7099
Wallaby Bar	9267 4118

Nightclub

Home	9266 0600

Function Centres

Dockside	9261 3777
L'Aqua	8267 0300

COCKLE BAY WHARF

Macleay Street Bistro

73A Macleay Street, Potts Point
Tel 9358 4891   Map 2

Contemporary

Score 14/20

For more than two decades, this unassuming little spot has produced solid comfort food for loyal locals. With ex Balzac protege Mark Flaherty now at the pans, the love's still there in spades, while the room has been subdivided into smaller spaces – with tables so close it's an eavesdropper's paradise. While the waiters appear run off their feet, the food is worth the wait. A special of steamed mussels is helped by the pungent addition of thyme and white wine sauce plus bread to mop up the juices. Beautifully house-made pork and fennel sausages sit well with polenta and sweet apple chutney sauce. Farmed barramundi comes with an elegant crab and fennel salad finished with a splash of lemon and herb vinaigrette. For dessert, Eton mess is sugary, fruity fun – crunchy meringue crushed into pieces with seasonal berries. Like an old friend, this bistro stands the test of time. And it's always there when you need it.

Hours Dinner daily 6–11pm
Bill E $17–$18.50 **M** $24.50–$36.50 **D** $13.50
Cards AE V MC
Wine BYO (corkage $3 pp)
Chef Mark Flaherty
Owner Carole Becka
Seats 46; outdoor seating
And...book an outside table for streetside action

Mad Cow

Ivy, Level 1, 330 George Street, Sydney
Tel 9240 3000   Map 1

Steakhouse

Score 14/20

Don't be perturbed by the name. It's all part of the fun at this cheery, loud steakhouse in the Ivy mega-watering hole. But do come if you're after a slab of top protein, beautifully cooked. The booth seating and exquisite white and lemon decor, in Doris Day-cute, subverts the usual big beefy bloke cliches. Service is equally funky. Chris Whitehead's (ex Opera Bar) menu reinvigorates classics with contemporary pizzazz – for example, a king prawn cocktail with feisty tomato chilli jam and soothing tomato consomme jelly. The hand-cut steak tartare with all the trimmings is textbook perfect, while roasted jewfish fillet on a stew-like bed of mussels, kipfler potato, zucchini noodles and diced tomato is classy, fine-diner fare. And then there's steak: not inexpensive, but certainly impressive – perhaps the wonderfully charred, flavoursome and unbelievably buttery wagyu skirt steak. For dessert, strawberry and passionfruit pav is part nostalgia, part fun and all pleasure.

Hours Lunch Mon–Fri noon–3pm; Dinner Mon–Sat 6–11pm; bookings essential
Bill E $19–$28 **M** $29–$57 **D** $18–$20
Cards AE DC V MC
Wine Impressive international and domestic list, but you'll pay for it; 25 by the glass
Chefs Peter Doyle & Christopher Whitehead
Owner Merivale Group
Seats 105; wheelchair access; outdoor seating (lunch only)
www.merivale.com
And...it can get loud and crowded on weekends

Mahjong Room

312 Crown Street, Surry Hills
Tel 9361 3985   Map 2

Chinese

Score 13/20

A cute, box-shaped room astutely arranged
with Maoist pop art and bric-a-brac lends an
eccentric bent to this quirky establishment,
perfectly suiting its spot on the cusp of
Oxford Street. Yes, those chunky lacquered
tables are for mahjong, unless you're herded
to the narrow plinths in the alley on the
way to the WC (where a picture of a benign
Chairman bears down upon the throne).
The menu is not the usual Cantonese tome
but a smallish list of well-balanced, mainly
northern favourites chided into the 21st
century. Sang choi bau of soft-shell crab
places the crustaceans in a delicate, spicy salt-
and-pepper-style batter with crisp vegetables
in a lettuce cup. Beijing sesame pockets are
DIY – fill them up with the accompanying mix
of roast duck and preserved radish. Sweet
vinegar pork belly was overly rich, yet scallops
steamed in the shell with glass noodles and
black bean are delicate and sweet with a
confident nod towards authenticity – a bit
like the staff, really.

Hours Dinner Mon–Sat 6–10.30pm

Bill E $4–$22 **M** $12.50–$28 **D** $8–$13.50

Cards AE V MC

Wine Small, precise list (plus Chinese beer);
9 by the glass

Chef William Hui

Owners Erika Chan & William Hui

Seats 60; private rooms

www.mahjongroom.com.au

And...mahjong play-lunches second Saturday of
the month, lessons included, bookings essential

Maitre Karl

197 High Street, Willoughby
Tel 9958 1110   Map 7

French (Alsace)/European   ♀

Score 13.5/20

Take a cosy bistro out of Strasbourg, plonk
it on busy High Street, hang some local
art and that's Maitre Karl. Lovers of porky,
smoky charcuterie, duck double-cooked and
flash-seared in its fat and those ubiquitous
doughy Germanic noodles, spaetzle, are
guaranteed satisfied stomachs here. You
can keep it light, too, if all you yearn for is
a plate of oysters, a slice of fortifying, thin-
crusted flammenkueche (wood-fired Alsatian
pizza) and a glass of chilled riesling. A fillet
of snapper served en papillote with shellfish,
potato fondant and house-made rouille is first
class; roasted duck with spiced red cabbage,
spaetzle and cranberries sums up all the glory
of Alsace's Franco–German blend. If you think
you're up to it, order the formidable French
bread-and-butter pudding. OK, we'd like to
see better table bread and the lovely green
salad not so overdressed, but terrific service
from knowledgeable career waiters gliding
between the dark bentwood chairs and tables
keeps everyone content.

Hours Breakfast Tues–Fri 8–11.30am,
Sat 8–11.15am; Lunch Tues–Sat noon–2.30pm;
Dinner Tues–Thurs 6–9pm, Fri–Sat 6–10pm;
bookings essential

Bill E $15.50–$19.50 **M** $26.50–$29.50 **D** $10.50

Cards AE DC V MC Eftpos

Wine Good local and European list, plus
half-bottles; 13 by the glass; BYO (corkage
$8 per bottle)

Chef Joel Baur

Owners Karl & Paivi Geissler

Seats 70; wheelchair access; outdoor seating

Child friendly Kids' menu; highchairs

www.maitrekarl.com.au

And...all-weather outdoor dining available

Malabar

334 Pacific Highway, Crows Nest
Tel 9906 7343   Map 5a
Also at 6/274 Victoria Street, Darlinghurst
Tel 9332 1755   Map 2

Indian (Southern)

Score 12.5/20

Malabar promotes itself as the dosa palace, with some justice if the Bangalore masala dosa is the benchmark. This thin, crisp crepe has the requisite bite of fermented rice and lentil flour batter and a lime-tinged potato filling, plus the heat of roasted coconut and sesame chutney. While the two-storey Crows Nest site has a decor so neutral that it borders on bland (we love Darlinghurst's regal mural), the distinctive flavours of the south are unmistakeable. A piping hot chicken biryani hosts melting nuggets of meat in richly aromatic yellow rice with high notes of cumin, clove and coriander. Slices of baby eggplant and diced potato bathe in a thick gravy strong on onion and tomato. Spinach chaat was a little overpowered by the flood of yoghurt and tamarind sauce topping, but pleasingly pistachio kulfi, a dessert that can often be cloyingly sweet, is restrained, allowing the creaminess of the reduced milk to complement the crushed nuts.

Hours Lunch Sun–Fri noon–3pm; Dinner daily from 5.30pm

Bill E $4.90–$14.90 **M** $14.90–$19.90 **D** $3–$5.90

Cards AE DC V MC

Wine Moderately priced range complementary to the food; 6 by the glass; BYO (corkage $3 pp)

Chef Paul Pandian

Owner Wilson Varghese

Seats 150; private rooms; wheelchair access

Child friendly Booster seats

Vegetarian From dosa to samosas and curries

www.malabarcuisine.com.au

And...mini dosa as entrees

The Malaya

39 Lime Street, King Street Wharf, Sydney
Tel 9279 1170   Map 1

Malaysian

Score 13/20

The Malaya made its name with laksa. That was more than 45 years ago. It has been turning up just the right amount of heat ever since, delivering a culinary journey around Asia with infinite skill and flavours that still pack a mighty punch. The large, modern space above King Street Wharf, with views over Darling Harbour, is slicker than your average neighbourhood Asian and priced accordingly. Service is crisp yet wise and upbeat. Start with otak otak, a spicy bundle of minced fish with chilli and spices wrapped in a barbecued banana leaf. Alas, steamed scallops on the shell in a puddle of soy sauce seemed overcooked for our tastes, but a main-course duck curry has a rich, deep sauce, based on the restaurant's original spice blend. Hot and spicy Singapore noodles combine dry-fried rice vermicelli with chicken, prawns, shallots, chilli and egg. And there's plenty to enjoy on the excellent cocktail menu.

Hours Lunch Mon–Sat noon–3pm; Dinner daily 6pm–late; bookings essential

Bill E $12–$22 **M** $17–$31; set menu $45–$48; 15% surcharge on Sundays

Cards AE DC V MC

Wine A considered list with appropriate wines; 7 by the glass

Chef Mustapa Jaffar

Owners Lance & Givie Wong

Seats 300; private rooms; wheelchair access; outdoor seating

Child friendly Highchairs

Vegetarian Set menu

www.themalaya.com.au

And...grab a gelato along the boardwalk for dessert

Manta

The Wharf, 6 Cowper Wharf Road,
Woolloomooloo
Tel 9332 3822   Map 2

Contemporary
Score 14/20

The finger wharf restaurant strip is sassy
Sydney at its best. In Manta's coolly modern
interior, the image of a ray floats on a teal-
coloured mural wall, yet most diners prefer
outside, where powerbrokers and B-list celebs
promenade to tables overlooking expensive
boats and the city skyline. It's no surprise that
seafood stars. Grilled scallops mingle with
zingy watercress, juicy orange and toasted
hazelnuts. Marron enhanced by the salty
richness of bottarga (dried mullet roe) butter
is as dazzling as the setting. Crisp-skinned
ocean trout with roasted tomatoes and olive
dressing doesn't make as big a splash as
skate and shellfish in a tomatoey roasted-
shellfish broth – although the accompanying
crouton was swamped in oil. Meat lovers
find contentment in a smart steak menu.
When the sauce from a chocolate fondant
runs seductively into lush banana ice-cream,
you'll forgive the fact that the friendly service
may not be as smooth or wise as hoped, and
happily stick around to see and be seen.

Hours Lunch daily noon–3pm; Dinner Mon–Sat
6–10.30pm, Sun 6–9pm
Bill E $24–$29 **M** $36–$48 **D** $16;
10% surcharge on Sundays & public holidays
Cards AE DC V MC Eftpos
Wine Thoughtful, four pages of Australasian
and European wines; 18 by the glass
Chef Daniel Hughes
Owner Rob Rubis
Seats 220; outdoor seating
Child friendly Kids' menu; highchairs
Vegetarian Full menu
www.mantarestaurant.com.au
And...tank-fresh lobster and crab

Marigold

Levels 4 & 5, 683 George Street, Sydney
Tel 9281 3388   Map 3a

Chinese (Cantonese)
Score 13.5/20

Marigold is many things to many people.
To some, it's the only place they'll queue
for yum cha. For others, it's dinkum Chinese,
pre- or post-theatre. And for most, this
nearly 20-year-old 800-seater is a destination
for truly authentic Cantonese with an
emphasis on seafood. (Well, you certainly
don't come for the tired scarlet and gold
decor.) Whoever you are, stick to the live
seafood presented still thrashing at the table
before being dispatched and returned as,
say, prawns steeped in wine, steamed barra
fragrant with ginger and shallots, or seared
scallops-on-the-shell freckled with salty black
beans. Crimson pork ribs with vinegar are
sticky, juicy and tangy all at once, while the
list of seasonal greens (maybe choy sum
or pea shoots) is always top notch. Not
everything goes to plan – a la carte steamed
prawns laced with garlic were past their use-
by date – but overall this majestic old lady
delivers on most fronts most of the time.

Hours Lunch daily 10am–3pm;
Dinner daily 5.30–11pm
Bill E $6.50–$17.80 **M** $18–$39 **D** $5–$8;
$2 pp surcharge on public holidays
Cards AE DC V MC
Wine Above-average list of mostly Australian
domaines, but no vintages listed; 2 by the glass
Chef Chen Bing Chung
Owner Nedosu Pty Ltd
Seats 800; private rooms
Child friendly Highchairs
Vegetarian 15 a la carte options; various choices
for yum cha
www.marigold.com.au
And...free parking for patrons after 6pm

Marque

4–5/355 Crown Street, Surry Hills
Tel 9332 2225   Map 3b

French Contemporary

靣靣靣 🍷
Score 18/20

Marque has had a makeover. After a decade in business, walls have gone glossy black and the dining room has been enlarged. Chef Mark Best, meanwhile, continues to create mini marvels. There's the cool, warm, syrupy vinegariness of an egg chaud-froid with twiggy salt grissini soldiers, and a sweet foie gras-buttered toast entree with yellowfin tuna, plus an earthy dusting of pulverised pork crackling and native pepper. The warm smoky pleasure of cured duck ham was cut by too much bitter witlof but a Japanese-inspired custard of pure crab liquor on dry ice is simply extraordinary. Roasted rabbit with slimy wakame, the slipperiness of baby zucchini flowers and the starchiness of raw cashews is textural bliss, so too roast pheasant with potato skins, roast onion rings and lentil custard. It's the extras that tip the scale – glorious rye crust and sourdough bread; a nutty sesame-oil after-note on delicate salad leaves; a line of salt caramel petits fours. Here's to 10 more years, please.

Hours Lunch Fri from noon; Dinner Mon–Sat from 6.30pm; bookings essential

Bill E $24–$30 **M** $42–$47 **D** $24; 8-course degustation $145 pp; a la carte menu not available on Sat

Cards AE DC V MC

Wine Oh what a list, from France and the world; 20 by the glass

Chefs Mark Best & Pasi Petanen

Owners Mark & Valerie Best

Seats 50; private room

www.marquerestaurant.com.au

And...marshmallow with lychee, citrus and white chocolate for dessert

MCA Café

140 George Street, The Rocks
Tel 9241 4253   Map 1

Contemporary

Score 13/20

Locations this good don't always come without a price tag, let alone decent food. So we're grateful the MCA Cafe doesn't take unfair advantage of its natural assets – in this case, a picture perfect Opera House outlook from the art deco terrace. True to its name, it serves some simple casual dining favourites executed with confidence. In a city swamped with salt-and-pepper calamari, this version stands up well: impressively tender and all the lighter for the accompanying chickpeas and roast capsicum. Wagyu beef burger with gruyere and chips is a solid lunch option, but was let down by an ordinary bun. Other classic standbys, such as a generous caesar salad and sirloin steak, present well. Desserts, including a parfait with Italian meringue, display some real panache. Service can be absent-minded, but it's easy to forgive and forget and while away the afternoon with a glass of white, sunshine and a busy harbour in front of you.

Hours Breakfast Sat–Sun 10–11.30am; Lunch daily noon–3pm

Bill E $18–$19 **M** $24–$32 **D** $8–$12; 10% surcharge on Sundays & public holidays

Cards AE V MC

Wine Well-priced Australian list; 8 by the glass

Chef Jason Faulconbridge

Owners Charles Wilkins, Simon Fox & Richard Brown

Seats 120; wheelchair access; outdoor seating

Child friendly Highchairs

www.culinaryedge.com.au

And...a one-course set lunch is excellent value for $35 with a glass of wine and tea or coffee

Nothing but the wine.

If only choosing
a restaurant was as easy.

Choosing a fresh, crisp, dry, lighter style and easy drinking white wine has never been easier.
Brown Brothers Pinot Grigio is fast becoming Australia's next big thing in white wine.

www.brownbrothers.com.au

Medusa Greek Taverna

2 Market Street, Sydney
Tel 9267 0799   Map 1

Greek

Score 13/20

Fabulous, rustic Greek fare at affordable prices in a smart city setting with chatty, attentive service seems almost as mythical as the fallen beauty for whom this taverna is named. As white as a Greek island villa, Medusa's base-of-an-office-block room is dominated by a mural of Santorini at sunset, allowing local office workers a brief moment of fantasy over their mezze. These can be the most divine taramasalata, squeaky, oregano-sprinkled haloumi, large chunks of marinated octopus, kalamata olives and tzatziki, mopped up with warm pita bread. A signature slow-roasted lamb shoulder, pungent with rosemary on a bed of roasted root vegies, is truly glorious, while moussaka is everything you imagine. Chilli-tinged prawn and swordfish skewers were let down by average prawns on a bed of equally dull baked potato wedges, but it's hard to beat the allure of the Medusa dessert: a cocktail glass of ouzo-soaked strawberries with pomegranate coulis and ouzo ice-cream with a tizz of shredded kataifi pastry on top.

Hours Lunch Mon–Fri noon–3pm; Dinner Mon–Sat 6–9.30pm

Bill E $7–$18 **M** $18–$32.50 **D** $10–$14

Cards AE V MC

Wine Modest range of decent value, familiar Australian brands, plus Greek quaffers; 7 by the glass

Chef Gregori (Greg) Akridas

Owner Peter Koutsopoulos

Seats 100; wheelchair access; outdoor seating

Vegetarian Yes

www.medusagreektaverna.com.au

And...fixed-price banquet menus for six or more

Milsons

17 Willoughby Street, Kirribilli
Tel 9955 7075   Map 5a

Contemporary

Score 15/20

Milsons just gets busier, sating both simple and sophisticated palates alike. The former revel in 400-day grain-fed tenderloin with baby spinach, savoyarde potatoes, foie gras butter and truffle jus; and the latter in a sensational galantine of quail wrapped around foie gras mousse, with shaved cuttlefish on baby leeks and chestnut mushrooms – an exciting yet subtle contrast of textures and temperatures. Macleay Valley rabbit is dramatically presented with the confit leg, cleverly concealed in brik pastry, forming a base for little turrets of perfectly cooked loin beneath a raft of crisp prosciutto. It's finished with parsnip puree and a tapenade of olive and pea. Sweet summer pudding is encased in a cube of meringue, with strawberry sorbet atop and coulis below. Everything else in this polished package supports the food, from exemplary yet unobtrusive service to comfortable chairs and generous spacing between double-clothed tables, and a fascinatingly varied international cheeseboard.

Hours Lunch Mon–Fri noon–3pm; Dinner Mon–Sat 6–10pm

Bill E $28 **M** $38 **D** $16; 2-course lunch $50 pp, 3 courses $75 pp

Cards AE DC V MC

Wine Well thought out, fairly priced global list with depth and interest; 16 by the glass; BYO Mon–Thurs, max. 8 people (corkage $12 per bottle)

Chef Lee Kwiez

Owner Ben Pollock

Seats 78; private room

www.milsonsrestaurant.com.au

And...ask about cooking classes with the chef

Mino

521 Military Road, Mosman
Tel 9960 3351   Map 7

Japanese

Score 13/20

Despite its unpretentious decor, Mino has quietly wowed locals and expats for many years now with its $42 five-course banquet. There are two mini kaiseki banquets (light dishes which traditionally accompany tea ceremonies): goshu and mino. With fewer raw options and more familiar tastes, such as a starter of steamed prawns, goshu won't deter less adventurous palates. Mino, on the other hand, kicks off with sea eel and crab tempura wrapped in tofu skin. Both are dressed with great acidic zing. Although sashimi is next, it's not where Mino's strength lies. Tempura and crumbed pork are hearty and crunchy, but it's the next dish that truly epitomises chef Nakoji's 26-year kaiseki expertise. Asparagus tempura is wrapped with thinly sliced duck and bursts with hot, creamy miso flavour. His signature scallop salad with salmon roe is nicely teamed with dill – a fusion take on an otherwise very Japanese dish. Green tea ice-cream and soy-flour-powdered chocolate make for a pleasantly light final course.

Hours Dinner Tues–Sun 6–10pm; bookings essential
Bill E $14–$18 **M** $22–$24 **D** $6–$8; 5 courses $42–$59 pp
Cards AE V MC
Wine Compact list of Australians, shochu and sake; 2 by the glass; BYO (corkage $2 pp)
Chef/owner Takaaki Nakoji
Seats 40
And...kaiseki banquet ($59 pp) offered daily; a la carte menu, too

Mirabelle

AMP Building, 33 Alfred Street, Circular Quay
Tel 9252 3553   Map 1

Modern European

Score 13.5/20

On the outskirts of the financial district and just a hop, skip and Cahill Expressway away from Sydney's sparkling harbour, Mirabelle nestles at the base of the AMP building. Possessing much of the attention to detail administered at its sister restaurant, Bambini Trust, Mirabelle is an under-estimated lunchtime oasis. In a simple dining space with red booths, white tablecloths and wooden chairs, waiters are precise and punctual as they serve up aces from the kitchen. Yellowfin tuna carpaccio is slightly seared and dressed with crisp shallots and a citrussy sauce vierge. Salt-and-pepper calamari is made for lovin' a smoked paprika aioli. Ultra-tender John Dee Gold beef fillet (from Queensland) is garnished with parmentier potato. Crisp Kurobuta pork belly is a delight on a slap of pureed fennel, with a peach and watercress salad for extra dimension. A wobbly buttermilk panna cotta wades in a puddle of rose-scented strawberries – consolation for having to return to the office.

Hours Breakfast Mon–Fri 7–11am; Lunch Mon–Fri noon–3pm; bookings essential
Bill E $18–$22 **M** $33–$35 **D** $12–$15
Cards AE DC V MC
Wine Short and sharp blend of Australian and European drops; 13 by the glass
Chef Luke Sankey
Owners Angela and Michael Potts
Seats 75; wheelchair access; outdoor seating
Child friendly Crayons and paper
www.mirabelle.com.au
And...breakfasts are popular, and the menu is just as interesting

Mission

3 Little Queen Street, Chippendale
Tel 9318 0815   Map 5b

Contemporary

Score 13.5/20

The original 19th century Sydney City
Mission building is now an art gallery,
restaurant and bar, tastefully restored by
architect Jason Blake, with chef Piera Potter
running the kitchen. Whether you're here
for lunch, a drink and bar snacks or perhaps
for dinner, expect to sit among pieces from
whatever exhibition is on show. The menu is
also a showcase for the appealing flavours of
Spain through to the eastern Mediterranean.
Balkan-inspired zucchini fritters are nicely
crisp outside and fluffy within, enlivened by
fresh herbs. Braised octopus is chargrilled
with a Moroccan-flavoured coating of
paprika, cumin and coriander. House-made
lamb pie with smashed peas is full of flakily
tender meat pieces and a rich, garlicky sauce
sweetened with carrot and zucchini. Ocean
trout comes with the requisite crisp skin and
a powerful, jammy, slow-cooked tomato
salsa. For dessert, a caramelised peach tart
with vanilla bean ice-cream continues the
robust Mediterranean theme.

Hours Tues–Fri 11am–10pm, Sat 9am–10pm

Bill E $9–$17 **M** $18–$28 **D** $12–$15

Cards V MC Eftpos

Wine A good small list; 12 by the glass

Chef Piera Potter

Owners Piera Potter & Nicky Ginsberg

Seats 40; private room; wheelchair access

Vegetarian Plenty of choices

www.missionbar.com.au

And...check out the exhibitions in the
NG gallery upstairs

Moncur Terrace

Woollahra Hotel, 116 Queen Street,
Woollahra
Tel 9327 9777   Map 4b

Contemporary/Pizza

Score 13/20

The trendy, low-key counterpart to Damien
Pignolet's iconic bistro, Moncur Terrace is
many things, most of them unexpected.
It opens, Tardis-like, into a sophisticated
upstairs bar and terrace filled with leather,
wood and stone. But huge pub flat-screens
blare relentless sport and music clips. It's
staffed by cheerful, casually competent
young things, but its clientele is mostly the
immaculate over-40s set. The food sounds
like pub grub with a gourmet twist. Take
the beef burger – wagyu beef, to be precise:
moist and velvety smooth. Or the ham
and mushroom pizza – meaty mushrooms,
delectable Kurobuta ham, tongue-snapping
taleggio cheese. A confit duck leg with saute
potatoes and swiss brown mushrooms begins
beautifully but leaves a hint of vinegary
aftertaste. Grilled spatchcock with chickpeas
is gorgeously plump and luxurious, and beer
battered fish maintains its piscine delicacy
within a crisp golden casing. House-made
ices – perhaps guava, blood orange and
coconut – zing with fruit and freshness.

Hours Lunch Sat–Sun noon–3pm; Dinner
Wed–Sat 6–10.30pm, Sun 6–9pm; no bookings

Bill E $8–$18 **M** $23–$32 **D** $15–$15.50

Cards AE DC V MC Eftpos

Wine Great global list to suit any budget;
30 by the glass

Chefs Damien Pignolet & Ben Hall

Owners Damien Pignolet & Ron White

Seats 160; wheelchair access; outdoor seating

www.woollahrahotel.com.au

And...an outdoor smoking section until rain
brings the retractable roof into play

MoS Cafe

37 Phillip Street (cnr Bridge Street), Sydney
Tel 9241 3636   Map 1

Contemporary

Score 14/20

It's incidental that this busy eatery is part of the Museum of Sydney, since the suited clientele are not history buffs but office dwellers drawn from their desks by good food and wine. It's obvious the kitchen and friendly waiters know their customers, as generous serves are dispatched quickly enough for everyone to enjoy lunch hour. There's a selection of entrees great for sharing, including bruschetta and crostini. A salad of pumpkin, peas and shallots is warm and fresh, but the dressing was too tart for our tastes. Mains include pork and fennel sausages and the popular Coopers beer-battered fish of the day. A full-flavoured pasta special of rigatoni with chicken chorizo, olives, chilli, parsley and napoletana sauce comes with a glass of wine. While a white chocolate cheesecake tries to seduce, the provision of two spoons for a dark chocolate and honeycomb mousse with honeycomb wafer wins our hearts. Please don't tell our dentist.

Hours Mon–Fri 7am–9pm, Sat–Sun 8.30am–5pm; bookings essential
Bill E $8–$19.50 **M** $26–$37 **D** $12–$19.50; 15% surcharge on Sundays & public holidays
Cards AE DC V MC
Wine Good range of varieties; 33 by the glass
Chef Grant Gordon
Owners Paul Lockrey & Ramy Shelhot
Seats 150; wheelchair access; outdoor seating
Child friendly Kids' menu
www.moscafe.com.au
And...make time to browse the MoS shop next door for unusual gifts

Mumu Grill

NEW

Shop 1–6, 70–76 Alexander Street, Crows Nest
Tel 9460 6877   Map 5a

Steakhouse

Score 13/20

Enthusiastic staff welcome you into this large room, fresh with mooing mural(!), pale woods, painted concrete floor and glass bi-fold doors open to outside tables. For a steakhouse, the menu is well varied, from tapas to specials, to duck, chicken, lamb shanks, seafood, pork and beef ribs. Dishes are sensibly simple and flavours burst through, particularly in a Black Russian tomato (kumato) salad with mozzarella and pancetta. There's finesse here: a special of whole roasted rainbow trout makes proper use of the wood-fired oven, as does the day's roast of full-flavoured Bangalow pork belly. Produce is of a uniformly high standard, from the olive selection to a fine range of grass-fed beef sourced from all over Australia. A subtly flavoured 150-gram fillet from the Hunter appears properly rested, with a lovely texture. The chocolate lover's delight appears overwhelming but sweetness is restrained. Order it after the 400-gram coffee bean-encrusted sirloin, though, and you'll wish you'd worn your mumu.

Hours Lunch Wed–Sun noon–3pm; Dinner 6–10pm
Bill E $6.50–$12 **M** $21–$36 **D** $15–$28; 10% surcharge on Sundays & public holidays
Cards AE V MC Eftpos
Wine Well-varied list ventures as far as Argentina and South Africa; 20 by the glass
Chef/owner Craig Macindoe
Seats 150; outdoor seating
Child friendly Kids' menu; highchairs
www.mumugrill.com.au
And...perch at the long bar for a cocktail or two and dine off the tapas menu

GET LOST IN THE MOMENT

COOKTOPS AND OVENS HAND MADE IN ITALY

nelsons brasserie

Lord Nelson Brewery Hotel, 19 Kent Street,
The Rocks
Tel 9251 4044   Map 1

Contemporary   ♀
                              Score 13.5/20

Moored in The Rocks since 1836, this
battleship of a building houses a buzzing
downstairs bar, while the care and produce
displayed in the food upstairs elevates it
above the usual pub fare. The sandstone
walls are marked by convict adzes and
memories of Nelson's victories, while the
wine list keeps you anchored to a surprisingly
comfortable naval-grey moulded chair. Fine
prosciutto, sliced a tad thickly, doesn't need
onion in the curly topknot of cress, just that
nutty parmesan and a touch of fruity olive
oil. Exemplary spatchcock is truly juicy and
succulent, while tender grass-fed steaks
are properly rested. So the champagne jelly
dessert was a little stiff, but a hint of Pedro
Ximenez lifts the thick double cream. Pears,
sweetly poached in Nelson's Blood Porter,
which is reduced to a syrup of chocolate
and caramel notes, is a standout. Tall vases
of flowers add an elegant touch in a restful
room that's light and airy, just like the service.

Hours Lunch Thurs–Fri noon–3.30pm;
Dinner Tues–Sat 6–10pm; bookings essential

Bill E $13–$17 **M** $28–$33 **D** $9–$13

Cards AE DC V MC

Wine Well-varied list, with a fine reserve
selection; 12 by the glass

Chef Ang Tendi Lama

Owners Blair R. Hayden & Partners

Seats 85; private room

Child friendly Highchair

www.lordnelson.com.au

And...beers from the brewery downstairs
to take away

Neptune Palace

Level 1, Gateway Building, cnr Pitt & Alfred
streets, Circular Quay
Tel 9241 3338   Map 1

Chinese/Malaysian   ♀
                               Score 14/20

The sea god might be surprised to see his
palace thus, with decor best described as
slightly shabby, hotel dining room circa 1988.
But were Neptune to set down his trident
and allow his brisk courtiers to spear him an
enormous lobster from the tank, he'd surely
approve. This is very good food indeed,
from the seafood, a specialty, to the smoky,
belachan-tinged zing of char tow kueh
(fried parsnip cake). Crowd pleasers such
as salt-and-pepper squid, punchy sambal
udang (chilli prawns) or a rich, zippy lamb
curry, served with roti, are all a cut above.
So too is murtabak (a roti parcel filled with
beef mince). Mentega dishes – fried with
butter and curry leaves – are something
of a specialty, transforming snake beans
into a dish to be savoured. We're not sure
this is what Roman gods eat but, with an
encyclopaedic wine list and service that mixes
efficiency with high spirits, it's more than
enough for us mortals.

Hours Lunch daily noon–3pm;
Dinner daily 5–10.30pm

Bill E $9.80–$27.80 **M** $20.80–$48
D $7.80–$9.80

Cards AE DC V MC

Wine Perhaps the best list in a Sydney Chinese
restaurant, sampling regions around the world;
14 by the glass

Chefs Kim Fai Lam & Fom Sau Tan

Owners Lee Ngann Ly & Derek Lim

Seats 200; private room

Child friendly Highchair

Vegetarian Separate menu

And...try the banquets from $42 pp

Nilgiri's

81–83 Christie Street, St Leonards
Tel 9966 0636   Map 5a

Indian

Score 14.5/20

A visit to this polished and professional pappadum and paratha heaven is a welcome reminder that Indian food in Sydney needn't come from the bain-maries of our ubiquitous north Indian diners. Here the spicing is considered, the flavours are memorable and the amenable floor staff eager to guide you through a menu that each month focuses on a different region of the subcontinent. A Kashmiri entree of sliced eggplant in tamarind, cumin and chilli batter is a lesson in texture and flavour that sets expectations high for what is to come. Excellent prawns arrive marinated in mustard oil, turmeric and aniseed, and in phool rogan josh, thinly battered cauliflower is given a kick from a spicy tomato and onion sauce. Slow-cooked goat served in a dark stew rich in cardamom, and Kashimiri-style chicken korma with crushed coriander, are mopped up with breads from the open kitchen's tandoor oven. Date and honey kulfi, one of six milky ices, is a divine revelation.

Hours Lunch Mon–Fri & Sun noon–3pm; Dinner daily 6–10pm

Bill E $15–$17 **M** $25–$27 **D** $9–$12

Cards AE DC V MC Eftpos

Wine Well-priced list of Australasian labels plus a Rhone Valley Hermitage; 18 by the glass; BYO (corkage $6 per bottle); plus India's Kingfisher lager

Chef Ajoy Joshi

Owners Ajoy & Meera Joshi

Seats 180; private rooms

Vegetarian Daily specials and banquet

www.nilgiris.com.au

And... Sunday buffets are great value at $27.50

North Bondi ★ Italian Food

118–120 Ramsgate Avenue, North Bondi
Tel 9300 4400   Map 9

Italian

Score 14/20

FAVOURITE FOOD-WITH-A-VIEW

Arriving at noon for a lazy weekend lunch provides a perfect insight into this hip beachside trattoria. Early on, it's family hour. Then the beautiful people arrive, followed by the fashion set. By early evening, the bar is jumping. Stylemeister Maurice Terzini's combination of ocean views, groovy (and good) Italian cucina and funky, upbeat waiters appeals to all comers. Baccala fritto – crisply fried salt cod balls with a lemon wedge and creamy aioli – is a prelude to more great things in a rustic, authentic Italian theme. Plate-sized veal saltimbocca alla romana is perfectly presented. Zampone (stuffed pig's trotter) is a splendid celebration of offal. For dessert, look no further than dolce della nonna, a decadent chocolate gelato with roast hazelnuts and chocolate and marsala zabaglione. Sydney may have a notoriously short attention span, but the eternally busy NBIF remains the place to see and be seen.

Hours Lunch Fri–Sun noon–4pm; Dinner daily from 6pm; no bookings

Bill Dishes range from $15–$29 **D** $14–$16; 10% surcharge on Sundays & public holidays

Cards AE DC V MC Eftpos

Wine Balanced, comprehensive list of Australian and Mediterranean; 22 by the glass

Chefs Robert Marchetti, Ben Horne & Marjorie Robertson

Owners Robert Marchetti, Maurice Terzini, Kimme Shaw & Tony Zaccagnini

Seats 120; wheelchair access; outdoor seating

Child friendly Highchairs; kids' dishes; blackboard

www.idrb.com

And...sip Campari and fresh orange juice at the bar

Nu's

178 Blues Point Road, McMahons Point
Tel 9954 1780   Map 5a

Thai

Score 14/20

Don't judge a book by its cover, or a contemporary Thai eatery by its heritage sandstone surrounds. At first glimpse, Nu's ignores the familiar Thai aesthetic, but spicy aromas inside reveal its secret. The room is a marriage of history and clean new lines while the extensive blackboard specials hint at the occasional Vietnamese and Chinese influence. Super-crisp prawn pancakes, akin to large ravioli, are spiked with coriander and complemented by a sultry tamarillo chilli dressing with a dulcet palm sugar accent. Betel leaves rolled around caramelised coconut, with the immutable crunch of peanuts and a tickle of ginger, are textured with slinky prawns. Stir-fried roast duck is simply voluptuous, marinated in honey, spices, garlic and ginger, heady with tum leung thai greens and a wisp of chilli. While service can waver when it gets busy, sassy desserts include pungently sour–sweet, thinly shaved nam doc mai mango soothed by sublime sticky rice and topped with toasted slivered almonds and black sesame seeds.

Hours Lunch Tues–Fri noon–3pm; Dinner Tues–Sun 6–11pm

Bill E $9–$16 **M** $19–$48 **D** $12–$18

Cards AE V MC Eftpos

Wine Concise, affordable list, includes several Thai-friendly whites; 10 by the glass; BYO Tues–Thurs & Sun only (corkage $10 per bottle)

Chefs Nu Suandokmai & Paul Webster

Owners Nu & Jane Suandokmai and Ruth Walsh

Seats 120; private room; outdoor seating

And...dishes are marked with 1, 2 or 3 chillies for timid diners

Ocean Room

Bay 4, Ground Level, Overseas Passenger Terminal, Circular Quay West, The Rocks
Tel 9252 9585   Map 1

Japanese/Seafood

Score 13.5/20

A wall of aquarium tanks and cascading lantern-shaped lights greet you in this swish, sexy, high-ceilinged room. With long-time chef Raita Noda now part-owner, the revamped menu is easy on the eye, too. The smaller plates are where his creative juices flow. Ocean's Eleven is a set of 11 sashimi shooters (alas, no George Clooney or Brad Pitt on the side), with distinctive dressings to match. Noda's marvellous signature tomato bomba is back, a staple from his reign at Rise. A whole tomato is caramelised to resemble agedashi (deep-fried) tofu, then served in rich, sweet dashi stock. Mains, on the other hand, are uncomplicated but also full of vigour and colour: a flounder basket is spectacularly presented as juicy fillets on the fish's crunchy deep-fried bones. The wide range of daily whole fish includes live seafood from the tanks. Experimental desserts are hit-and-miss – the "orange" plate's fine parfait was overpowered by sweet citrus cakes and candied bits – but ensure a finale with plenty of wow.

Hours Lunch Tues–Fri noon–3pm; Dinner Mon–Sat 6–10.30pm; bookings essential

Bill E $14–$26 **M** $35–$42 **D** $15–$17; 10% surcharge on Sundays & public holidays

Cards AE DC V MC

Wine Extensive list of well-selected mostly Australian wines; 14 by the glass

Chef Raita Noda

Owner Zetton Ocean Room Pty Ltd

Seats 200; private room; wheelchair access; outdoor seating

Child friendly Kids' meals; highchairs

www.oceanroomsydney.com

And...good views unless a liner is docked in front

Oceanic Thai

309 Clovelly Road, Clovelly
Tel 9665 8942   Map 9

Thai

Score 13.5/20

Ah, sweet mystery of mee grob, at last I've found thee…light as fairy floss, delicately nuanced with garlic chives, fragrant with plum sauce – and in coastal Clovelly. In this suburban Thai bistro, with the bus stop outside the door, chef Max Mullins shows off his finesse with imaginative, bright food, devoid of terrible chilli and coconut cliches, coaxing us into understanding the briskness and subtlety of our sour palate. You can ride the gentle waves of a salmon larb with its roasted rice and crisp rice crackers. You can sail a course through a heady jungle curry of crisp pork belly and pickled bamboo. Though the rice wasn't exceptional, the dessert platter is, with its surprising chocolate and coconut pandan dumplings in spiced coconut milk, and yellow bean and star anise cake. Also exceptional is the grace with which host Sally Lynch looks after everyone in this handsome, dark room with bistro chairs and table stools.

Hours Dinner Tues–Sat from 6pm

Bill E $14–$16 **M** $17–$24 **D** $18 (plate for 2); 4-course banquet $55 pp

Cards V MC

Wine Food-friendly, mainly Australian list with foreign touches, including a Thai highlands drop; 8 by the glass; BYO Tues–Thurs (corkage $3.50 pp)

Chef Max Mullins

Owners Max Mullins & Sally Lynch

Seats 40; wheelchair access

Vegetarian Six vegan dishes

www.oceanicthai.com.au

And…the house cocktail, a ginger, lime and lychee caipiroska, is a blast

Oliveto

Brays Bay Reserve, 443 Concord Road, Rhodes
Tel 8765 0006   Map 6

Italian

Score 13/20

A wood-fired oven greets you as you enter, heralding a warm welcome ahead. Despite fairly austere surrounds and some under-staffing, the team from Leichhardt's Grappa knows how to make you feel at home. That oven produces thin, bubbly pizza with some nice charring. It's also used for several seafood and meat dishes. Deep-fried calamari in a dark crunchy batter is deliciously salty and soft, and scallops on a bed of carrot puree with pancetta are pretty and subtle. House-made lobster and cannellini bean ravioli were limp and a little flavourless, although generously filled with lobster. An outstanding sage and parmesan-crusted pork chop is beautifully presented with bitter chicory and caramelised witlof – perfect with a glass of chianti. The peaceful river view lulls you into relaxation and, at night, the restaurant's white surfaces glow. So stay for dessert, especially when the espresso granita with mascarpone and fluffy brioche both soothes and invigorates.

Hours Lunch Mon–Fri & Sun noon–3pm; Dinner Tues–Sat 6–10pm; bookings recommended

Bill E $17.50–$26 **M** $21.50–$38 **D** $14.50

Cards AE DC V MC Eftpos

Wine An interesting Australian-dominated list, lacking in enough Italians; 20 by the glass; BYO (corkage $4.50 pp)

Chef Chris Georgakopolous

Owners Tony Colosi, Charlie Colosi, Alessandro & Carmen Milozzi

Seats 150; wheelchair access; outdoor seating

Child friendly Kids' menu; highchairs

www.oliveto.com.au

And…a great choice for dinner or lunch before a Homebush event

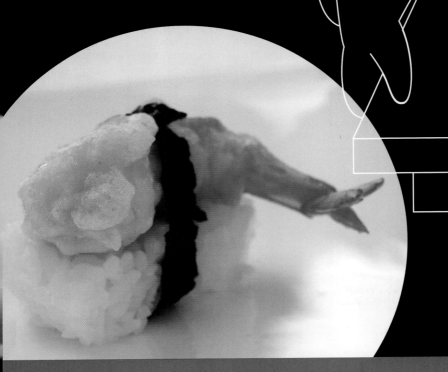

Onde

346 Liverpool Street, Darlinghurst
Tel 9331 8749   Map 2

Modern French

Score 14/20

The full-length windows at Onde (French for wave) reveal a pared-back bistro filled with the perfect Darlinghurst cross-section of older couples, dates, mates, young families and even solo diners. Caring service ensures everyone gets just the right amount of attention, but try for a banquette table along the feature wall to reduce noise a little. Fried zucchini flowers come (unfilled) straight from pan to plate, with a quick stop for a generous grating of parmesan over their ultra-crisp batter. Confit pork with pickled apple and mesclun arrives as a pleasantly light salad – each forkful teams shreds of delicately spiced meat with bitter leaves and the fruit's acidic bite. Mains are simple and spot-on, from a textbook T-bone with red-wine butter and frites to plump roast chicken on chunks of pine mushroom and roast potato. Finish with a piping-hot plum crumble and you'll realise why Onde is still riding high on a wave of popularity after 13 years.

Hours Dinner Mon–Thurs 5.30–10.30pm; Fri–Sat 5.30–11.30pm; Sun 5.30–10pm; no bookings

Bill E $13.50–$16 **M** $19–$26 **D** $9

Cards AE DC V MC

Wine Very reasonably priced, mostly Australian with a few European; 24 by the glass

Chef Laif Etournaud

Owners Laif Etournaud & Simone Lai

Seats 36

And...if you're waiting for a table, have a cocktail at the Victoria Room around the corner

Opera Bar

Lower Concourse Level, Sydney Opera House, Sydney
Tel 9247 1666   Map 1

Contemporary

Score 12/20

It's the great Faustian bargain of Sydney dining: how badly do you want the view? Enough to sacrifice peace and quiet, shelter from the weather, and any semblance of crowd control? If so, the famously buzzy, fabulously funky Opera Bar is for you. It's incredibly noisy, largely open air (at least for view seekers), and absolutely jam-packed. But in exchange, the metal seats and casual cafe tables give you one of world dining's iconic views: the bridge, the Opera House, the city and harbour. With such a visual feast at hand, any menu will struggle to compete, but there's plenty to graze on. The pre-theatre tasting plate includes tender lamb cutlets and tasty pork belly skewers, though samosas, cured fish tortilla and fig and rocket salad were all a little tired. Main course chargrilled scotch fillet lacked both style and substance, but miso-marinated blue-eye with bok choy and shimeji mushrooms is pleasing. And there's always a dozen Sydney rock oysters and more champagne. Let the party begin!

Hours Daily noon–11pm; no bookings

Bill Dishes from $6–$27; tasting plate for two $46

Cards AE DC V MC Eftpos

Wine Comprehensive list, mostly Australian; 40 by the glass

Chef Brian Martinez

Owner Solotel Hotel Management

Seats 450; wheelchair access; outdoor seating

Vegetarian Mezze plate, pizza, pasta, risotto & salads

www.operabar.com.au

And...live jazz funk every night – stop talking and boogie

Oscillate Wildly

275 Australia Street, Newtown
Tel 9517 4700   Map 8

Contemporary

Score 15/20

Hugely talented young chef Daniel Puskas is on the next stage in his culinary journey, introducing an eight-course degustation. Prices have doubled, but it's still decent value and this cute shopfront restaurant continues to be booked out months in advance. This thrilling experience can hit heady heights with its outlandish flavour combinations and presentation. There's salmon roe perched on a creamy dollop of cauliflower and white chocolate; and a modern take on gazpacho: a pile of icy cold tomato granita on a smear of cottage cheese with specks of cucumber and beetroot. Soft-as-butter beef cheek partners watermelon foam and turtle bean. Sometimes it goes too far. Vanilla sponge with jewfish and chickpeas didn't marry successfully, and cinnamon toast overpowered duck and sweet potato. Our faith is restored with a triumphant dessert of hibiscus granita, long pepper, ginger and coriander. If dining out is about taking your tastebuds where they've never been before, Puskas is the chef to do it.

Hours Dinner Tues–Sat 6–10pm; bookings essential

Bill 8-course degustation $95 pp

Cards AE V MC Eftpos

Wine A concise list chosen with great care, including some aged beauties, almost bottle shop prices; 7 by the glass; BYO (corkage $3 pp)

Chefs Daniel Puskas & James Parry

Owner Ross Godfrey

Seats 28

Vegetarian Vegetarian degustation

And...excellent coffee and tea included in the price

Osso

19 Lawson Street, Penrith
Tel 4722 6102   Map 6

Contemporary

Score 12.5/20

Modern, stylish and comfortable sums up both Osso and its food. This oasis in the backstreets of downtown Penrith dares to serve some challenging entrees. Beautifully fresh butterflied prawns are paired with wasabi vichyssoise. Pork belly is served on a bed of whitebait fritters, albeit with rather too much caramelised balsamic vinegar. A well-made, strongly flavoured goat's cheese tart is topped with deboned quail, while there's a decent pasta menu, too. Main courses are less experimental, with a simple lamb rump, slow-roasted beef fillet and pork loin with polenta. Duckling is simply roasted but needed a sauce to lift the flavour score. A mushroom risotto special has plenty of honest taste. Desserts are simple, such as the house chocolate plate, lemon and lime baked ricotta and a panettone trifle. Osso is a welcome blend of culinary sophistication and friendly professional service. Its great bar makes things even better.

Hours Lunch Mon–Fri from noon; Dinner Tues–Sat from 6pm

Bill E $15.50–$37.50 **M** $25–$36.50 **D** $12.50–$25

Cards AE V MC Eftpos

Wine Mid-sized list with good choice of premium labels at a fair price; 13 by the glass

Chef Clayton Jude

Owners Tony & Norman Italiano & Clayton Jude

Seats 100; outdoor seating

Child friendly Kids' menu; highchairs

www.osso.com.au

And...share a tasting plate of the four more exciting entrees

Osvaldo Polletti

148 Norton Street, Leichhardt
Tel 9560 4525   Map 5b

Southern Italian

Score 13.5/20

If you have a sense of humour and a hunger for rustic south Italian cuisine, look no further. Host Franco Napoliello welcomes you like family, with formalities dismissed and big hand gestures aplenty. Jeans-and-T-shirt clad waiters work the noisy room, dashing up and down the stairs and between the dark-timber tables. The menu changes regularly but may include antipasto of golden olive fritte: crumbed, fried green olives stuffed with goat's cheese. Pasta dishes are invariably fantastic, all fresh and house-made. Try tagliatelle with rabbit, peas and tomato, a simple and effective flavour and texture combination. Better still is squid-ink tortellini with a smooth salt-cod filling in a shallow pool of fish broth. Mains are best ordered with side dishes (sauteed carrots or green beans perhaps). Crisp-skinned trout was fresh but unevenly cooked, while spatchcock – roasted breast and confit legs – is just right. Tiramisu is gorgeous topped with almond praline crumbs.

Hours Dinner Mon–Thurs 6–9pm, Fri–Sat 6–10pm

Bill E $8–$18 **M** $25–$30 **D** $6–$11

Cards V MC Eftpos

Wine Affordable Italians; 8 by the glass; BYO (corkage $5.50 per bottle)

Chefs Franco Napoliello & Luca de Martin

Owners Joe & Franco Napoliello

Seats 60

Child friendly Kids' menu; highchair

And...one of the cheeky boys pictured on the wall is probably your waiter

Otto Ristorante

Area 8, 6 Cowper Wharf Road, Woolloomooloo
Tel 9368 7488   Map 2

Italian

Score 15/20

Summer's prevailing nor'easter whistles through the rigging of the squillion-dollar flotilla out front, the city skyline scowls back at you and the sun winks on the water. You chortle with the other sun-glassed suits on the corso of the Finger Wharf, where Otto sets the benchmark for a symphony of style and substance. Service here is oft copied but rarely bettered, mixing flawless efficiency with sweet charm. Poached Spencer Gulf prawns laze on white polenta with a salt-cod stuffed zucchini flower sweetened by raisins and pinenuts. Prosciutto comes with peach puree to temper tart Woodside goat's curd. Mains include rack of lamb with eggplant and chickpea puree or barramundi partnered by the earthy flavours of beetroot with apple balsamic. Otto's take on tiramisu, in a naff martini glass, layers mascarpone sabayon, chocolate panna cotta and amaretto jelly with espresso granita on the side. La vita don't get much more dolce than this.

Hours Lunch daily noon–3.30pm; Dinner daily 6–10.30pm

Bill E $20–$29 **M** $35–$42 **D** $18–$20; 10% surcharge on Sundays & public holidays

Cards AE DC V MC

Wine Super list with super mark-ups, predominantly Italian & Australian; 22 by the glass

Chef James Kidman

Owner Leon Fink

Seats 150; private rooms; wheelchair access; outdoor seating

Child friendly Kids' menu; highchairs

Vegetarian 3-course vegan menu

www.otto.net.au

And...valet parking available at Blue

Ottoman Cuisine

Pier 2, 13 Hickson Road, Walsh Bay
Tel 9252 0054   Map 1

Turkish

Score 15/20

Turkish-born chef Serif Kaya is the master of supple textures and subtle tastes, extracting lingering, exquisite flavours from his courtly cooking. Service is getting better all the time, and we feel like sultans in the dark, plush space illuminated like a mosque by a dazzling display of tulip-shaped hanging lights. From a long and fascinating menu that journeys through the Ottoman empire, start with yaprak dolma – refined, cigarillo-sized vine-leaf rolls stuffed with rice, gorgeous pinenuts and sweet currants. The more modern kabak mucver are dark-golden puffs of zucchini with a creamy, garlicky yoghurt sauce. Kaya's lemony, juicy spatchcock is deboned and grilled, skin on, while a buttery cracked wheat pilaf is perfumed with roasted capsicum. Even the traditional kofte (minced lamb torpedoes) are smoother and finer than most, white beans offering crunchy contrast. As for dessert, raspberries with cardamom ice-cream (and a touch of stretchy salep) are divine, while kazandibi, a wobbling baked custard with mastic, is suitably sublime.

Hours Lunch Tues–Fri noon–3pm; Dinner Tues–Sat 6–10pm

Bill E $18–$22 **M** $29–$35 **D** $6–$14

Cards AE DC V MC Eftpos

Wine Distinguished reserve list, handsome Australians, Mediterranean section; 15 by the glass

Chef Serif Kaya

Owners Serif & Gulbahar Kaya

Seats 200; private rooms; wheelchair access; outdoor seating

Vegetarian Several entree & main options

www.ottomancuisine.com.au

And...a sweeping, glorious view from the Harbour Bridge to Luna Park

Palace Chinese

Level 1, Piccadilly Tower,
133–145 Castlereagh Street, Sydney
Tel 9283 6288   Map 1

Chinese (Cantonese)

Score 13/20

Chinatown it ain't. Nor is it your standard neighbourhood joint. Perhaps it's the marble-stair walk up to the Palace's first-floor entrance off a smart shopping arcade. Maybe it's the Castlereagh Street address, the plushly carpeted floors, gold and green decor and genial, informed service. Weekdays are for the white-collar lunchtime clientele eyeing off the yum cha trolleys. But by night it's a family affair, with a menu that's strictly a la carte and from the tank. Steamed duck dumplings are juicy, plump and meaty. Baby spinach with king mushrooms, soaked in oyster sauce gravy, is glorious to share. A generous serve of braised scallops in XO chilli sauce with bean sprouts and snow peas also pays homage to Cantonese authenticity but chicken in Sichuan sauce with green peppers didn't reach similarly great heights. Perhaps live coral trout, lobster or crab is a more spectacular choice. Come with a gang and do both.

Hours Lunch daily 11am–3pm; Dinner daily 5–10.30pm

Bill E $8.80–$25.80 **M** $18.80–$58 **D** $5.80–$6.80

Cards AE DC V MC

Wine Premium Australian list; 19 by the glass

Chefs Ma Song & Li Ming

Owner Lee Ngann Ly

Seats 250; private rooms

Child friendly Especially nights and weekends; highchairs

Vegetarian Multiple options

www.palacechinese.com.au

And...$7 parking voucher available weeknights & weekends

emirates.com/au

A matter of taste.

The Emirates fine-dining menu.

Every time you fly on Emirates you'll enjoy a delicious multiple course menu created by world-class chefs. And to make sure your selections are always fresh, our menus change regularly. Bon Appétit.

Fly Emirates. Keep discovering.

Emirates

Palisade Dining Room

Palisade Hotel, 35 Bettington Street,
Millers Point
Tel 9251 7225   Map 1

Contemporary

Score 14.5/20

Fancy fit-outs aren't the only vehicle for superior food. Here, deep in The Rocks, is palpable proof. Anyone trying to emulate Palisade's determinedly no-frills pub design had better be armed with the impressive cooking skills of long-time double-act chefs Matthew Quinn and Brian Sudek. In a simple, whitewashed dining room upstairs from a lively public bar, you'll find a menu of intelligence and integrity with impressive Asian and Mediterranean flourishes. Confident, attractively presented dishes include king prawn wontons with lemongrass broth and glass noodles, and Balmain bug salad with chilli, Vietnamese mint and coconut vinegar. Mains range from wonderfully juicy Glenloth chicken, with puy lentils, speck and eschallots to non-standard meat dishes such as choice sirloin fillet, sliced, slow-roasted and succulent, with king brown and chestnut mushrooms and a restrained bearnaise. The mastery continues in a mixed berry summer pudding (the fruit forms the basis of the entire dessert) with white chocolate creme anglaise. Trendier, glossier, pub-grub cousins take note.

Hours Lunch Tues–Fri noon–3pm; Dinner Tues–Sat from 6pm; bookings essential

Bill E $18–$22 **M** $32–$36 **D** $14

Cards AE DC V MC Eftpos

Wine Balanced, interesting list; 10 by the glass

Chefs Brian Sudek & Matthew Quinn

Owner Palisade Properties Pty Ltd

Seats 50

www.palisadehotel.com

And... Sydney Theatre Company is just a short walk away

Pendolino

Shop 100, Level 2, The Strand Arcade,
412–414 George Street, Sydney
Tel 9231 6117   Map 1

NEW

Italian

Score 14/20

Pendolino is an olive oil lover's heaven. Nino Zoccali, founding chef at Otto, runs a moody, modern Italian ristorante and olioteca (oil shop) atop the fashionable Strand Arcade. Out front is a crowded casual cafe, while inside hosts the shop, plus a cleverly lit brick room with dark carpets, timbers and leather banquettes. Many dishes are listed with an accompanying oil, which is drizzled, for example, to give a peppery kick to char-grilled, grass-fed sirloin on a malty oxtail and pearl barley risotto. House-made pappardelle slither around a succulent, creamy slow braise of marjoram-scented White Rocks veal shin. A pretty yellowfin tuna carpaccio is slashed with a clever tonnato dressing. But porchetta – shredded and fennel-crusted pork shoulder on cotechino sausage, with a white bean and potato puree, and fennel and orange salad – is a little too busy and overworked. Your inner sweet tooth will thrill to nougat, Ligurian honey and almond milk semifreddo with candied almonds.

Hours Breakfast Mon–Sat 9–11.30am; Lunch Mon–Fri noon–3pm; Dinner Tues–Sat 6–10pm; bookings essential

Bill E $19–$26 **M** $27–$36 **D** $12–$15; 10% surcharge on public holidays

Cards AE V MC Eftpos

Wine Small, clever mix of Australian classics and Italians at decent prices; 23 by the glass

Chef Nino Zoccali

Owners Nino Zoccali & SG Foodservice Pty Ltd

Seats 140; private room

Vegetarian A third of the menu

www.pendolino.com.au

And...taste (and buy) oils and vinegars in the Olioteca

Penny's Lane

Cnr Kings Cross Road and Penny's Lane,
Kings Cross
Tel 9356 8177   Map 2

Contemporary French

Score 14/20

This irregular, bistro-style space is tucked
away under the Diamant Hotel (and Coke
sign). It's a blend of faux wooden tables,
soft leather banquettes and comfortable
string chairs on a chequerboard floor that's
not nearly as personable as the welcoming,
informative and charming waiter. British chef
Robert Crichton is behind the stoves, having
previously worked with owner Manuel
Spinola at his QVB Tearooms. His solid bistro
fare ranges from a classic chicken liver parfait
to an outstanding dish of rabbit loin cleverly
served like yin and yang with black pudding
beside spaetzle and tomato coulis. Perhaps
the bearnaise with otherwise delightful steak
frites lacked acid balance. Poached king
salmon in a tomato and corn broth, however,
is a miracle of textural contrast beneath
wafer-thin roesti, and the flavour lingers on.
A beautifully executed fine apple tart delights
with its light puff pastry and thinly sliced
apple set off by silky pomegranate ice-cream.

Hours Breakfast daily from 7am; Lunch daily
from noon; Dinner daily from 6pm

Bill E $17 **M** $28 **D** $12

Cards AE DC V MC

Wine Well-chosen, interesting, varied global list,
reasonably priced; 16 by the glass

Chef Robert Crichton

Owner Manuel Spinola

Seats 120; wheelchair access

Child friendly Kids' portions

www.pennyslane.com.au

And...$25 lunch and $31 dinner specials
are good value

Perama

88 Audley Street, Petersham
Tel 9569 7534   Map 8

Greek

Score 15/20

If you're still wondering why one of Sydney's
best Greek restaurants is in Little Portugal,
don't sweat it. Just count your lucky
dolmades if you bag a table on Saturday
night. While you're there, thank the gods
for David Tsirekas. A few things about
Perama feel like the Old Country –
whitewashed stucco walls, wooden arches,
Byzantine pottery, friendly, distracted staff.
But the chef's restless, creative muse defies
the Hellenic cliches. A lobster moussaka
special is a mini masterpiece of fresh shellfish
and rich, oozing bechamel; and a pastitsio
of braised lamb with fennel and onion salad
sings like a siren to a sailor. Regulars know
that Tsirekas's savoury filo pastries (his mum
Jenny's, actually) are extraordinary, so be sure
to follow your mezze or barbecued calamari
with one of Jenny's pites, or perhaps a
sumptuous pork belly baklava. Come dessert,
enjoy the sensational, complex interplay
of sweet and tart accents in a pineapple
bougatsa (custard parcel). Coffee please.

Hours Dinner Tues–Sat 6–10.30pm;
bookings essential

Bill E $14–$19 **M** $25–$29.50 **D** $2.50–$12.50;
10% surcharge on public holidays

Cards V MC Eftpos

Wine Quality Greek wines featured; 13 by the
glass; BYO wine only (corkage $5 per bottle)

Chef David Tsirekas

Owners David & Belinda Tsirekas

Seats 110; private room; outdoor seating

Vegetarian Several entrees, a main, sides
and salads

www.perama.com.au

And...good luck finding parking nearby

Pier

594 New South Head Road, Rose Bay
Tel 9327 6561   Map 9

Contemporary/Seafood   ♨♨♨ ♆
Score 18/20

It's easy to see why there has been nothing but applause for chef Greg Doyle's shrine to the sea. Awash with nautical tones, the elegant room struts the length of a pier, jutting into Rose Bay and displaying stunning harbour views from every well-dressed table. It's an irresistible lure, so sit back, imagine money is no object and savour some of the city's finest seafood. Doyle's obsessive focus on quality results in standout freshly opened oysters and gorgeous pan-roasted scallops, superbly teamed with cauliflower and truffle risotto. Service is flawless, with the kind of care that shines on the plate. Crisp-skinned ocean trout displays heavenly texture, matched with tomato fondue, baby zucchini flowers, basil and black olive puree. Bass grouper is cooked sous vide (sealed, in water, at low temp) and decorated with golden baby beetroot and samphire, white balsamic and ginger foam. Katrina Kanetani's desserts impress: sour cherry and custard doughnuts are lavished with creme fraiche sauce, cinnamon and kirsch.

Hours Lunch daily noon–3pm;
Dinner Mon–Sat 6–10pm, Sun 6–9pm
Bill E $36–$45 **M** $49–$85 **D** $28; $10 pp surcharge Sundays, $12.50 pp public holidays
Cards AE DC V MC
Wine Extensive, notable list of international and local varietals – at a price; 15 by the glass
Chefs Grant King, Katrina Kanetani & Greg Doyle
Owners Greg & Jenny Doyle
Seats 120; private room
Child friendly Kids' menu
Vegetarian Separate menu
www.pierrestaurant.com.au
And...take home the Pier cookbook, too

Pier Tasting Room

594 New South Head Road, Rose Bay
Tel 9327 6561   Map 9

Contemporary/Seafood   ♨ ♆
Score 15.5/20

This must be one of the best views and best food you'll find while perched on a Sydney barstool. Calming grey and white tones leave you to focus on the water from the long white bench in Pier's converted foyer. Supremely knowledgeable waiters bring scaled-down versions of the main restaurant's fare. It's Pier lite, even if the prices are not, especially when some morsels are so small that sharing them almost requires microsurgery. Choices range from sublimely simple – pristine Sydney rock oysters with a squeeze of lemon, to simply sublime – crisp-skinned barramundi with the marmalade bitterness of caramelised witlof and orange. Cured salmon "pastrami" with cauliflower panna cotta and tiny beetroot is another highlight, but Murray cod tartare with soy and mirin fell a little flat. Desserts deserve their own degustation. Standouts include a creamy pistachio millefeuille beneath a slab of toasted marshmallow, and mango parfait beside a green mango and coconut salad with sweet native finger lime pearls.

Hours Lunch daily noon–3pm;
Dinner Mon–Sat 6–10pm, Sun 6–9pm
Bill Tasting dishes $9–$28 **D** $15; $7.50 pp surcharge on Sundays, $10 pp on public holidays
Cards AE DC V MC
Wine Long, high-end international list; 15 by the glass
Chefs Grant King, Katrina Kanetani & Greg Doyle
Owners Greg & Jenny Doyle
Seats 20
Child friendly Kids' menu
Vegetarian Separate vegetarian menu
www.pierrestaurant.com.au
And...you can ask for wines matched to each tasting plate

Pilu at Freshwater ★

End of Moore Road, Freshwater
Tel 9938 3331   Map 7

Italian (Sardinian)

♔♔ ♈
Score 16.5/20

FAVOURITE EXTRAVAGANCE

Pilu is the best of both worlds: the vibrant, thrilling, sunshiny flavours of chef Giovanni Pilu's Sardinian homeland, combined with some irresistible Sydney sand and surf. The water beckons below as you peer from the breezy heritage beach house, but that would mean tearing yourself away from Pilu's polished fare, such as evocatively saffron-scented malloreddus – Sardinian shell pasta – with vongole, zucchini flowers and salty bottarga. Pancetta-wrapped quail, stuffed with chicken livers and the aniseed perfumes of fennel and tarragon, is equally sensual on a bed of eggplant caponata. The signature slow-roasted suckling pig and its seductive crackling may induce swooning, assuming you're not entranced by the lush, tomato-based soup brimming with seafood, accompanied by poetically named carta di musica (crackly flatbread sheets). Desserts are a showcase of Sardinian specialties, but it's hard to beat the elegance of sheep's milk gelato with warm berry compote and savoiardi – as lovely as a day at the beach.

Hours Lunch Wed–Sun noon–2.30pm; Dinner Tues–Sat 6–10pm

Bill E $24–$26 **M** $35–$42 **D** $16

Cards AE DC V MC Eftpos

Wine Outstanding and well-annotated range of Australian and Italian varietals; 23 by the glass

Chef Giovanni Pilu

Owners Giovanni Pilu & Marilyn Annecchini

Seats 110; private rooms; outdoor seating

Child friendly Kids' menu; highchairs; colouring-in books

www.piluatfreshwater.com.au

And...7-course Sardinian degustation for $95

Pink Peppercorn

122 Oxford Street, Darlinghurst
Tel 9360 9922   Map 2

Modern Laotian

Score 13/20

This is a delightful dose of eye candy at the not-so-sweet end of Oxford Street. Wedged between Leather Connection and Adult World (after dessert, thanks), Pink Peppercorn is adorned with rosy shades and scenes of Dalai Lama-look-alikes in saffron robes. The crowd is equally appealing – one part smart suit to two parts Mardi Gras glam – and the service, while perfunctory, is pleasant enough. The food, billed as modern Laotian, is also eye-catching. There are all the specialties of old Laos (salads and grills), plus more mod ones such as steamed salmon in banana leaves. Crab and chicken rolls arrive as crisp cigarillos, while chicken larb comes as nuggety pieces of bird laced with fragrant herbs and the tang of chilli and lime. Laotian-style beef was not as successful due to less-than-tender strips of meat in a bland coconut sauce. Dessert ends on a high note though. A chocolate volcano – choc pudding with white chocolate sauce – prompts excited squeals from the dining divas.

Hours Dinner daily 6pm–late

Bill E $12.50–$14.50 **M** $21–$24.50 **D** $11.50; 10% surcharge on public holidays

Cards AE V MC Eftpos

Wine Limited list of big-name brands; 10 by the glass; BYO (corkage $3 pp)

Chef Anouvong Kaseum

Owners Anouvong Kaseum & Peter Barker

Seats 65; outdoor seating

And...for those who like a passing parade, seats on the footpath

ASTRAL

Discover Level 17

Sean Connolly

Chef's Hat 2007 & 2008, Sydney Morning Herald, Good Food Guide Awards

Chef of the Year 2008, Sydney Morning Herald, Good Food Guide Awards

Chef of the Year 2006, 2007 & 2008, Australian Hotels Association

Restaurant of the Year 2007 & 2008, Australian Hotels Association

Best Fine Dining Restaurant in a Hotel,
Restaurant and Catering Awards for Excellence, NSW 2006

Discover the Astral phenomenon. Level 17, 80 Pyrmont Street Pyrmont Sydney
For reservations call 1800 700 700 or visit www.astralrestaurant.com.au

Pizza e Birra

Shop 1, 500 Crown Street, Surry Hills
Tel 9332 2510   Map 3b

Italian/Pizza

Score 13.5/20

Pizza and beer not only sound sexier in Italian, they feel sexier too in this ever-bustling, dimly lit space where the beautiful people go for a night off the no-carbs. You may have to wait – and wait – for a table (no bookings, alas) but one bite of these wood-fired, Neapolitan-style beauties will make it worthwhile. With bases this good, many opt for the simplicity of a margherita, but we also love the creamy comfort of quattro formaggi (four cheeses) and the flavour punch of sausage with porcini mushroom. Other offerings are also appealingly authentic, from pasta to olives all'ascolana (fat green olives filled with mince, crumbed and fried). Zucchini flowers stuffed with goat's cheese and anchovies could have done with a little less salt, and a vanilla panna cotta dessert was low on wow. Service is cheerful if sometimes a little pushed. But a glass of pale ale from Victorian boutique brewer Holgate will help you relax into it.

Hours Mon–Wed 6–11pm, Thurs–Sun noon–11pm; no dinner bookings
Bill E $6–$20 **M** $18.50–$33 **D** $11.50–$14.50; 10% surcharge on Sundays & public holidays
Cards AE DC V MC
Wine Reasonable and effective Australian and Italian list; all 50 by the glass
Chefs Vishel Rummun, Gianluca Vinci, Gianni Cristiano & Nino di Donato
Owners Khali Khouri, Mauro Marcucci & Sabina Buoncompagni
Seats 100; wheelchair access; outdoor seating
Vegetarian Choices from pizza, pasta, risotto and salad
And...there's Pizza e Birra in Melbourne now, too

Pomegranate Thai

191 Darling Street, Balmain
Tel 9555 5693   Map 5b

Thai

Score 13/20

Looking like an overdressed Lord Jim set with an open kitchen, this Prasit's offshoot has plenty of authentic Thai dishes. There's a small regular menu, which locals seem to know by heart, and a bigger blackboard list of enticing specials, albeit at times a little one-dimensional in flavour. Choor muang – steamed violet dumplings stuffed with delicate minced fish – have become an instant classic. Notching up the spice scale, Balmain rolls are a strongly spiced crab and pork mix inside a bean curd skin. Pla grob (deep-fried whitebait with roast coconut) is served on a betel leaf with chilli jam and plenty of heat. Gang thai pho (fried pork belly with kaffir lime) has the punch of Bangkok street food, while pad thai was a touch on the sweet side. Desserts include taro cake with coconut ice-cream and a gentle yok manee – tapioca pudding with fresh coconut, sweetcorn and coconut ice-cream.

Hours Lunch Fri–Sun noon–3pm; Dinner Tues–Sun 5.30–10pm
Bill E $10.50–$12.50 **M** $21.50–$27.50 **D** $7.50–$8.50
Cards AE V MC Eftpos
Wine Small list well suited to the spicy tastes; 7 by the glass; BYO (corkage $3 pp)
Chef Supachai Kongkham
Owner Eric Sudardja
Seats 60; wheelchair access
Child friendly Kids' menu on request
And...order desserts as a takeaway for later

Pony Lounge & Dining

14–15, The Rocks Centre, Playfair Street,
The Rocks
Tel 9252 7797   Map 1

Contemporary
Score 14.5/20

To dismiss this extremely pleasing diner for its touristy location would be to miss out on good food and real hospitality. Exposed brick walls, an open kitchen and a warm welcome create an immediately exciting, appealing vibe. Seafood, pasta and a fine meat selection from the wood-fired grill are boosted by food that's great fun to share and friendly, knowledgeable service. We make light work of a tasting plate of manchego cheese, olives, cumquat and pear chutney, and squabble over chorizo and tomato and butter bean salad. A second entree of crisply fried prawns, served with soy sauce and Sichuan spice for dipping, leaves us wanting more. Crisp-skin snapper arrives in a colourful tomato broth bobbing with plump Boston Bay mussels, celery, potatoes and peas. An enormous 600-gram beef rib special is a bit unwieldy, but the potato hash with bacon is an interesting side. A bitter chocolate tart and a raspberry and white chocolate cheesecake conclude an evening we don't want to end.

Hours Lunch daily noon–3pm;
Dinner daily 6pm–late

Bill E $19–$24 **M** $26–$45 **D** $8.70–$15.50;
small plates $3.40–$18.90; 10% surcharge on Sundays and public holidays

Cards AE V MC Eftpos

Wine Appealing Australian and European list;
20 by the glass

Chef Damian Heads

Owners Nick & George Kyprianou & Damian Heads

Seats 74; wheelchair access; outdoor seating

Vegetarian Lots of small plates

www.ponydining.com.au

And...arrive early for a drink on the ultra-cool deck

Post Restaurant

Lower Ground Floor, GPO,
1 Martin Place, Sydney
Tel 9229 7744   Map 1

Seafood/Contemporary   ♉
Score 14/20

The corporate types who lunch at this slick CBD brasserie no doubt find the fit-out – muted colours, restrained artwork – comfortingly similar to their company boardrooms. Indeed, as the sister restaurant to the meat-focused Prime, Post is so focused on quick-turnaround business lunches that its staff sometimes fail to recognise customers keen on a more leisurely experience. As the name suggests, fish caught using the ike jime (instant kill) spiking process are the main feature of the menu although a small number of meat dishes are popular with the mostly male crowd. Steamed barramundi rolled into a roulade with zucchini ribbons is lifted by a subtly flavoured fennel puree. Salty seaweed helps cut through Balmain bug linguine served with prawn bisque. An intriguing green tea brulee with lentil ice-cream and a sweet lentil cake seemed to prove that lentils are best in savoury dishes, but we admire the kitchen's sense of adventure in an otherwise staid world.

Hours Lunch Mon–Fri noon–3pm;
Dinner Mon–Sat 6–10pm

Bill E $16.50–$19.50 **M** $28–$37.50 **D** $15.50

Cards AE DC V MC Eftpos

Wine Substantial Australian-focused list;
20 by the glass

Chef Iwao Yamanishi

Owner Peter Petroulas

Seats 240; wheelchair access

Child friendly Highchairs

www.gposydney.com

And...rock and Pacific oysters with some of the city's more inventive accompaniments

Prime

Lower Ground Floor, GPO,
1 Martin Place, Sydney
Tel 9229 7777   Map 1

Steakhouse/French

Score 13/20

There's no subtext to the menu in this vaulted, historic, sandstone dining room beneath the GPO. It's all about beef and the choicest grade your corporate plastic will stand. For CEOs with a few stock options still in the money, the special wagyu menu offers an F1 wagyu-holstein cross (marble score 6) or full-blood wagyu (marble score 9) in individual fillets or as an imposing chateaubriand for two. We'll happily settle for a juicy, grilled angus-hereford yearling, black angus sirloin, rib-eye or T-bone cooked on the rare side of medium–rare with a nice char. Add a classic sauce and mash or a good potato gratin and it's love and marriage (going together like a friendly takeover). The few non-carnivorous dishes include a so-so truffled goat's cheese souffle, a well-executed snapper fillet with ratatouille, and a lovely mascarpone tart for dessert. Service can be nervy but is never less than polite. Atmospheric lighting, private alcoves and leather banquettes ensure a clubby, discreet business lunch or dinner.

Hours Lunch Mon–Fri noon–3pm;
Dinner Mon–Sat 6–10pm

Bill E $24–$28 **M** $30–$48 **D** $17.50

Cards AE DC V MC Eftpos

Wine Patrician list of bordeaux and burgundy with some more affordable appellations, plus local and Spanish; 20 by the glass

Chef Iwao Yamanishi

Owner Peter Petroulas

Seats 140; private room; wheelchair access

Child friendly Highchairs

www.gposydney.com

And...a spacious private function room

Qmin

5/207b Pacific Highway, St Leonards
Tel 9966 5557   Map 5a

Indian

Score 14/20

The clean lines, spaciousness and subdued earthy colours set the tone for Qmin's contemporary take on Indian dishes. Forget the red yoghurt-and-spice crust of the usual tandoor-cooked chicken tikka for the signature tulsi ke tikke, marinated chicken with a more subtle and cooler flavouring of basil, garlic and cashews. Eggplant dumplings are soft, delectable balls combining mashed potato, shredded eggplant and light spicing in a rich tomato and cream sauce. Goat bhuna is a drier-style curry with melting chunks of slow-cooked goat spiced with strong notes of cumin and coriander, to emphasise the darker flavour of this meat. Bindhi (okra) cooked with mango is a fabulous creation, while a side order of Punjabi salad – lettuce, tomato, sliced Spanish onion, whole green chillies and limes – brightens the palate in preparation for a richly eggy, cardamom-perfumed baked custard. Service is attentive without being intrusive, and wait staff are delighted to show off their knowledge of the dishes.

Hours Breakfast Mon–Fri 8–10.30am; Lunch Mon–Fri noon–3pm; Dinner Mon–Sat 6–10pm

Bill E $13–$17 **M** $17–$28 **D** $10–$12

Cards AE DC V MC Eftpos

Wine A small but varied, well-chosen range; 10 by the glass; BYO (corkage $7 per bottle)

Chef/owner Anil Ashokan

Seats 70; wheelchair access

Vegetarian A good range of creative choices

www.qmin.com.au

And... Get Ashokan's secrets in his *Qmin* cookbook

Save me from my mortgage

(I'm drowning in fees!)

Find out if you could be saving on your home loan

Could your repayments be lower? Are you paying unnecessary fees? Is your interest rate really competitive? Find out by calling ING DIRECT. You'll soon see if you're being looked after. It's your money.

Call 1800 353 378 or visit ingdirect.com.au

ING DIRECT
It's your money

Quay ★

Upper Level, Overseas Passenger Terminal,
Circular Quay West, The Rocks
Tel 9251 5600   Map 1

Contemporary

Score 18/20

RESTAURANT OF THE YEAR

The mind-blowing location pales into
insignificance beside Quay's sculptural food.
Chef Peter Gilmore's cooking is bold and
evolutionary yet never tricky, served with
finesse and pride by polished staff. Dinner's
quartet of courses (choose from five dishes
per course) rethinks traditional dining with
alacrity. It might begin with the sultry texture
of ethically harvested Australian shark fin
with egg yolk, turnips and duck consomme,
followed by the textural contrast of crisp,
succulent pork belly and handmade silken
tofu beneath a whisper of shaved abalone
and Japanese mushrooms. Blue-eye trembles
under a brioche crust contrasted by celery
heart, hazelnuts and buttery young leeks.
Desserts are as glamorous as the setting,
including a sensual white peach granita
with white peach snow egg. Chocolate cake
features eight layered textures in a perfect
disc with hot ganache melting seductively
through the middle. Gilmore's ability to
astound and delight keeps us enthralled.

Hours Lunch Tues–Fri noon–2.30pm; Dinner daily
6–10pm; bookings essential

Bill 4–course a la carte dinner menu $145 pp;
2-course lunch $75 pp, 3 courses $90 pp;
10% surcharge on public holidays

Cards AE DC V MC

Wine Appealing, extensive international list with
prices to match; some half bottles; 13 by the glass

Chef Peter Gilmore

Owner Leon Fink

Seats 220; private rooms; wheelchair access;
outdoor seating

Child friendly Kids' menu

www.quay.com.au

And...2- and 3-course set lunches are great value

Rambutan

96 Oxford Street, Darlinghurst
Tel 9360 7772   Map 2

Thai (Southern)

Score 13/20

Unlike the curiously spiky fruit from which
it takes its name, Rambutan is all chic good
looks, with an open kitchen behind backlit
marble, solid timber tables, including a
communal version, moody lighting and
strong incense. Accomplished chef Mai
Busayarat (ex China Doll and Jimmy Liks)
cooks for a hip crowd used to shared food
and chirpy Thai flavours. Smoked trout on
betel leaf with grilled chilli eggplant is a
popular party starter, while the Chinese
influence in jasmine tea-smoked quail with
an addictively salty black pepper sauce is
superb. The eponymous tropical fruit appears
in a dish of crisp duck with a surprisingly
sweet tamarind sauce, while gaeng om –
a lush, northern-style veal shank curry with
apple eggplants and coriander – is good
preparation for a night on the town. And if
a soupy caramel and coconut flavoured bao
loy with pandan leaf, taro and pumpkin is
too much of an acquired taste for dessert,
there are always those cocktails.

Hours Dinner Tues–Sun 6–11pm; Supper tasting
menu Fri–Sat 6pm–2am

Bill E $3.50–$15 **M** $18–$35 **D** $6–$10;
10% surcharge on Sundays & public holidays

Cards AE V MC Eftpos

Wine Small, food-friendly, affordable list;
9 by the glass

Chef Mai Busayarat

Owners Joe & Milena Natale

Seats 120

Vegetarian A third of the menu

www.rambutan.com.au

And...funky downstairs bar serving amusingly-
named cocktails

Ratu Sari

470 Anzac Parade, Kingsford
Tel 9662 8788   Map 9

Indonesian

Score 12/20

Ratu Sari is one of the smarter joints in a neighbourhood that's packed with affordable, good-quality Asian eateries. The simple but pleasant room has a white-tiled floor, comfortable chairs, and Indonesian batiks adorning the walls, but unassuming surrounds belie feisty flavours fiery with chilli. Bringing a group is ideal to try a range of dishes from the large menu, and to help stop you polishing off the bowl of addictive fried anchovies and peanuts by yourself. Just as more-ish are pieces of crisp-skinned quail with deliciously moist flesh. There are lots of vegetable options, from a classic gado-gado salad to velvet-soft and caramelised eggplant fried with belachan (dried shrimp paste). A house specialty of meltingly flaky beef rendang hits just the right note, and tiger prawns stir-fried with pungent petai beans (also known as stink beans, an acquired taste) come in a rich, blisteringly hot chilli sauce. Afterwards, a cooling, multi-coloured shaved-ice dessert will quell the fire.

Hours Lunch Tues–Sun noon–3pm; Dinner Tues–Sat 5.30–9.30pm, Sun 5.30–9pm

Bill E $6.50–$9.50 **M** $11.90–$18.90 **D** $6.50–$8.50

Cards AE DC V MC Eftpos

Wine BYO (no corkage)

Chef Rohana Halim

Owners Michael & Rohana Halim

Seats 70; wheelchair access

Child friendly Highchairs; kids' banquet

Vegetarian Several dishes (check for shrimp paste)

And...stock up on Asian groceries while you're in the 'hood

Red Chilli

Shop 3, 51 Dixon Street (entry via Little Haymarket Street), Haymarket
Tel 9211 8122   Map 3a

Chinese (Sichuan)

Score 13/20

Overlooking the hustle, bustle and flickering neon nightlife of Chinatown, Red Chilli stands out from the pack. Its Sichuan-style cuisine delivers a bigger knockout than a George Foreman right hook with its liberal use of chillies (fresh and dried) and mouth-numbing Sichuan pepper. Don't be fooled by the at-times impassive service or the functional decor. This is all about the food. Wickedly gelatinous slices of pork belly are steamed then lightly battered, arriving crisp and golden brown. Whole steamed barramundi is decorated with ginger and shallots – the silky flesh falls from the spine. Aromatic lamb with cumin shows off regional subtleties, as does stickily slippery, chilli eggplant. Salt, pepper and chilli king prawns get your spice receptors working before you leap into real tongue-numbing delicacies, such as deep-fried chicken with very (*very*) hot dried chilli. And if you're really game, head to the upper level for cook-your-own super-chilli hotpots. After all, fortune favours the brave.

Hours Lunch daily 11.30am–2.30pm; Dinner daily 5–10.30pm

Bill E $3.20–$11.80 **M** $10.80–$78.80 **D** $3.20–$16.80; $2 pp surcharge public holidays

Cards AE DC V MC Eftpos

Wine Simple and small list; 2 by the glass; BYO (corkage $3 pp)

Chefs Zhou Ping, Luo Zhen, Shu Jie & Liu Yimin

Owners Cheng Jian, David Zhang & Teresa Dai

Seats 190; private room

Child friendly Highchairs

www.redchillirestaurant.com.au

And...avoid the queues and book ahead, but don't be late

Red Lantern

545 Crown Street, Surry Hills
Tel 9698 4355   Map 3b

Vietnamese

Score 13/20

Snaring a seat between Red Lantern's vivid vermilion walls can be harder than getting onto the UN Security Council. Once ensconced, you'll enjoy efficient, informed service and decent Vietnamese fare. Cha gio is a super-duper spring roll filled with pork, chicken, glass noodles, carrots and wood-ear mushrooms, while the meat in bo tai chanh, fine slices of lemon-cured sirloin with saw-leaf coriander, holy basil, rice paddy herb and crushed peanuts, was a little too tartare for our tastes. Seafood and poultry dominate the mains, such as fleshy fish fillets cooked in a clay pot with tomato, black pepper and chilli; and roast duck with wok-seared Asian greens and plum sauce. Desserts adhere to the Indo–Chinese theme, including a refreshing tapioca pudding with banana and cassava; and black sticky rice with taro and coconut milk. Some may prefer the sparkling Vietnamese authenticity of Cabramatta, Marrickville or Bankstown, but long may Red Lantern's easy, approachable and buzzy inner-city style reign, and shine.

Hours Lunch Tues–Fri 12.30–3pm; Dinner Tues–Sun 6–10pm; bookings essential
Bill E $12–$18 **M** $21–$30 **D** $11–$12; 10% surcharge on Sundays & public holidays
Cards AE DC V MC
Wine Short but good choice of Australasian reds and whites; 10 by the glass
Chef Mark Jensen
Owner Luke Nguyen
Seats 50; outdoor seating
Vegetarian Separate menu
www.redlantern.com.au
And…two chef's choices menus for $40 and $50

Rengaya

73 Miller Street, North Sydney
Tel 9929 6169   Map 5a

Japanese

Score 14/20

Beef a bit overcooked? Chicken a tad tough? Vegies a little underdone? Stop complaining. At this real-deal Japanese yakiniku joint, you've only yourself to blame. Yakiniku means table barbecue – a place where the diner is the chef. And Rengaya's excellent ingredients make it hard to go wrong. They include F1 black wagyu beef, no less – a Japanese black/Australian angus cross. Start with excellent sushi and sashimi and then fire up the barbie grill in front of you, choosing from more wagyu cuts than you can wave your tongs at. There are chicken and pork grilling options, too, as well as soup, noodle and rice dishes. After more than 15 years in business, Rengaya continues to lift its game, rating as one of our more enjoyable Japanese nights out. The lucid, illustrated menu, complete with colour pics, is a joy. Helpful service is abundant, too, with more floor staff than at restaurants where chefs do all the cooking.

Hours Lunch Tues–Fri noon–3pm; Dinner daily 6–9.30pm
Bill E $3.80–$39.80 **M** $8–$39.80 **D** $9–$23.90; set menu $65 pp; 10% surcharge on Christmas & New Year holidays
Cards AE V MC
Wine Simple list; 7 by the glass; try Japanese beers and sake
Chef Yoshihiro Akiba
Owner Yoshiro Inoue
Seats 96; private rooms; outdoor seating
Child friendly Highchairs; booster seat
www.yakiniku.com.au
And…enlist the friendly staff's help and advice if you're unsure

Republic Dining

Republic Hotel, cnr Bridge & Pitt streets,
Sydney
Tel 9252 6522   Map 1

European
                                    Score 12.5/20

A solid, upstairs hideaway in the CBD,
Republic sure knows its audience – suits, and
predominantly male ones at that. So expect
plenty of good red meat, buckets of great
red wine, crumbed veal the size of a plate
and some slightly cheeky service from the
mostly all-female floor crew in a bistro-style
room of paper-on-cloth tables, banquettes
and windows with the occasional bridge
view. While the food was once a cut above,
now it's fairly standard pub fare. For starters,
the oysters seemed a little dull, chargrilled
calamari was a little bit chewier than it
ought to be, and no one should expect to
find bones in a duck sausage. Wagyu sirloin
steak (grade 7–8), however, is exemplary
and cooked to order, while barramundi
with mash, capers, lemon and spinach also
impresses. The wine list, of predominantly
Aussie classics, is fairly priced and well
chosen – suiting the suits to a tee, especially
with the Aussie and European four
cheeses plate.

Hours Lunch Mon–Fri noon–3pm;
bookings essential
Bill E $19–$21.50 **M** $33–$38 **D** $12.50
Cards AE DC V MC
Wine Well-chosen list of predominantly
Australian classics with some old-world
treasures; 21 by the glass
Chef Chris Coolahan
Owner Patrick Ryan
Seats 80; private room; wheelchair access
www.republichotel.com
And...try the lounge or downstairs bar for better-
than-average snacks

Restaurant Arras

Ground Floor, 24 Hickson Road,
Walsh Bay
Tel 9252 6285   Map 1

British
                                    Score 15.5/20

Yorkshire lad Adam Humphrey has turned
a historic wool bond store into a smart and
stylish fine diner. His cooking blends droll
English humour with refined French style
for fabulous entrees, such as the opulent
crab bread-and-butter pudding; and vitello
tonnato cleverly reconstructed into a terrine
as handsome as Heathcliff striding across
the Moors. The gently lit room is a sexy mix
of exposed brick walls and mottled coats
of paint amid heavy timber beams, while
Alon Sharman (ex Quay) runs a crisp and
effervescent floor team. "Rack on black"
alternates slices of house-made black
pudding and lamb saddle beside a mound
of decadent pommes anna, leek "ravioli"
and gravy. Pappardelle with brussels sprouts,
chestnuts and parsnip veloute is wintry,
Christmas-like pleasure. Desserts don't come
much better than Yorkshire cream tea, a
trifle-like concoction of scone, clotted cream,
strawberry jam and tea jelly, assuming the
brimming and decadent cheese trolley hasn't
caught your eye first.

Hours Lunch Tues–Sat noon–2.30pm; Dinner
Tues–Sat 6–10pm; bookings essential
Bill E $21–$27 **M** $27.50–$48 **D** $17–$17.50
Cards AE DC V MC Eftpos
Wine Affordable, global boutique list;
18 by the glass
Chefs/owners Adam Humphrey & Lovaine Allen
Seats 60; private room; wheelchair access
Child friendly Highchairs; colouring pens
www.restaurant-arras.com.au
And...don't park around there after midnight
or you'll be booked

The Restaurant at 3 Weeds

197 Evans Street, Rozelle
Tel 9818 2788   Map 5b

Modern European

Score 14.5/20

You know something's going on when, even on a Saturday night, pub patrons are more focused on eating than drinking. The bar menu alone gives some restaurants a run for their money, but in the adjoining glass-encased eatery, John Evans offers a precise and sophisticated reworking of the bistro theme. Slow-cooked pork belly with morcilla (Spanish blood sausage), caramelised apple and spinach is so beautifully cooked it reminds you why it became a Sydney staple. An Asian raviolo of crab and coriander with soy and mirin dressing is so brilliantly sweet, light and spike-sharp you'll hope it becomes similarly ubiquitous. Our only quibble with saltwater char (ocean brown trout) is that the accompanying eggplant puree is so deeply, darkly smoky that it threatened to overwhelm the perfectly seared fish. Service has the same extra shine as the food, and the decor's green earth tones are easy on the eye. Bags the last bite of baked ricotta cheesecake with strawberry salad.

Hours Dinner Tues–Sat 6pm–late; bookings essential

Bill E $17–$23 **M** $28–$33 **D** $15–$17

Cards AE DC V MC Eftpos

Wine Well-chosen, interesting list sourced globally; 15 by the glass

Chef John Evans

Owner Rylely Pty Ltd

Seats 75; wheelchair access

www.3weeds.com

And…a good selection of draught beers to try, too

Restaurant Atelier

22 Glebe Point Road, Glebe
Tel 9566 2112   Map 5b

Modern European

Score 14.5/20

There's no lack of eating opportunities in Glebe, but fine diners are thin on the ground. This heritage-style red-walled cottage with linen-clothed tables and friendly, informed staff fills the niche, with generous, creative, contemporary cooking, albeit at times overworked. Pig's trotter croquettes are a generous serve of gelatinous meat and prawn chunks encased in a crisp coating, lifted by a vibrant piquillo pepper puree, although the accompanying citrus and seafood salad seemed redundant. Slowly caramelised tomatoes and tangy goat's cheese work well in a warm tomato tarte Tatin, yet the crust was a touch soggy. Roasted Queensland squab is rare and beautifully tender, the accompanying crisp salsify and slippery shiitake providing great textural contrast before a twist of linguine with Chinese truffles again tipped the accompaniments into excess. Come dessert, caramel souffle with salted caramel ice-cream and whisky anglaise is a seamless assembly of flavours and a fine finale.

Hours Lunch Fri noon–2pm; Dinner Tues–Sat from 6pm; bookings essential

Bill E $16–$22 **M** $30–$34 **D** $15; 3-course menu (Tues–Thurs only) $59 pp

Cards V MC Eftpos

Wine Interesting selection of local and imports, many under $50; 13 by the glass; BYO Tues–Fri only (corkage $8 per bottle)

Chef Darren Templeman

Owners Darren & Bernadette Templeman

Seats 80; private room; wheelchair access; outdoor seating

www.restaurantatelier.com.au

And…3-course weeknight special is great value

Restaurant Balzac

141 Belmore Road, Randwick
Tel 9399 9660   Map 9

Modern European/British

Score 16/20

If the doughty figure of Captain Cook were to spin on his pedestal and peer through the window of the imposing two-storey sandstone building behind, he'd see happy diners in a charmingly understated room. The good captain would surely admire the banquettes, the sturdy wooden chairs and the diligent service, and salute Matthew Kemp's English influence on the French-inspired menu. The kitchen coaxes clarity and intensity of flavour from daringly juxtaposed, and often humble, ingredients. All work gloriously well. A dollop of salt cod mousse primes succulent, seductive aged serrano ham; a tumble of shaved cuttlefish and chorizo graces a block of pork belly; a slew of curried vongole cushions a lovely piece of bream. In anticipation of the next seasonal and produce-driven menus, we'll forgive the closeness of the tables and a bombe Alaska that, one night, coldly resisted cutlery. Have faith that Kemp's contemporary sensibility and classic techniques promise seriously good eating.

Hours Lunch Fri noon–2.30pm; Dinner Tues–Thurs 6–10pm, Fri–Sat 6–10.30pm; bookings essential

Bill E $20–$25 **M** $28–$36 **D** $12–$16; 2-course pre-theatre menu $50 pp; 9-course degustation $85 pp

Cards AE DC V MC

Wine A terrific, thoughtful, wide-ranging list; 16 by the glass; BYO Tues–Thurs & Sun only (corkage $14 per bottle)

Chefs Matthew Kemp & Wade Brown

Owners Matthew Kemp & Lela Radojkovic

Seats 110; private room; wheelchair access

Child friendly Booster seats

www.restaurantbalzac.com.au

And...street parking is easy

Restaurant Sojourn

79 Darling Street, East Balmain
Tel 9555 9764   Map 5b

Modern European

Score 14.5/20

The classically trained, husband-and-wife team of Paul and Kim Camilleri brings a touch of culinary class to the ferry end of Darling Street. Romancing couples and gourmet groups pack this two-storey terrace of warm sandstone walls to see what the fuss is about. It's foremost in an entree of corpulent scallops (all the way from Nova Scotia, no less) adorned with tiny sticks of Iberico jamon and tomato "caviar", but unfortunately the result was more disappointing than dazzling. It's a rare off-note on a menu that features a magnificent grain-fed Victorian beef fillet poached in a veal and beef stock until it's so tender that it slices like butter. Farmed Humpty Doo barramundi is similarly spectacular, with a delightfully crisp skin over pearl-white flesh, paired with steamed clams, pureed jerusalem artichoke and smoked bacon veloute. Kim's desserts are equally enticing. In fact, the millefeuille of fig with cinnamon pastry cream and blackberry sorbet is irresistible.

Hours Lunch Fri noon–3pm; Dinner Tues–Sat 6–10pm; bookings essential

Bill E $22–$26 **M** $35–$39 **D** $16–$18; 10-course degustation $95 pp; 10% surcharge on public holidays

Cards AE V MC

Wine Very savvy international list; 14 by the glass

Chefs Paul Camilleri & David Wright

Owners Paul & Kim Camilleri

Seats 55; private room; wheelchair access

www.restaurantsojourn.com.au

And... Sojourn's 10-course degustation menu is now available every night

Ripples at Chowder Bay

NEW

Deck C, Chowder Bay Road, Mosman
Tel 9960 3000   Map 7

Contemporary

Score 13/20

Ripples have spread around the harbour, from Milsons Point (where the original Ripples, beside Luna Park, remains a great breakfast spot) to pretty Clifton Gardens, to create this picturesque gem in an historic old naval building. Its harbourside location with outdoor veranda seating and affordable bistro food is backed up by friendly and professional service. Lunch is when the harbour sparkles but, day or night, Ripples offers all-round delightful dining. The broadly appealing, Italian-leaning menu ranges from tempura-style soft-shell crab served on slightly-too-sweet fennel coleslaw to chargrilled calamari and chorizo with risoni pasta and rocket. A generous serve of grilled quail sits on parsley-spiked crushed potato with salad to the side. Roast kingfish fillet is well matched with tomato compote and green olive tapenade. For dessert, a tangy goat's curd tartlet with strawberries and lemon is as irresistible as the setting.

Hours Breakfast Mon–Fri 9–10.45am (summer only), Sat–Sun 8–10.30am; Lunch Mon–Fri noon–3pm, Sat–Sun noon–4pm; Dinner Mon–Sat 6–9pm, Sun 6–8.30pm

Bill E $15–$19 **M** $22–$29 **D** $11–$14; 15% surcharge on public holidays

Cards AE DC V MC

Wine An appealing, comprehensive list; 26 by the glass; BYO (corkage $8 per bottle)

Chefs Jeff Turnbull & Vaclav Dvorsky

Owner Bill Drakopoulos

Seats 164; private rooms; outdoor seating

Child friendly Kids' meals; highchairs

www.ripplescafe.com.au

And...pop in anytime for coffee

Rocket

1–5 Railway Street (cnr Help Street), Chatswood
Tel 9411 8233   Map 7

Contemporary

Score 14/20

Floating above the muted rumble of passing trains and exposed through floor-to-ceiling glass, this modern, friendly space lends itself to contemporary fare, served by young, accommodating staff. A tiny pot of complimentary creamy artichoke vichyssoise gets the night off to a pleasant start, although later on, some portions seem a little on the small side. A warm salad of crunchy asparagus with dollops of Kytren goat's cheese and mini beetroot is bolstered by a kalamata tapenade. Solid mains tout strong flavours: grain-fed beef Rossini is a star, rich with port and truffle salsa. Flavoursome seared lamb loin and babaghanoush is perfectly tender, offset by a lively tabouli, even if the eggplant is overpowered by yoghurt. White peach souffle presented in a petite copper saucepan, accompanied by vanilla bean ice-cream, is a knockout, while a kaleidoscopic seasonal fruit plate with cubes of elderflower jelly and quenelles of lychee sorbet looks as pretty as it tastes.

Hours Lunch Mon–Fri noon–2.30pm; Dinner Mon–Sat 6–9.30pm; bookings essential

Bill E $18–$22 **M** $31–$35 **D** $9–$17

Cards AE DC V MC Eftpos

Wine Very representative Australasian list; 14 by the glass; BYO (corkage $7–10 per bottle)

Chef Richard Allsop

Owners Peter & Theresa Fletcher

Seats 80; private rooms; wheelchair access; outdoor seating

www.rocketrestaurant.com.au

And...complimentary parking under the building (evenings only)

Rockpool (fish)

107 George Street, The Rocks
Tel 9252 1888   Map 1

Seafood

Score 16.5/20

Neil Perry has kept his finger on Sydney's pulse for almost two decades at Rockpool, cajoling our palates, setting trends and capturing the city's zeitgeist. Now he's taken off his fine diner's tie and jacket to create a more casual, yet still smart, seafood diner and a brighter, more open space with leather-topped tables. The oyster bar is back and the service is impeccable. Then there's Perry's principled advocacy of the finest, sustainable produce. Such devotion doesn't come cheap, but its value is obvious in raw, live scallops, opened to order, with a ginger and chilli-infused black bean dressing. Snapper fillet with a thin bread crust lolls on a lush roast tomato sauce. The sprawling menu comes ashore for a masterful combination of slow-cooked egg with mushy peas and mint on crisp bruschetta, while slow-roasted Barossa chook is perfectly moist. Among a series of extraordinary desserts, the iconic date tart remains a lovely way to remember the past as the revamped Rockpool (fish) sails smoothly on.

Hours Lunch Mon–Fri noon–3pm; Dinner Mon–Sat 6–11pm

Bill E $16–$39 **M** $36–$56 **D** $16

Cards AE DC V MC

Wine World-class list; 24 by the glass

Chefs Neil Perry & Michael McEnearney

Owners Neil Perry & Trish Richards

Seats 120; private room

Child friendly Highchair

www.rockpool.com

And…splurge on lobster, mud crab and abalone fresh from the tank

Royal Bar & Grill

Royal Hotel, 237 Glenmore Road, Paddington
Tel 9331 5055   Map 4b

Contemporary

Score 12.5/20

The ceilings soar but the menu of bistro favourites is down to earth in this airy, second-floor pub dining room. It's popular with groups, but the twos and threes can retreat through French doors to the iron-lace veranda and take in the district views. Waiters weave in and out, but sometimes it's a challenge to attract their attention. A warm duck salad is more duck than salad – light on spinach, with a tasty whole leg served under a haystack of fried leek. It's perhaps too substantial to precede the flavoursome angus rump, cooked beyond the requested medium, with plenty of garlic butter to soak up with crunchy house-made wedges. Chargrilled salmon is contrasted by a Thai-dressed salad of green beans and tomatoes. Desserts ply classic-hits territory, and while we'd prefer the mudcake-like flourless chocolate cake to be a little less chilled, it's a minor point at the end of a sun-soaked weekend lunch.

Hours Lunch Mon–Fri noon–3pm; Dinner Mon–Fri 6–10pm; Sat noon–10pm; Sun noon–9pm

Bill E $8.50–$17.50 **M** $18.50–$29.50 **D** $9.50; 10% food-only surcharge on public holidays

Cards AE V MC Eftpos

Wine Good selection goes beyond the average pub list; 23 by the glass

Chef Keith O'Leary

Owner Foodsmith Pty Ltd

Seats 110; outdoor seating

Child friendly Highchairs

www.royalhotel.com.au

And…half-price cocktails at the Elephant Bar until 6.30pm

The Royal Oak

The Mean Fiddler, cnr Commercial
& Windsor roads, Rouse Hill
Tel 9836 5036 Map 6

Contemporary

Score 13/20

The white paper-topped linen tablecloths, comfortable banquettes and spacious yet elegant interior of the Royal Oak are a welcome respite from the jangling, somewhat confused attractions of what has become the Mean Fiddler pub theme park. This is a brave and ultimately successful pitch at fine dining, complete with white gloves and amuses bouche. An entree quail salad was a little heavy on walnut dressing and a little light on quail, but an intensely flavoured roast pumpkin and sage soup is perfectly pitched against a neatly formed blue swimmer crab sausage. Pork belly rounds stuffed with house-made black pudding, plus roasted quince, prawn colcannon (mash) and balsamic jus is a joyous mix of sweetness and richness. A 100-day grain-fed aged rib-eye fillet with bearnaise is easy to say but not to cook to this state of fresh, soft pinkness. Pear and passionfruit crepe with vanilla ice-cream cinnamon foam is a beautiful belly-buster.

Hours Lunch Wed–Sat noon–3pm,
Sun 11.30am–3pm; Dinner Wed–Sun 6–10pm

Bill E $15–$18 **M** $27–$30 **D** $8–$18

Cards AE DC V MC Eftpos

Wine Affordable list of locals with some internationals; 16 by the glass

Chef Angelo Velante

Owner Drinx Group Pty Ltd

Seats 140; wheelchair access; outdoor seating

Child friendly Kids' menu; highchairs; playground; kids' entertainment Wed–Fri & Sun

www.meanfiddler.com.au

And…the regular rotisserie showcases meat and game from the Oak's own ageing room

Safi

55 Ridge Street, North Sydney
Tel 9954 6146 Map 5a

Middle Eastern

Score 13/20

A cottage calm hangs over this brick-paved heritage strip, housing contemporary art galleries and tiny eateries. Safi fits right in, with cafe-style outdoor seating and a clean, red-and-grey lettered menu that puts a fresh gloss on classic Middle Eastern mezze. Plain white walls with only the odd folkloric touch – jugs, rugs and a nargileh (water pipe) – match a detectable lightness through dips, salads, vegetarian and meat dishes. Besides chickpea-rich hummus and gently nutty felafel, there are addictively good muhammara – a crumbly chilli-red walnut paste speckled with pine nuts; and slender potato kibbeh – crushed wheat patties with coriander. Not everything is comfortingly familiar – a liberal use of sumac (a citrussy, slightly floral spice) over-sharpened an already tart fattoush salad, and lemony notes also dominated yeasty spinach pockets. Smiling, obliging waitresses are not always as attentive as hoped. But crisp, just-sweet pistachio-nest baklava with a glass of perfumed chai or ahweh (Arabic coffee) hits just the right delicate note.

Hours Lunch Tues–Fri noon–2.30pm;
Dinner Tues–Sat 6–10pm

Bill Shared plates $9.50–$17 **D** $2–$3;
14-dish banquet menu $35 pp

Cards AE V MC Eftpos

Wine BYO (corkage $3 pp)

Chef/owner Vic Ossian

Seats 70; private room; outdoor seating

Child friendly Booster seat

Vegetarian Ideal, with plenty of choices

www.safidining.com

And…it's justifiably popular, and tiny, so make sure you book

Sailors Thai Canteen

Street Level, 106 George Street, The Rocks
Tel 9251 2466   Map 1

Thai

Score 14/20

Long-time Sailors chef Pacharin "Air" Jantrakool's stamina is matched only by her talent for enticing vivid, feisty Thai flavours from the open kitchen at this casual communal eatery. Every day this historic sandstone cottage brings fresh waves of eager diners vying for a place at the long, well-worn 50-seat zinc table to watch the chopping, wokking and sizzling action and enjoy evocatively perfumed fast food that costs little more than nearby parking. Deep-fried whole trout salad is lively with green mango, chilli and lime, while a decadently rich red peanut curry of beef packs a kick-boxer's punch. Traditional condiments of dried chilli, peanuts and fish sauce are on the table but pad thai-style stir-fried rice noodles with dried prawns, peanuts and bean sprouts are nicely sweet–sour and spicy even without them. Sticky, crunchy, deep-fried pork spare ribs with a hot and sour sauce are so addictive you'll be back in tomorrow's queue if you have the stamina.

Hours Mon–Sat noon–10pm; no bookings

Bill E $10–$12 **M** $17–$30 **D** $10

Cards AE DC V MC

Wine A dozen spice-friendly, affordable drops; 12 by the glass

Chef Pacharin Jantrakool

Owner Peter Bowyer

Seats 56; outdoor seating

www.sailorsthai.com.au

And...try to score one of the four small outdoor tables

Sailors Thai Restaurant

Lower Level, 106 George Street, The Rocks
Tel 9251 2466   Map 1

Thai

Score 15/20

So David Thompson, now expat and Michelin-starred in London's Nahm, has officially left this historic sandstone building. Thankfully, his former business partner, Peter Bowyer, and chef Ty Bellingham carry on the Thai fine-dining tradition. Starched linen tablecloths, splashes of bold colour and highly professional waiters, well versed in the intricacies of this carefully conceived cuisine, make Sailors Thai a special place to eat. Every dish is about balance and layers of flavours. Betel leaves topped with a sweet yet briny king prawn burst with the creamy crunch of rich, toasted peanuts. Toasted rice adds texture to a beef salad of smoky, caramelised wagyu rump. Both the duck and fish dumpling curries deliver waves of complex flavours yet never overpower their main ingredient. Broccoli salad is revved up with chilli and garlic. And while the desserts are not always pure Thai, the coconut dumplings deserve every milligram of their legendary status.

Hours Lunch Mon–Fri noon–2.30pm; Dinner Mon–Sat 6–10pm

Bill E $24–$28 **M** $34–$42 **D** $10–$12; tasting menu $85 pp

Cards AE DC V MC

Wine A list that perfectly matches the spicy food; 14 by the glass

Chef Ty Bellingham

Owner Peter Bowyer

Seats 80; private room

Vegetarian Good range

www.sailorsthai.com.au

And...a range of quality Chinese teas to soothe the palate

Sails on Lavender Bay

2 Henry Lawson Avenue, McMahons Point
Tel 9955 5998 Map 5a

Contemporary

Score 14/20

One of Sydney's finest locations has had an elegant makeover since the arrival of new owner Greg Anderson (of Sugaroom), complementing the million-dollar views of Lavender Bay, Luna Park and the harbour bridge. Subtle tones, dark, sexy lighting, clothed tables and smart padded chairs, a striking new bar and outdoor dining area have given Sails the polish it deserves. With cruisers and ferries gliding in right to the front door, the only thing missing is a float-through takeaway. The menu should lure diners to dry land with daily seafood specials and freshly shucked Port Lincoln oysters. An earthy, textured terrine of foie gras, chicken and prunes is seriously more-ish, served with prosciutto and crisp toast. Slow-roasted suckling pig is executed with style, teamed with bok choy, cracked wheat and apricot puree. Tender grilled lamb rump is sliced pink and matched well with ratatouille, black olive and tarragon jus. A delicate dessert of watermelon jelly is superbly flavoured with pomegranate, basil and ginger beer sorbet.

Hours Lunch Tues–Fri, Sun noon–3pm; Dinner Mon–Sat 6pm–late

Bill E $20–$28 **M** $35–$39 **D** $15–$17; 10% surcharge on Sundays & public holidays

Cards AE DC V MC Eftpos

Wine Impressive, appealing local and global list; 23 by the glass

Chef Steven Skelly

Owners Greg Anderson & Patricia Nunes

Seats 95; private room; wheelchair access

www.sailslavenderbay.com

And...arrive by ferry or splash out on a water taxi

Sakana-Ya

336 Pacific Highway, Crows Nest
Tel 9438 1468 Map 5a

Japanese

Score 13.5/20

The decor is far from flash and the menu a touch unwieldy, but this "fish shop" has been packed for nigh on 20 years with Japanese expats hankering for a home-style meal and locals wanting their seafood fix. Order an Asahi and dive straight into the full-page "today's fish" list, studded with stars to indicate the chef's recommendations. Sablefish is moist and invitingly charcoal-grilled, with a miso flavour that is clean and gentle. A nimono of kingfish (simmered in sweet sake and soy broth) is equally carefully executed and reasonably priced. The usual suspects, such as sushi hand rolls and a chunkily cut sashimi platter, are well portioned. For something different, try pressed sushi. The refreshing flavours of vinegared mackerel prove a nice contrast to the many tempura options. Deep-fried soft-shell crab and oysters offer a burst of ocean flavour, nicely tempered with shochu or sake to sip on. A home-style sesame pudding with brown honey sauce never fails to please.

Hours Lunch Mon–Fri noon–2.30pm; Dinner daily 6–10.30pm

Bill E $5.50–$29 **M** $13.50–$39 **D** $7.50–$8; 7-course menu $60 pp, 9 courses $90 pp

Cards AE DC V MC JCB

Wine Basic list, plus Japanese beer, sake and shochu; 2 by the glass; BYO wine only (corkage $5.50 per bottle)

Chef Toshi Goto

Owner Yasu Yasuoka

Seats 75; private rooms

Child friendly Highchairs; kids' sushi

Vegetarian Six courses for $39

And...expats order bara-zushi – a box of sushi rice sprinkled with salmon and more

Salon Blanc

2/6 Cowper Wharf Road, Woolloomooloo
Tel 9356 2222   Map 2

Contemporary

☿

Score 13/20

Well positioned at the start of this finger
wharf's popular dining strip, Salon Blanc's
starkly elegant white room begs your
attention, especially the dramatic Missoni
mural engulfing an entire wall. Perhaps the
mix of bar and formal and informal dining
confuses, because the service isn't always
on song and chef Alex Ensor's ambitious
efforts occasionally misfire. The faintest
wisp of a sourdough wafer is artistically
perched on a moulded blue swimmer crab
salad piled on diced avocado topped with
tomato concasse. Unfortunately, pan-fried
john dory, topped with lemon and parsley-
sharpened green asparagus, seemed too well
cooked on a swirl of butternut puree. A silky
roasted cashew nut semifreddo combines
creaminess with the crunch of caramelised
hazelnuts, and while plump raspberries are
an exquisite accompaniment, the vivid green
veil of pistachio pashmak (Persian fairy floss)
disappointed. Yet the views never fail to
delight, and you can always recline on vibrant
striped couches for cocktails and tasty tapas.

Hours Lunch daily noon–3pm; Dinner daily
6–10.30pm; bookings essential
Bill E $22–$35 **M** $36–$45 **D** $14–$18; 3-course
menu $70 pp, 4 courses $80 pp; 10% surcharge
on Sundays & public holidays
Cards AE DC V MC
Wine Extensive international list; 20 by the glass
Chef Alex Ensor
Owners Paul Cheika, Danny Douehi,
Colin Selwood & George Gavalas
Seats 150; private rooms; outdoor seating
Child friendly Highchairs
www.salonblanc.com.au
And...enjoy dessert with a matched wine

Sanders Waterfront Restaurant

D'Albora Marina, 138 Cabarita Road, Cabarita
Tel 9736 2468   Map 6

Contemporary Seafood

Score 13/20

You'd be hard pressed to find a more
appealingly located restaurant along the
inner shores of the harbour than this gem in
the marina at the tip of Cabarita Park. Chef
Belinda Geary serves up a veritable United
Nations of influences in her fish-biased
menu but manages to carry it off. A nicely
textured ocean trout tartare is paired with
a quirky beetroot jelly and a watercress and
horseradish salad that packs a delightful
peppery punch. A delicate black sesame and
soy blue swimmer crab omelette sits in a
subtle brown miso broth. A main of steamed
mussel pot was the only mis-timed moment,
due to an overly salty broth and anorexic
mussels. Crisp-skinned salmon reclines
on a warm potato salad punctuated with
little bursts of salmon roe. And there's no
sweeter ending than a frozen Baileys parfait
sandwiched between chocolate rice bubble
wafers and coffee anglaise, for an amusing
take on an Australian staple.

Hours Breakfast Sun 9–11am; Lunch Wed–Sun
noon–4pm; Dinner Wed–Sun 6pm–midnight
Bill E $18–$21 **M** $29–$35 **D** $15;
10% surcharge on Sundays & public holidays
Cards AE V MC Eftpos
Wine Short but interesting list; 9 by the glass;
BYO (corkage $5 pp)
Chef Belinda Geary
Owner Grant Scott Philipp
Seats 80; private room; wheelchair access;
outdoor seating
Child friendly Kids' menu; highchair;
colouring-in books
www.sandersrestaurant.com.au
And...take the RiverCat to Cabarita Wharf

The Sardine Room

NEW

Shop 2, 31 Challis Avenue, Potts Point
Tel 9357 7444   Map 2

Seafood

Score 12/20

When the effusive Angela Heracleous cosies up beside your table to explain the menu and wines, you can't help but fall under her charming spell at this small slip of a bistro-style fish cafe. It's a cheerful, casual space that spills out onto Challis Avenue's perennially popular footpath. The modest menu mainly plies Mediterranean shores while occasionally dipping its toe in Asia. The results can be mixed, especially when the flavours end up more complex than necessary. Sardine fillets are paired with fattoush (a summer salad with Lebanese bread croutons) but also the surprising and unnecessary addition of chickpeas. Salt-and-pepper squid with aioli borrows some Asian spicing while maintaining its crowd-pleasing status. The signature mixed seafood pie – a puff pastry-capped melange of prawns, mussels and fish in runny gravy with crisp ribbons of sweet potato – was let down by average quality seafood. But a quick shot of affogato with an Italian liqueur, and you're ready to tackle the nearby nightlife.

Hours Brunch Sat–Sun 10am–3pm; Dinner Tues–Sun 6–10pm

Bill E $14–$16 **M** $24–$28 **D** $12; 10% surcharge on public holidays

Cards AE V MC Eftpos

Wine Small, affordable, yet interesting international list; 10 by the glass; BYO (corkage $4 per bottle)

Chef Andrea Nardi

Owners Andrea Nardi & Angela Heracleous

Seats 40; outdoor seating

www.thesardineroom.com.au

And...takeaway menu, too

Sea Treasure

46 Willoughby Road, Crows Nest
Tel 9906 6388   Map 5a

Chinese (Cantonese)

Score 13/20

Dozens of beady eyes meet you as you walk past the tanks brimming with live lobsters, crabs and prawns and into Sea Treasure's pleasant dining room dotted with yellow tablecloths. Quality seafood is a highlight of this local fave, which also does a brisk yum cha trade each day. Service varies, so try to get the right waiter to help navigate the vast a la carte menu – the daily list of what's fresh from the markets is a good start. Steamed scallops are sublime with a dressing of XO and soy, and succulent drunken prawns provide tableside theatre – flames leap from the saucepan as they cook in aromatic Chinese rice wine. Beijing-style pork ribs, coated in sweet, smoky sauce, were slightly spongy, although glossy, crunchy sugar snap peas offer a good balance. Barbecued pigeon is lifted by the accompanying spiced salt and sharp vinegar and is a good alternative to the always delicious duck.

Hours Lunch Mon–Fri 11am–3pm, Sat–Sun 10am–3pm; Dinner daily 5.30–11pm

Bill E $4.80–$36.80 **M** $8.50–$288 **D** $5–$24.80; $2.50 pp surcharge (children $1) public holidays

Cards AE DC V MC

Wine Four pages of well-priced Australasian drops, plus a good selection of big-ticket reds; 7 by the glass; BYO (corkage $5 pp)

Chef Lau Yui Wah

Owner Sea Treasure Pty Ltd

Seats 280; private rooms; wheelchair access

Child friendly Highchairs

Vegetarian Dishes in a la carte & set menus

And...six banquet options, including vegetarian

Sean's Panaroma

270 Campbell Parade, Bondi Beach
Tel 9365 4924 Map 9

Contemporary

Score 15.5/20

Dining at Sean's is like eating with your extended family – hard to find a suitable time, sometimes too close for comfort but with a cosy, surrounded-by-friends feel, and food Mum would love. The tone is beachside chic: sea urchin shell lamps, swinging blackboards promising seasonal offerings, and bowls of fruit on the bench above the squeezy open kitchen. The team's friendly, informal charm belies their supreme professionalism. Beetroot ravioli are perfectly formed pillows encasing beetroot puree, nestling beside beetroot leaves, finished with parmesan and crisp onion. Mains are presented simply, on large plates reminiscent of the Sunday roast: Murray cod is encased in a salt crust, carefully served at the table to reveal moist flesh, and balanced with tarragon mayonnaise. Then there's the legendary roast chook with its jus, spinach and mustard sauce. Desserts may include rhubarb from Sean's farm, roasted with figs, blood plums and blackberries beneath a whisper of crumble with peach leaf ice-cream.

Hours Lunch Fri–Sun noon–3pm; Dinner Wed–Sat 6–9.30pm; bookings essential

Bill E $23–$28 **M** $26–$42 **D** $16–$19; 6-course tasting menu $110; $7 pp surcharge on Sundays & public holidays

Cards V MC

Wine Succinct, creative list of boutique locals plus champagne; 24 by the glass; BYO ($20 corkage)

Chefs Sean Moran & Griff Pamment

Owners Sean Moran & Michael Robertson

Seats 70; outdoor seating

Vegetarian Entree, main and mixed plate options

www.seanspanaroma.com.au

And...have a drink in the new reception room

Selah

12 Loftus Street, Circular Quay
Tel 9247 0097 Map 1

Contemporary

Score 13/20

You gotta love little places that take an unpretentious aim at their clientele and consistently hit the bullseye. This smart, minimalist bistro with walls of sandstone and red terracotta, inoffensive artwork and dark timber floors and tables (beware – it gets noisy) serves price-perfect, beautifully presented fare. Targeted squarely at the lunchtime business crowd and pre-theatre diners, Selah does bright, contemporary dishes and spares no room for flair or failure. Sensationally moist, plump, seared scallops bring a little sea sweetness on top of Chinese pork, lifted with the crunch of young coconut. Ocean trout fillet sits on robust prawn and ginger "ravioli" and paddles in a gentle pool of star anise and Asian mushroom consomme. Belgian chocolate fondant oozes satisfaction next to chocolate ice-cream, praline, nutmeg-poached orange segments and an orange-cream-filled tuile. Smiling, beguiling and rapid service completes the pleasing picture.

Hours Lunch Mon–Fri noon–3pm; Dinner Mon–Sat from 5.30pm

Bill E $17 **M** $24–$30 **D** $13

Cards AE DC V MC Eftpos

Wine Short, sharp list of Australasian tipples offering decent value; 15 by the glass

Chef Gavin Foster

Owner Sam Pask

Seats 50

Child friendly Highchairs; kids' options

www.selah.com.au

And...ideal pre-theatre spot considering the pricier alternatives

Sevardi Cucina Italiana

1/12 Hannah Street, Beecroft
Tel 9980 1150   Map 6

Italian

Score 13/20

There's a decent, unassuming vibe to this homely (if not slightly cramped) trattoria where ultra-friendly service and unfussy food of huge proportions make it consistently popular. The black-and-white photos adorning the walls are by the eponymous 19th-century chef who inspired this decade-old Italian. An entree of four huge pancetta-wrapped scallops, with a lemon and parsley dressing cutting through any hint of saltiness, is so generous that it makes a main course of eye fillet morsels (also wrapped in pancetta) impossible to finish. Another entree – a small mountain of chicken livers, caramelised onions and mushrooms on toast – just slipped in under the too-dry line. Slow-cooked pork belly may look a little like chunky salmon steaks, but they'd never have crackling this good, or such sweet flesh accompanied by caramelised apple and seeded-mustard sauce. A huge affogato keeps up the size motif, as do three scoops of fruity house-made gelato.

Hours Dinner Tues–Sat 5.30–10pm
Bill E $14–$22 **M** $24–$32 **D** $8–$12; 15% surcharge on public holidays
Cards AE V MC Eftpos
Wine BYO (corkage $3 pp)
Chef Livio Commissione
Owner Antonio Abassi
Seats 60; private room; wheelchair access
Child friendly Pasta dishes; highchair
www.sevardi.com.au
And...hope you get the charming Leonardo as your waiter

Shanghai Yangzhou House

177 Forest Road, Hurstville
Tel 9580 9188   Map 8

Chinese (Shanghai)

Score 12.5/20

Even if you're not in the know, the crowds will tell you that this brightly lit shopfront is the place to head for on this busy casual Asian dining strip. With a counter of cold dishes, live seafood tanks and a photographic menu of epic proportions, the options can be overwhelming. Sit at one of the simple laminate tables, then start with a no-brainer – Shanghai's famous xiao long bau (listed as steamed pork buns) – plump dumplings that release a burst of flavoursome stock with each bite. Less intimidating than it sounds, jellyfish salad comes as transparent, crunchy ribbons – the perfect mild conduit for its sesame oil dressing. Sichuan hot-pepper prawns, in a thick batter, weren't quite as they were pictured, but a special chilli eggplant hotpot is a silky-smooth delight. And if your decision-making powers fail, you can always follow the crowd again and point to an intriguing dish bubbling away at the next table.

Hours Lunch daily 11am–3pm; Dinner daily 5.30–10pm
Bill E $4.80–$48 **M** $9.80–$38.80 **D** $4.80–$5.80; $1.50 pp surcharge on public holidays (80c for children)
Cards Cash only
Wine BYO (corkage $1.50 pp)
Chefs Tony Jiang & Hanshi Li
Owners Tony Jiang & Dianna Yan
Seats 70
Child friendly Highchairs
And...grab cold dishes from the counter to take away

Silvas

Shop 1, 82–86 New Canterbury Road,
Petersham
Tel 9572 9911   Map 8

Portuguese

Score 13/20

Hungry? The rapier-like skewer poised over your table is loaded with hunks of beef rump. Along come fluffy, grilled polenta, garlic bread and a platter overladen with chargrilled pork belly, salad and terrific chips. Then follows one of five bacalao (salt cod) dishes, swimming in garlic, ringed by six golden, soft-centred spuds. Specials include chargrilled spatchcock and veal rack, while Portugal's reputation for seafood is well served by pipis, limpets, john dory and super sardines. This is big, boisterous, full-flavoured food, perfect to share in small groups. Subtlety mellows marinades and tempers a caldo verde soup – the smooth, carefully seasoned potato base laced with shredded kale hiding a smoky sliver of chorizo. In this clean, tiled, corner room a bustling takeaway counter doesn't intrude but adds to the relaxed, good-time atmosphere. Smiling service ensures that you waddle out replete and happy, but not before "pudim" (a dense slice of creme caramel) and/or chocolate mousse.

Hours Tues–Thurs & Sun 10.30am–9pm, Fri–Sat 10.30am–9.30pm; bookings essential
Bill E $11.90–$15 **M** $19.50–$26.90 **D** $5–$7.50
Cards V MC Eftpos
Wine Basic, inexpensive, perfectly adequate list; 12 by the glass; BYO (corkage $2.50 pp)
Chef Osvaldo Da Silva
Owners Osvaldo & Guida Da Silva
Seats 55; wheelchair access
Child friendly Highchair
www.silvas.com.au
And...takeaway chargrilled chicken, with piri piri (chilli sauce) is great, too

Spice I Am

90 Wentworth Avenue, Surry Hills
Tel 9280 0928   Map 3a

Thai

Score 13/20

This is no-frills dining at no-frills pricing in a no-frills stretch of Surry Hills. It's all polished tables, noisy tile floors and disparate walls, no bookings, no licence, cash only and with abrupt service from orange T-shirt-clad staff. Yet something keeps us coming back. That would be the food and its authentic, fiery flavours. All the standards, including a refreshing pad thai and lush beef massaman curry, feature in a broad menu but there are more adventurous routes to follow. Grilled, finely sliced marinated pork is piping hot, spicy and full flavoured. Fried rice with crab meat may be a little dry but pad prik pork belly is a thick, satisfying curry with green beans, chilli and kaffir lime. It's all about texture and as much heat as you like in a green papaya (som tum) salad with cherry tomatoes, peanuts and cabbage. There are no desserts, so refresh with lemon ice tea, then depart with a spring in your step.

Hours Lunch Tues–Sun 11.30am–3.30pm; Dinner Tues–Sun 5.45–10pm; no bookings
Bill E $7.90–$13.90 **M** $13.90–$25.90 **D** $13.90
Cards Cash only
Wine BYO (no corkage)
Chef Sujet Saenkham
Owners Padet Nagsalab & Sujet Saenkham
Seats 45; outdoor seating
www.spiceiam.com
And... great drinks, such as young coconut juice and Thai tea

Starfish Avalon

23 Avalon Parade, Avalon Beach
Tel 9918 2077   Map 7

Modern Asian

Score 13/20

By day, it's a cafe for wagyu burgers and beachy, casual tucker. At night, this otherwise plain shopfront transforms into a restaurant, offering some deceptively good Asian and Italian flavours at bare, white, candlelit tables that spill out on to the footpath. Don't let the paper napkins and occasionally nonchalant service fool you. This is serious cooking that begins with a small amuse bouche, perhaps salt-and-pepper tofu, followed by an tamarind-tart Indonesian-style spicy squid stir-fry on a jicama salad. Sugar-cured ocean trout with pickled daikon, shiso and Vietnamese dressing is just as lively and impressive, while crisp pork belly with chilli caramel is cleverly matched with an Asian-accented apple salad punchy with ginger. The warm scents of cinnamon and star anise drift from crisp yet tender duck and figs with a sweet-and-sour sauce that errs on the side of sweet, but soft-centred chocolate pudding with pistachio ice-cream is everyone's sweet dream come true.

Hours Breakfast Sat–Sun 8.30–11am; Lunch Tues–Sun 11am–3pm; Dinner Tues–Sat 6–9pm; bookings essential on weekends

Bill E $15–$18 **M** $23–$33 **D** $12–$14; 10% surcharge on Sundays & public holidays

Cards V MC Eftpos

Wine Concise and affordable Australasian list; 12 by the glass; BYO (corkage $7 per bottle)

Chefs Joji Shikama & Phillip Martin

Owners Shin Young-An, Phillip Martin & Joji Shikama

Seats 65; outdoor seating

Child friendly Highchairs; kids' menu

And...the Italian flavours are just as polished

Strangers with Candy

96 Kepos Street (cnr Phillip Street), East Redfern
Tel 9698 6000   Map 3b

Contemporary

Score 13/20

When you invite friends to a restaurant in Redfern that has no licence – and only accepts cash – expectations may not be high. But that underestimates the creativity in the kitchen at this popular neighbourhood restaurant. Sit in the cosy front room – or in the lantern-lit brick courtyard – and peruse a promising menu that draws on Asian, Italian and Greek influences. A delicate steamed prawn wonton in lemongrass broth with earthy Chinese mushrooms and coriander pesto is a success, but minced chicken and prawn betel leaves were bland and the foliage was too tough. A wagyu pie on a bed of mashed potato won't satisfy pastry lovers but the flavours are robust and the accompanying tomato and lime chutney is a nice touch. Spaghettini with blue swimmer crab was lukewarm and slightly soggy but small black mussels are flavoursome. Portions are generous, and innovative meat-free dishes mean that vegetarians are not forgotten. Nor are dessert lovers – sauternes custard with raspberries and bitter caramel is outstanding.

Hours Breakfast Sat–Sun 9.30am–3.30pm; Lunch Sat–Sun 11.30am–3.30pm; Dinner Wed–Sat 6–9.30pm; bookings essential

Bill E $14.50–$18.50 **M** $23.50–$29.50 **D** $4.50–$14.50

Cards Cash only

Wine BYO (corkage $3.50 pp)

Chef Veronica Stute

Owners Justin Wells & Veronica Stute

Seats 40; private rooms; outdoor seating

Vegetarian Some creative choices

www.strangerswithcandy.com.au

And...try the innovative breakfast bruschetta

Subsolo

161 King Street (cnr Castlereagh Street), Sydney
Tel 9223 7000   Map 1

Spanish/Portuguese
Score 13.5/20

Why was everyone asking for intimate Melbourne-style wine bars when Sydney already had one (the former Omega site) tucked away in this subsolo (basement in Portuguese)? With contemporary tapas and a wine bar with decent cocktails, it's also a brooding restaurant in sultry flamenco reds and browns, with leather chairs and banquettes. The menu balances tradition with modern appeal in crunchy bacalao (salt cod) croquettes and paella-filled squid awash with anchovy-spiked burnt butter. The gazpacho might occasionally be wan but it matters not when confit rabbit salad – a pale jumble of citrus-dressed celeriac, celery hearts, apple, cannellini beans and lush, salty meat – is so sublime. Then there's a credible paella, plus scene-stealing espetadas – the Portuguese version of sis kebab – speared with seafood, meat or vegetables, including sherry-glazed quail. A coffee, chocolate and almond ice-cream torte with jammy sangria compote is as colourful and striking as a piece of Gaudi architecture.

Hours Lunch Mon–Fri noon–2.30pm; Dinner Mon–Sat from 6pm

Bill E $8–$24 **M** $15–$39 **D** $14

Cards AE DC V MC JCB Eftpos

Wine Great Spanish and Portuguese drops at occasionally excessive mark-ups; 12 by the glass

Chef Jacqui Gowan

Owners Richard Nichols, Marcello & Iolanda Lantelme

Seats 200; private room

Vegetarian Numerous decent options

www.subsolo.com.au

And...interesting Spanish beers and sherries, too

Sugaroom

Shop 2, 1 Harris Street, Pyrmont
Tel 9571 5055   Map 5b

Contemporary
Score 13/20

Sydney's harbourside restaurants are a mixed bag. Enough said, but let's pay credit where it's due to this smart bar and restaurant on Jackson's Landing. Take pre-lunch or dinner drinks in the compact, banquette-lined bar adjoining the dining room or outside on the terrace overlooking secluded Elizabeth Macarthur Bay. The decibels climb on Friday and Saturday nights but early in the week the mood is more intimate with candlelit tables, that old devil moon on the water and a menu that is safe but desirable. A baked eschallot tart is beguiling; pan-roasted barramundi with pumpkin and sweetcorn puree slipped into slightly more exciting territory dressed in a chorizo and clam sauce; and a jumbo pork chop, a rustic trotter crepinette balancing atop, is porcine bliss, despite a gluggy calvados sauce. Our rose-scented peaches with elderflower jelly and citrus powder tilt towards the abstract but aren't difficult to eat. And the service is unfailingly smiling and professional.

Hours Lunch Tues–Sun noon–3pm; Dinner Mon–Sat 6pm–late

Bill E $15–$16 **M** $28–$30 **D** $14–$15; 10% surcharge on Sundays & public holidays

Cards V MC Eftpos

Wine Succinct, interesting boutique Australasian list; 16 by the glass; BYO Mon–Thurs only (corkage $10 per bottle)

Chef Brad Sloane

Owners Greg Anderson & Patricia Nunes

Seats 120; wheelchair access; outdoor seating

www.sugaroom.com.au

And...it's great for business lunches, too

Summit Restaurant

Level 47, Australia Square, 264 George
Street, Sydney
Tel 9247 9777   Map 1

Contemporary

Score 14/20

It hasn't stood still in 40 years, rotating at a
metre a minute, 47 spectacular floors above
the city. As the grey–pink veil of evening
envelops the sunset, the plush room acquires
a warm, translucent glow from watermelon
pink lamps and myriad Campari bottles. A
scaffold of slim olive oil breadsticks is perched
over paper-thin shaved jamon scattered with
intensely sweet, roasted baby tomatoes, as
well as slightly insipid shaved marmande
(beefsteak) tomatoes. Sweet, lemon-brined
organic chicken is appealingly tender, with
a perky crisp-skinned leg, luscious garlic
butter potatoes and a drizzle of chianti
pan juices that elevate it to greatness. An
elegant and divine stonefruit "bellini frappe"
is handsomely presented in an ice bowl,
consisting of vanilla spiked white peach
granita, and poached stone fruits splashed
generously with champagne. Michael Moore's
professional, attentive and knowledgeable
team take the Summit back to its rightful
place at the top of Sydney dining.

Hours Lunch Mon–Fri noon–3pm; Dinner daily
from 6pm; bookings essential

Bill Lunch **E** $26–$31 **M** $36–$42 **D** $18–$24;
Dinner 2 courses $78, additional courses from
$18; 10% surcharge on public holidays

Cards AE DC V MC

Wine Gratifying Australian and international
list with some big shots; 20 by the glass

Chef/owner Michael Moore

Seats 250; wheelchair access

Child friendly Kids' menu; highchair

Vegetarian Several options

www.summitrestaurant.com.au

And…the famous Lenotre desserts

sushi e

Level 4, Establishment Hotel,
252 George Street, Sydney
Tel 9240 3041   Map 1

Japanese

Score 14/20

No, it's not a nightclub. Just the coolest sushi
joint around – left of the sultry next-door
bar – spotlit out of the ambient dimness by
copper mirror lights, with wide stool seating
up at a thick marble counter. Sushi master
Ura-san and his team are ready to roll, sear,
shape and slice at your command. Begin with
kingfish sashimi, "cooked" ceviche-style in
ponzu (citrus-soy), and something from the
kitchen menu, if you will (although Balmain
bug tempura was pricey, over-battered and
bland). The real finesse is at the counter.
Sushi rolls (futomaki) are big with the after-
work, pre-night-out crowd – fat logs of
mostly cooked ingredients (soft-shell crab,
avo and mayo anyone?) sliced into mouth-
sized discs. But nigiri-zushi shines: apricot-
pink salmon belly scored and torched; sweet,
milky bonito; stickily good eel; delicately fishy
snapper sashimi with a peppery shiso leaf
tucked beneath…each fish-of-the-day pick
is gleamingly sea-fresh and craftsman-sliced
onto quickly shaped beds of vinegared rice.
Dip in soy and savour.

Hours Lunch Mon–Fri noon–2.30pm; Dinner
Mon–Thurs 6–10.30pm, Fri–Sat 6.30–10.30pm;
bookings essential

Bill E $9–$31 **M** $26–$45

Cards AE DC V MC

Wine Smart mixed list; 10 by the glass; Japanese
beers and sake in ceramic pitchers

Chef Nobuyuki Ura

Owner Merivale Group

Seats 38; wheelchair access

Vegetarian Sushi rolls; salads

www.merivale.com

And…Hemmesphere awaits next door for cocktails

Swordfish

Level 2, South Sydney Junior Leagues Club,
558A Anzac Parade, Kingsford
Tel 9344 4404   Map 9

Italian
Score 13/20

There's a tinkle of poker machines, the dull thud of a "variety spectacular" and an asteroid-patterned carpet. It's clearly home to the Bunnies (well, the baby Bunnies anyway). But just up the escalators is a peaceful Italian seafood eatery with white linen tablecloths and relaxed hospitality. The menu is skewed towards seafood, but the Cipris brothers are just as good with meat and they keep the menu interesting with daily specials. Prosciutto-wrapped figs on a light gorgonzola sauce capture the change of seasons as summer ends. A fine tuna carpaccio with olive oil is given a pleasant twist thanks to a touch of soy. Strozzapreti (house-rolled "priest strangler" pasta tubes) with swordfish and eggplant is intensely rich. Meatballs with mozzarella and tomato sauce pack a similar punch, yet they could use an accompaniment to make them less daunting. The portions are fit for a prop forward, but see if you can tackle chilled crepes with mascarpone before the full-time siren sounds.

Hours Lunch Tues–Fri & Sun noon–3pm; Dinner Tues–Fri & Sun 6–10pm, Sat 5.30–10pm

Bill E $15–$18 **M** $21–$28 **D** $10.50

Cards AE DC V MC Eftpos

Wine Great, affordable mix of domestic and Italian wines; 12 by the glass

Chef Carmelo Cipri

Owners Carmelo, Anthony & Joe Cipri

Seats 250; private rooms; wheelchair access; outdoor seating

Child friendly Kids' menu; highchairs; pencils

Vegetarian Various entrees and pasta

www.southsjuniors.org.au

And... Swordfish is a great option for groups

Szechuan Garden

Shop 1, 599 Pacific Highway, St Leonards
Tel 9438 2568   Map 5a

Chinese (Sichuan, Hunan & Peking)
Score 13/20

Dressed in today's fashionable colours – muted browns and earthy ochres – this is not a (fortune) cookie-cutter Chinese. The glass-fronted restaurant, with ample space between tables, is serene considering the high-rise wind tunnel that surrounds it. The food is a cut above, too, taking its cue from China's north with specialties from Sichuan and Hunan provinces – areas known for simple, hearty, rustic fare awash with chilli oil. Aware of its daytime clientele, the kitchen mostly tempers such authenticity but there's still bona fide fire in the succulent, super-fresh, flash-fried prawns with Sichuan pepper and whole chilli. Spiced, dry-fried string beans with pork mince and chilli are a standout, while the recommended chicken in a wok comes bathed in a pungent hot and sour sauce. Service is outstandingly efficient and friendly, smoothly appearing to top up a glass or whisk away an empty plate and then vanishing into thin air – like those prawns.

Hours Lunch Mon–Fri noon–3pm;
Dinner daily 6pm–late

Bill E $6.90–$16.90 **M** $13.90–$32.90
D $8–$8.80; 10% surcharge on public holidays

Cards AE DC V MC

Wine Reasonably priced, food-friendly list, plus small, pricey vintage list; 5 by the glass; BYO (corkage $3.80 pp)

Chefs Mark Deng & John Yue

Owner Mark Deng

Seats 130; wheelchair access; outdoor seating

Child friendly Highchairs; kids' portions

Vegetarian Plenty of options

www.szechuangardenrestaurant.com.au

And...all but a few clearly marked dishes are MSG-free

Tabou ★

527 Crown Street, Surry Hills
Tel 9319 5682   Map 3b

French   ⚱
                        Score 14.5/20

FAVOURITE BISTRO

There's been a changing of the kitchen guard
after many years, but Tabou's finely crafted
French panache continues, starting from the
classic bistro decor. There's a modern touch
to Alisdair McKenna's subtle and appealing
cooking, which eschews overpowering
sauces or elaborate combinations. The small,
classic menu features favourites such as
steak tartare, cheese souffle and the gigantic
rib of beef. Four generous pieces of veal liver,
simply grilled medium rare, are mild and
sweet but enriched by a bone marrow sauce.
McKenna's influence is particularly noticeable
in the more adventurous daily specials
list. Perfectly poached King Island marron
with trumpeter mushrooms retains clear,
distinctive flavours. Crisp-skinned jewfish
on a bed of prawns and lentils is an earthy
yet pleasing combination. Creme brulee
sets a benchmark others would do well to
emulate, and there's always a platter of fine
French cheeses, the selection scrawled on
the huge mirror. For a touch of France with
contemporary creativity, Tabou keeps
on keeping on.

Hours Lunch Mon–Fri noon–2.30pm;
Dinner Sun–Fri 6.30–10pm, Sat 6–10pm;
bookings essential

Bill E $17–$24 **M** $26–$35 **D** $13–$16

Cards AE DC V MC

Wine Well-chosen, medium-sized list with plenty
of French depth; 15 by the glass

Chef Alisdair McKenna

Owners Rod & Julie McPherson

Seats 80; private room

Child friendly Crayons and paper tablecloths

And….in the 1950s it was a dentist's surgery

Taiki

96 Longueville Road, Lane Cove
Tel 9428 1007   Map 7

Japanese

                        Score 13.5/20

There's more to this haunt of business
lunchers and evening Japanophile groups
than co-owner Yoshiki Fukunaga's sushi
counter, but regulars book out stool seating
well in advance anyway. From the ochre and
indigo noren (half-curtains) at the entrance
to the plain sand-coloured interior, it's great
for nibbling edamame with an Asahi or
heading straight for a selection of expertly
shaped sushi and finely sliced sashimi.
Appealingly presented on fine ceramic plates,
uzukuri of kingfish comes with slightly
spicy daikon and the house ponzu (citrus
soy). Jumbo rolls include nori-wrapped
spiced salmon belly and the house special
of kingfish, snapper, salmon, cuttlefish and
bonito (or whatever's fresh that day) with
the peppery sting of wasabi and fresh shiso.
A salad of spinach with house-made sesame
(goma) dressing is one of Sydney's best. And
carefully made miso broths (including a pipi
special) add just the right contrast. Taiki is
about gathering together to eat well.

Hours Lunch Tues–Fri noon–2.30pm; Dinner
Tues–Sun 6–10pm; bookings essential for sushi
counter and Fri–Sat dinner

Bill E $7.80–$36.80 **M** $18.80–$39.80
D $7.80–$16.80; 10% surcharge on Sundays
& public holidays

Cards AE V MC JCB

Wine Small, leading brand Australian, plus good
sake; 13 by the glass; BYO bottled wine only
(corkage $10 per bottle)

Chef/owner Yoshiki Fukunaga

Seats 70; outdoor seating

Child friendly Highchairs; kids' cutlery
and bowls; colouring-in

www.taikijapaneserestaurant.com.au

And…taiki means "big tree" in Japanese

Tan Viet Noodle House

2–3/100 John Street, Cabramatta
Tel 9727 6853   Map 6

Vietnamese

Score 13/20

Whether for a quick pit stop or longer, floods of diners ebb and flow among the serried ranks of tables in this big, clean, no-nonsense room where authentic Vietnamese is the order of the day. Tea arrives gratis, then it's decision time, conjuring a meal from your choice of soup noodles or rice with pork, beef, chicken or duck. Fresh tastes leap from herbs, both familiar and unfamiliar, including perilla, polygonum (Vietnamese mint), coriander and saw-tooth herb. A delicate broth with a swirl of whiter-than-white rice noodles and pieces of boiled chicken makes an invigorating, nourishing meal. Fatter "drop" noodles cosset bouncy fish cakes; egg noodles surface seductively around strands of red-simmered duck, dark with star anise. Sides of crisp-skinned chicken and a small bowl of goat curry are hard to resist. Finally, grab a sweet, smooth, red bean milk or soothing medicinal elixir from the cool cabinet. After all, you still have some shopping to do.

Hours Daily 9am–7pm; no bookings

Bill M $10–$12 **D** $3–$3.50

Cards Cash only

Wine BYO (no corkage) but why bother, with a great list of soft drinks, teas and coffee

Chef/owner Hung Kiem Lam

Seats 90; wheelchair access

Child friendly Highchairs

And...cheap parking nearby

Taste on Sussex Lane

Unit 10, 275 Kent Street,
Westpac Place, Sydney
Tel 9299 0888   Map 1

French

Score 13.5/20

If you build it, they will come and eat. Since it opened in late 2006, hordes of hungry souls have arrived in this new CBD development east of King Street Wharf, all needing lunch. The dining infrastructure has followed and this bar–restaurant with Vietnamese decor and a French accent stands out from the crowd. We really like the bar menu, perhaps more than the pricier a la carte. You can dine from both whether you're in the bistro or the swankier restaurant annex. At the posh end, enjoy foie gras, boudin blanc and armagnac-soaked prunes to start, then, from the bar menu, bouillabaisse with haul-in-the-nets fishy intensity; and coq au vin that warms and comforts. Desserts are appealing, particularly a ganache with honeycomb, cherry jelly and creme de griotte (liqueur cherry) ice-cream. You can try rocking up without a booking, but then you'll have to queue with the countless bankers and money men in the neighbourhood.

Hours Lunch Mon–Fri noon–2.30pm;
Dinner Thurs–Fri 6–10pm

Bill E $16–$20 **M** $25–$30 **D** $16–$20

Cards AE V MC Eftpos

Wine A classy French and Australian list;
16 by the glass

Chef Darryl Martin

Owners Hieu Luong & Madeleine Cheah

Seats 30; wheelchair access; outdoor seating

www.tastefood.net.au

And...the bar is a civilised after-work option on Thursday and Friday nights

The Tea Room Gunners' Barracks

Gunners' Barracks, end of Suakin Drive,
off Middle Head Road, Mosman
Tel 8962 5900   Map 7

Contemporary

Score 13/20

The downhill walk from the car park is soon
forgotten as the panorama unfolds from this
135-year-old sandstone fortification. On a
sunny day, the view across Sydney Harbour
from the wooden deck makes The Tea
Room's genuinely good food almost seem a
bonus. Slivers of succulent, seared swordfish
impress alongside a crisp, creamy salt cod
croquette, while zingy salmon ceviche
dotted with pomegranate seeds, baby cress,
smooth Persian fetta and crisp fried shallots
is a textural delight. Main courses were a
little less exciting. Chicken and mushroom
pie lacked depth and cohesion, arriving as a
casserole inside a little copper pot with a crisp
pastry disc perched on top. Service can range
from theatrical to indifferent, but watching
yachts skip across the harbour, sipping good
espresso (or, of course, tea) and enjoying
shortbread with house-made grapefruit
sorbet and tea jelly will put you in a forgiving
mood. It's what living in Sydney is all about.

Hours Lunch daily noon–3pm; Morning &
afternoon tea daily 11am–3pm; bookings essential

Bill E $20 **M** $35 **D** $15; Morning & afternoon
tea $27–$55 pp; 15% surcharge public holidays

Cards AE DC V MC

Wine Interesting list of domestic and imports,
with some big-spender icons; 16 by the glass

Chef Marc Philpott

Owner Manuel Spinola

Seats 100; private room; wheelchair access;
outdoor seating

Child friendly Kids' menu; highchairs

www.thetearoom.com.au

And...morning and afternoon tea with fine china

The Tea Room QVB

Level 3, QVB (Market Street end),
455 George Street, Sydney
Tel 9283 7279   Map 1

Contemporary

Score 13.5/20

Where else would you find a gaggle of girls
with a champagne flute in one hand and a
teacup in the other? Actually, it's hard to find
a bloke among the throng of women who
descend on this majestic 1890s ballroom at
noon. They come for sandwiches, petits fours
and steroidal scones on Royal Albert china,
and a cracking good time. All that's missing
is the tinkling of a baby grand. Others in the
know arrive just after the morning tea rush
for a little lunch: a fine galette arranged with
slices of fig and a dollop of onion jam, or
maybe a perfectly pink salmon fillet studded
with coriander seeds and moated by fennel
veloute. Those with heartier appetites should
try the rib-eye with a punchy tabbouleh and
horseradish cream. There are gluten-free
desserts, but for those who like it high GI,
spiced plum and frangipane tart with sheep's
milk yoghurt sorbet is a fine finish.

Hours Lunch daily noon–3pm; Morning &
afternoon tea Mon–Fri from 11am, Sat–Sun
from 10am

Bill E $17 **M** $27 **D** $12; Morning and afternoon
tea $21–$50 pp; 10% surcharge on weekends
and public holidays

Cards AE DC V MC

Wine Balanced list of well-known whites, lighter
reds and sparklings; 17 by the glass

Chefs Mark Holmes & Keith Murray

Owner Manuel Spinola

Seats 200; wheelchair access

Child friendly Kids' menu; highchairs

Vegetarian Separate section on a la carte menu

www.thetearoom.com.au

And...$70 tea-for-two gift vouchers

Temasek

71 George Street, Parramatta
Tel 9633 9926   Map 6

Malaysian/Singaporean

Score 13/20

Don't think you can just rock up here
for the signature Hainan chicken or chilli
squid (sambal sotong). Weekend tables are
nabbed well in advance by large groups,
each with a platter of glistening chicken rice
and cucumber and ginger-shallot dipping
sauce, a fat oyster omelette, teensy satays
and bursting minced pork-stuffed bean-skin
rolls. If you get a seat, order all of the above
with plenty of the jammy house sambal (a
tomato–chilli relish) and a basin-sized bowl
of Assam fish – jewfish cutlets, pineapple
and tomato chunks in a sweet-sour broth
filmed with chilli. If you're on your own for
lunch, there's good nasi goreng with a frilly
egg and green onion on top; and prawny
har mee – hokkein noodles in a sweetish
broth, swimming with crisp-fried garlic, fish
cake slices and just-cooked baby bok choy
leaves. Service is good-hearted but needs the
occasional crash-tackle from impatient diners.
Snaffle a serve of pandan-flavoured sago
with gula melaka (palm sugar) syrup before
it sells out.

Hours Lunch Tues–Sun 11.30am–2.30pm; Dinner
Tues–Sun 5.30–10pm; bookings essential

Bill E $4.80–$16.80 **M** $10.80–market price
D $4–$4.80; $2 pp surcharge on public holidays

Cards AE DC V MC Eftpos

Wine BYO (corkage $1.50 pp)

Chefs Susan Wong & Jeremy Cho

Owners Susan Wong, Jeremy Cho
& Mei Ling Wong

Seats 170; private room; wheelchair access;
outdoor seating

Child friendly Highchairs; lollies

Vegetarian Separate menu

And...it's down the old Roxy arcade

Teppanyaki

Ivy, Level 2, 330 George Street, Sydney
Tel 9240 3000   Map 1

NEW

Modern Japanese   ♈

Score 14/20

While the grill is its hearth, Ivy's Teppanyaki
is much more than its name suggests.
Dine in the dark, sexily lit restaurant at the
communal table in front of the open kitchen
or repair to the adjacent Ivy lounge with its
New York-meets-Raffles feel. Depending on
your perspective, attentive young waitresses
in oh-so-short kimonos will either delight
or confront. The menu's varied enough for
snacking with drinks, or for a serious meal,
lending Japanese accents to a broader Asian
palate, such as Thai-style betel leaves with
ponzu-dressed blue swimmer crab. Lightly
seared new-style snapper sashimi, dressed
with sesame and olive oils, tastes every bit as
beautiful as it looks and beats Nobu's efforts
hands down. Crunchy, deep-fried Balmain
bug tails were overwhelmed by white pepper
and seemed a little pricey, but 100 grams of
buttery, grilled wagyu striploin, cut by grated
horseradish, beside a nutty, earthy mix of
mushrooms with roasted buckwheat and
fresh edamame beans is worth every penny.
Banana spring rolls score points for novelty,
but the exotic fruit platter is a better bet.

Hours Lunch Tue–Fri noon–3pm; Dinner Tue–Sat
6–11pm; bookings essential

Bill E $14–$28 **M** $22–$57 **D** $16–$28

Cards AE DC V MC

Wine Wide-ranging international list of boutique
labels, plus sake; 19 by the glass

Chefs Shaun Presland & Adam Lane

Owner Merivale Group

Seats 60; wheelchair access

www.merivale.com

And...fine cocktails in the adjacent Den

The Terrace On Pittwater

Newport Arms Hotel, cnr Beaconsfield
& Kalinya streets, Newport
Tel 9997 4900   Map 7

Contemporary

Score 13.5/20

A delicate smoked salmon amuse bouche
is delivered by chirpy, young staff. They
enthuse about a menu of fresh seafood,
steaks from the grill and much more. Are
we really at that iconic northern beaches
watering hole, The Arms? The Terrace is
an elegant, tiered semicircle perched above
the green, landscaped beer garden, where
glass doors roll back in summer to welcome
grandstand views of Pittwater. An entree of
spice-crusted Hervey Bay calamari is simply
complemented by mustard-pickled carrot,
cucumber and a sweet mirin dressing. Steak
lovers appreciate the broad range and quality
on offer. A 400-gram grain-fed rump, seared
to succulent perfection, is served with shiraz
jus and dauphine potatoes. Twice-cooked
King River baby lamb, teamed with white
asparagus, roast tomato and paris mash,
melts in the mouth. And sweet tooths will
swoon over a florentine sandwich filled with
honeycomb parfait and caramel sauce.

Hours Lunch daily noon–3pm; Dinner Mon–Thurs
6–9pm, Fri–Sat 6–9.30pm

Bill E $19.90–$21.90 **M** $26.90–$37.90 **D** $13.90;
10% surcharge on weekends & public holidays

Cards AE DC V MC Eftpos

Wine Impressive, rare collection and well-priced
premium locals; 24 by the glass

Chef David Bell

Owners Mark, Wayne & Neville Bayfield

Seats 200; private room; wheelchair access

Child friendly Kids' menu; highchairs

Vegetarian Small separate menu

www.theterraceonpittwater.com.au

And…there's accommodation, too

Tetsuya's

529 Kent Street, Sydney
Tel 9267 2900   Map 3a

Japanese/French

Score 18/20

The best is the best; and on the rare
occasions we find it, we have to take it the
way it is. Tetsuya Wakuda has maintained
an almost implausibly high standard for
other Sydney restaurants to match, yet
rarely exceed. Every so often we hear
quibbles about the bread, the wine list's
limited range of half-bottles and haughty
moments during the otherwise overwhelming
service. None of this amounts to a hill of
edamame after the first sublimely fresh oyster
dressed in Wakuda's perfect vinaigrette; an
ethereal baked custard with caramelised
leeks and crab served with an elegant
beechwood spoon; then scampi showcased
in four astonishing ways. The twelve-course
degustation is a sybaritic experience, and at
each step there's subtlety, precision of flavours
and mystery. Defining peaks include wagyu
with lime and wasabi, and a mesmerising
chocolate terrine in cognac anglaise. The
delicate ceramic art and calming Japanese
garden are essential to the magic. And this
really is magical dining.

Hours Lunch Sat noon–2.30pm; Dinner Tues–Sat
6–9.30pm; bookings essential

Bill Set degustation menu $195 pp

Cards AE DC V MC

Wine Compelling, comprehensive European and
new world list with particular depth in burgundy
and Bordeaux; 15 by the glass

Chef/owner Tetsuya Wakuda

Seats 120; private rooms

www.tetsuyas.com

And…valet service available or parking station
next door

Thanh Binh

52 John Street, Cabramatta
Tel 9727 9729   Map 6

Vietnamese

Score 13/20

Container of chopsticks at the ready? Check. An array of chilli-spiked condiments? Check. Thermos of tea? A nondescript, mirrored room turning over tables at a rate of knots and a mile-long menu of Vietnamese and Chinese dishes? Check. Check. Check. Whatever did we do before the advent of the Vietnamese cafe? Thanh Binh is a cut above the rest: the mountains of herbs and bean sprouts are shimmeringly fresh; pho is slippery and satisfying; and sugarcane prawns are sweet and fragrant. It's the fresh rolls though, that you will want to return for, as well as their ceremonial wrapping. Dampen a round of rice paper, lay the crisp roll on it, embellish with herbs, pickled carrots and lettuce, then wrap into a parcel and dip in nuoc cham sauce. If that's not enough to keep you happy, consider also the quail in spicy salt, glistening claypot pork and, yes – you know you really want it – the addictive Chinese-sausage-studded fried rice.

Hours Daily 9am–9pm

Bill E $8–$20 **M** $8–$35 **D** $4–$6

Cards V MC Eftpos

Wine BYO (corkage $1.50 pp)

Chef Tien Dung Cao

Owner Thanh Can Huynh

Seats 70

Child friendly Highchairs

And...for that Hoi An holiday feel, try a sweet lemon soda or luridly green pennywort drink

Tilbury Hotel

12–18 Nicholson Street, Woolloomooloo
Tel 9368 1955   Map 2

Contemporary/Italian

Score 12.5/20

This pub was once a venue for Australia's most famous cabaret stars. Tastefully restored some years ago, a sense of theatre remains, with a funky cocktail bar upstairs and the big open bar underneath leading to an elegant dining room of white linen tablecloths and tan leather banquettes. Then there's the adjoining terrace out the back. At night, it's noisy but lunch is a more tranquil affair. An entree of Wallis Lake oysters with red wine shallot vinegar more than satisfies. Scallops on sweetcorn puree are heightened by punchy, crisp pancetta. Marinated spatchcock with leeks and asparagus lost some subtlety in the cooking; however, tiny sweet peas are a fine match for blue-eye, with a slice of jamon for further texture. For dessert, a generous serve of semifreddo with honey, pistachio and almond toffee is good to share, while the cheerful service and ambience ensure that everyone leaves happy.

Hours Breakfast Sun 10am–noon; Lunch Tues–Sat noon–3pm, Sun noon–5pm; Dinner Tues–Sat 6–10pm, Sun 5–8pm

Bill E $17–$19.50 **M** $27.50–$32 **D** $12–$13.50

Cards AE V MC

Wine Quality, big-name Australian list; 15 by the glass

Chefs Bryan O'Gallaghan & Geoff Haines

Owner Mac Whitehouse

Seats 100; wheelchair access; outdoor seating (lunch only)

www.tilburyhotel.com.au

And...parking nearby is tricky

Toko Surry Hills

490 Crown Street, Surry Hills
Tel 9357 6100   Map 3b

Japanese

Score 13/20

Toko is all about atmosphere, energy and exuberance. While groovers and movers wax lyrical in the cocktail bar, diners pull up stools at communal tables that dominate a dimly lit but sleek space. Sultry back-row tables for two offer a little more intimacy. Service can be a little lacklustre but the open kitchen provides a sense of theatre as chef Keita Abe and his team prepare a mixed take on contemporary Japanese cuisine. Sashimi of salmon, kingfish and tuna is spot-on, served on a bed of ice; so too are hand rolls of tuna, kingfish, tobiko (flying fish roe) and chives. Skewers of pork belly are lathered in sweet-chillied miso before hitting the robata grill; while, from the kitchen beyond, silken tofu comes adorned with a spicy avocado salad. Braised wagyu beef cheeks are soft and gelatinous, but the accompanying ginger sauce lacked substance. Conclude with a simple brulee trio and a quick quiz to guess the flavours.

Hours Lunch Wed–Fri noon–3pm; Dinner Mon–Sat 6pm–late; no dinner bookings

Bill E $5.80–$16.80 **M** $16.80–$48 **D** $11.20–$15.80; 10% surcharge on public holidays

Cards AE DC V MC

Wine Compact, apt and affordable; 22 by the glass; plus 21 sakes (7 by the glass)

Chef Keita Abe

Owners Daniel, Alan & Matthew Yazbek

Seats 126; private room; wheelchair access; outdoor seating

Child friendly Highchairs; books

Vegetarian Sushi and rolls; salads; tofu; vegetable skewers

www.toko.com.au

And…the bar is open until 11pm

Tran's

523 Military Road, Spit Junction, Mosman
Tel 9969 9275   Map 7

Vietnamese

Score 13/20

There's more than a touch of old Indochine about the glowing lanterns, ornate dark timbers and sunflower yellow walls at Tran's. The French colonial influence lingers not just in the colour scheme but also on the menu, where veal is cooked in a clay pot and turmeric fish is flavoured, Hanoi-style, with dill and chives. Lanna and Tri Tran's cosy restaurant is a longstanding favourite, with glowing testimonials from its celebrity clientele, but our enthusiasm is a little more muted. Dishes such as quail with pickles and boned duck seemed overcooked and uninteresting. The signature crisp rice pancake was filled with a desultory number of prawns and pork slices. Thankfully, the goat curry, dry and aromatic, is a worthy highlight, while desserts shine, such as a slippery tapioca pudding with banana and black rice that isn't too sweet or coconut creamy. The lovely waitresses are heavenly in their slinky ao dai (Vietnamese traditional tunic and trousers) and the intimately lit room is as romantic as they come.

Hours Dinner Tues–Sun from 6pm

Bill E $8–$14 **M** $17–$28 **D** $8–$11

Cards AE DC V MC Eftpos

Wine BYO (corkage $2 pp)

Chef Lanna Tran

Owners Lanna & Tri Tran

Seats 100; private rooms

Vegetarian Numerous options

www.transrestaurant.com.au

And…takeaway available, too

Twelve Spices

197 St Johns Road, Canley Heights
Tel 9609 1465   Map 6

Thai/Lao

Score 13/20

Translucent, soft and glistening, tossed with fresh Vietnamese mint and peppermint leaves, sliced spanish onion, lemon juice and a little fish sauce, tripe is a dish for offal lovers to swoon over. There are other sound reasons for your palate to rejoice at this no-fuss cafeteria-style eatery decorated with Buddhas and woven hangings. It might be harshly lit and noisy when crowded, which is all the time, but this is Lao- and Thai-influenced fare at its most authentic. Som tam lao won't win prizes for presentation – a humped island of shredded green papaya with outcrops of sliced cherry tomatoes, lapped by a pungently fishy sauce – yet here this much-loved salad reaches exhilarating flavour heights. Red roast duck curry boasts thick chunks of meat and sliced mushrooms in a gravy of coconut milk and fresh turmeric tangy with galangal and lemongrass. Nibble on fresh vegetables and ball up sticky rice from woven baskets as you eat. And don't miss the juicy, lemongrass-laden Lao pork sausages.

Hours Daily 11am–3pm, 5–10pm
Bill E $8 **M** $10–$16 **D** $5
Cards Eftpos
Wine BYO
Chef Somboon Angsananon
Owner Bountang Mounivong
Seats 50
Child friendly Highchairs
And…have an avocado fruit shake for dessert

Uchi Lounge

15 Brisbane Street, Surry Hills
Tel 9261 3524   Map 2

Modern Japanese

Score 13/20

Whether following tradition or playing with it, new century Japanese eating is out and proud across Sydney. Yet this arty, bohemian-fringed hideaway does its thing quietly, as it has for more than a decade, with strains of jazz and sake cocktails downstairs, bare boards and ethereal gauze room divider above. Squirreled away off the tail end of Oxford Street, there's still something vaguely experimental about Uchi's quirky menu, from competently cut john dory sashimi with a sweetish–salty umeboshi plum dressing to grilled snapper crusted with miso, and a refreshing daikon and konbu salad beneath a perhaps too mayo-ey dressing. Service can be clumsy or a touch dreamy and not every creation is a masterpiece – endearingly cute ball-shaped sushi was overly sticky and house-made tofu with avocado curiously grainy. But there's lots to marvel at – including lickings of azuki (red bean) ice-cream or green tea and cinnamon brulee – and atmosphere to burn.

Hours Dinner Mon–Sat 6.30–11pm; no bookings Fri–Sat
Bill E $6.50–$12.50 **M** $15–$26 **D** $9–$9.50; 10% surcharge for groups of 8 or more
Cards AE V MC Eftpos
Wine Small and affordable locals; 6 by the glass; plus a serious sake list; BYO (corkage $3 pp)
Chefs Takashi & Wataru Ohuchi
Owner Takashi Ohuchi
Seats 50
Vegetarian Some decent options
www.uchilounge.com.au
And…warm sake cocktails for an alternative dessert

Universal Restaurant

Republic 2 Courtyard, Palmer Street, Darlinghurst
Tel 9331 0709   Map 2

Contemporary

♟♟♟
Score 16/20

Chris Manfield is back and Universal reminds us how much we missed her edgy, vibrant cooking. It's a thin, orange-glowing space, spilling into a courtyard and filled with funky colour-backed chairs and handsome black booths. Her intrepidly global menu is a whistlestop tour of small to medium-sized plates, from delicately wrapped pork and cabbage dumplings in Chinese golden broth to Moroccan veal sweetbreads, chickpeas and kofte balls with a tangy, tomato perfume. Amiable waiters, who crouch as they counsel you, are your culinary tour guides. Meltingly soft braised beef shin, bathed in a powerful yet subtle pea and eggplant green curry, evokes Manfield's old Thai stamping ground. Spicing on the roasted hapuka with anchovy sauce is mellow magic. Dessert visits planet childhood with "sugar plum fairies" – over-salted brioche, sugar plums and unbelievably smooth basil ice-cream – and "totally nuts", a super-salty caramel parfait with chocolate. Manfield is having fun. So are we.

Hours Lunch Fri noon–2.30pm;
Dinner Mon–Sat from 6pm

Bill Tasting dishes $18–$29; 10% surcharge on public holidays

Cards AE V MC

Wine A fascinating, peripatetic journey around the world; 24 by the glass

Chefs Christine Manfield & Jessica Muir

Owner Christine Manfield

Seats 80; wheelchair access; outdoor seating

Vegetarian Six savoury plates plus vegan options

www.universalrestaurant.com

And...monthly full moon dinners

U-Thong Thai

439 Miller Street, Cammeray
Tel 9922 6087   Map 5a

Thai

Score 12.5/20

With newer, flashier Thai joints opening regularly on this buzzy strip, there are solid reasons why locals pack this long-term classic. Despite recent renovations, U-Thong remains true to its original 1982 style, with its welcoming elephant and water feature opening up to busy back quarters. The extensive menu of more than 70 salads, stir-fries, curries and chargrills makes it easy to find familiar dishes such as satisfying prawn pad Thai. Golden moneybags – sweet minced pork and prawn wrapped in crunchy pastry – are a stand out, along with fish cakes, karom jib (Thai dim sims) and curry puffs. Choosing the anointed "favourites" is equally rewarding – cabbage salad with chicken, prawns and coconut milk is an interesting and appealingly fresh combination, and U-Thong's secret nam jim (chilli dressing) adds a punchy touch to chargrilled marinated chicken. Unlike the nam jim, there's no secret to why diners stay loyal – U-Thong delivers everything we love about suburban Thai.

Hours Lunch Tues–Fri noon–2.30pm;
Dinner Tues–Sun 6–10pm

Bill E $8–$12 **M** $15–$32 **D** $4.50–$9;
$2.50 pp surcharge on public holidays

Cards AE V MC Eftpos

Wine Small predictable selection; 3 by the glass;
BYO wine only (corkage $4 per bottle)

Chef Sue Kietprasert

Owners Manop & Sue Kietprasert

Seats 120; private rooms

Child friendly Highchairs

Vegetarian Standout options

And...sit up the front for a more traditional Thai feel

Verandah Restaurant

Mezzanine Level, 60 Castlereagh Street, Sydney
Tel 9238 0214   Map 1

Contemporary European

Score 14/20

Steak and fish are undoubtedly power lunch staples. There are three of both on offer at this smart first-floor newcomer. The long room in blond and dark timbers takes its name from the narrow veranda overlooking the Castlereagh Street throngs. The menu promises straightforward bistro-style food that ticks all the corporate boxes, with a few daily specials for extra interest. It's designed for executive suits stopping by for a quick refuel between hostile takeovers. Grain-fed steak fillet, served perfectly pink with just-crunchy beans and mash, offers a good reason to pause. But glossy mahi mahi fillet with fried prawns and flavoursome cubes of roast pumpkin arrived – without warning – on spinach instead of the promised creamy leeks, making it altogether less interesting. The choux pastry in the "freshly baked" profiteroles was too unyielding to live up to the menu's promise, but creamy Toblerone ice-cream is the star of jazzed-up affogato.

Hours Lunch Mon–Fri noon–3pm; Dinner Mon–Fri 6–9pm

Bill E $19–$22 **M** $34–$40 **D** $15–$17

Cards AE DC V MC

Wine A solid Australasian list; 30 by the glass

Chef Jonathan Ingram

Owner Dean Haritos

Seats 100; wheelchair access; outdoor seating

www.verandah.com.au

And...after dark it turns into a wine bar with tasting platters

Verde

115 Riley Street, East Sydney
Tel 9380 8877   Map 2

Italian

Score 13/20

A trio of Calabrian cousins has restored this heritage-listed Victorian-era building (formerly Two Chefs on Stanley). The stylish ground-floor dining room is a warm and sassy mix of exposed timbers, soft lighting and white-linen-topped tables. Co-owner Louie Kallas leads an enthusiastic team. The menu gives contemporary pizzazz to classic Italian combinations, sometimes to curious effect, as in garlic prawns with green olives and puzzling "rocks" of rusk-like bread. Pan-fried baby squid on baked baccala (salt cod) has a chilli and garlic zing. Larger dishes include house-made pasta, such as a handful of tagliatelle with a hearty sauce of spiced pork leg and fennel seeds. An earthy mix of puy lentils with celery hearts and baby leeks provides contrast to the delicacy of baked barramundi. And while buffalo milk gelato with honey and fresh berries lacked the milk's distinctive tartness, tiramisu is as good as nonna's – probably because it's her recipe.

Hours Lunch Wed–Fri noon–3pm; Dinner Tues–Sat 6–10.30pm

Bill E $14.50–$18.50 **M** $24–$36 **D** $12

Cards AE DC V MC Eftpos

Wine A solid and wide range of local and Italian wines; 15 by the glass

Chefs Antonio Ruggerino & David Page

Owners Antonio Ruggerino & Louie Kallas

Seats 100; private room; wheelchair access; outdoor seating

Child friendly Kids' menu; highchairs; crayons

Vegetarian Separate menu

www.verde.net.au

And...start your night in the upstairs lounge bar looking out from the Juliet balcony

Vicini

37 Booth Street, Annandale
Tel 9660 6600   Map 5b

Italian

Score 12.5/20

This distinctive two-storey corner terrace (formerly Zenith on Booth) is the sort of place where neighbours (i.e. vicini) become good friends. You're greeted by a casual cafe and pizzeria beside the open kitchen, but climb the stairs to a welcoming and smart ristorante of dark timbers and white linen tables. Smiling service makes you feel right at home. The blackboard menu of Italian favourites seems more reliable than exciting, delivering the steady comfort you want from a loved local. Steamed black mussels with tomato, chilli and garlic are a well-executed classic, but otherwise pleasant Sicilian-style mushrooms with baby spinach might leave you pondering their $16 price tag. Fettuccine laced with rabbit ragu is satisfyingly dreamy, while lamb cutlets are happily matched with roast capsicum, radicchio and eschalots. Desserts range from classics, such as vanilla panna cotta with blueberry compote, to a crowd-pleasing chocolate tart with vanilla bean ice-cream.

Hours Breakfast Tues–Fri 8am–noon, Sat–Sun 9am–noon; Lunch Tues–Sun noon–2.30pm; Dinner Tues–Sat from 6pm

Bill E $16–$18 **M** $20–$29 **D** $12–$14; 10% surcharge on public holidays

Cards DC V MC Eftpos

Wine Small, affordable Antipodean range, plus some Italians; 13 by the glass; BYO (corkage $7 per bottle)

Chef Brett Jeffrey

Owners Natalie Keon & George Hatzimihail

Seats 80; outdoor seating

Child friendly Kids' menu & drinks; highchairs; colouring-in

www.vicini.com.au

And…ask for the veranda in warmer weather

Vini

3/118 Devonshire Street, Surry Hills
Tel 9698 5131   Map 3b

Italian   ♉

Score 14/20

Black is still the new black at this perpetually hopping enoteca (wine and food bar). The walls, floor and furniture are black, and the waiters are dressed in black, as are most of the patrons. Stop by for antipasti and a glass of vino or squeeze in for dinner. Select a few daily specials from the black (naturally) board and you'll see the food comes in many colours. Torn basil and grated grana padano garnish comforting potato gnocchi (made to a family recipe from Friuli) with roasted cherry tomatoes and zucchini and dollops of Milawa goat's cheese for an unusual lift. Chargrilled sirloin offers elegant simplicity, perfectly cooked and rested, with eggplant and piquant salsa verde. House-made tagliatelle tossed with tender, oven-baked veal and succulent field mushrooms, plus a scintilla of rosemary and garlic, is an absolute purler. So is creamy, crunchy honeycomb ricotta semifreddo with balsamic strawberries. Sip a shot of grappa for a perfect conclusion.

Hours Lunch Tues–Fri noon–4pm; Dinner Tues–Sat 6–10.30pm; no bookings

Bill E $6–$16 **M** $16–$28 **D** $9–$12

Cards AE DC V MC Eftpos

Wine A cook's tour of Italy from the heel to the Alps, plus grappa and liquori; 25 by the glass

Chefs Andrew Cibej & Daniel Johnston

Owner Andrew Cibej

Seats 60; private room; wheelchair access; outdoor seating

Child friendly Highchair

And…no bookings but call, or call in, to go on the nightly waiting list

Wasavie

8 Heeley Street, Paddington
Tel 9380 8838   Map 4b

Japanese

Score 13.5/20

Creative specials and well-executed classics ensure that diners are willing to wait for a spot in this converted terrace. And queue they do. The communal table feels uncrowded although the functional stools hardly encourage lingering. They've even squeezed in a sushi bar, so start with something from there – maybe miso-marinated fish that you sear on a hot stone at your table. Also marinated misoyaki-style, grilled prawns curl on their bed of black rice under a blanket of salty–sweet bisque sabayon. Sticky slabs of braised pork belly – hard to negotiate with chopsticks – are a flavour hit, lifted with a dab of hot mustard. Cod, mussels and Japanese mushrooms in a mild broth are delicate by contrast and arrive in a neatly stapled baking-paper parcel that's cut open at the table. To finish, dig your spoon into one of the parfait-like "glass desserts", such as black sesame mousse with orange jelly. Then relinquish your seat to the next wave of eager diners.

Hours Dinner Mon–Sat 6–10pm, Sun 6–9pm; bookings essential

Bill E $6–$14 **M** $11–$25 **D** $5–$10

Cards AE V MC Eftpos

Wine BYO (corkage $3 pp)

Chef Matsumoto Satoru

Owner Saqura Investment & Consulting Pty Ltd

Seats 60; outdoor seating

www.wasavie.com.au

And...seats are a little easier to come by thanks to a recent expansion

Watermark

2A The Esplanade, Balmoral Beach
Tel 9968 3433   Map 7

Asian   ♀

Score 13/20

Daytime dining at Watermark is always going to be a highlight. After all, it sits right on one of Sydney's prettiest beaches. There are appealing brekkie options before the full menu kicks in from lunchtime. Then again, the bright evening ambience and glass-encased dining room may appeal to those who struggle with dim lighting. A seafood tasting plate highlights the menu's Asian bent, with delicious glazed eel on sweet coconut rice, but matching delicate scallops with an earthy beetroot and goat's cheese sauce (labelled a "sherbet") was less elegant. Luscious shredded pork belly is encircled by tomato slices and paired with peach and apple compote. Double-roasted duck is tender, but sadly lacked crisp skin. John dory sits well with a tousle of paper-thin squid, carrot and slinky black fungus, although the promised chinese cabbage was missing. A stunning walnut and honey creme brulee and double-chocolate tart crowned with mint-spiked ice-cream signal it's time to join passers-by for a beachside stroll.

Hours Lunch daily noon–3pm; Dinner daily 6.30–10pm

Bill E $23.50–$26 **M** $28.50–$44.50 **D** $18–$27

Cards AE DC V MC Eftpos

Wine Impressive, vast, mainly Australian list with lots of boutique drops; 15 by the glass

Chefs Ringo Au & Harnady Susantio

Owner Peter Miric

Seats 170; outdoor seating

Child friendly Kids' menu; highchairs; booster seats; colouring books; toys

Vegetarian Degustation option

www.watermarkrestaurant.com.au

And...degustation menu with matching wines

Drink
better
wine

"Head to NSC for an excellent and interesting **hand-selected range** of top boutique and selected imports at all price points...**This is a nice place to buy wine...**"
Matthew Jukes & Tyson Stelzer, Taste Food & Wine 2007

"Great staff"
Gary Walsh, winorama.com.au

"One of the more interesting merchants in Sydney **run by a trio of keen young wine-lovers...**"
SMH Foodies Guide To Sydney 2008

For Australia-wide delivery phone 1300 768 979 or visit our new shop at 189 Miller Street (Cnr Berry St, opp Rag & Famish Hotel) North Sydney. Open 7 days or shop 24 hours at **northsydneycellars.com**

North Sydney Cellars Market Cafe

Welcome Hotel

91 Evans Street, Rozelle
Tel 9810 1323   Map 5b

Modern European   ♀
                                    Score 14/20

Never was a pub more aptly named.
Drag yourself away from the bar and into
the discreet dining room with its clean,
elegant, traditional lines, tones of cream
and mahogany and padded wooden chairs,
or out to the (heated in winter) tree fern-
lined conservatory. Warm, house-baked
soda bread, softened butter and iced water
quickly arrive with Graham Johns's well-
balanced, well-crafted menu, which hints at
his Irish heritage. Capers stud a meaty, tightly
textured ham hock terrine. Black pudding
adds a clever, savoury edge to scallops,
as does chorizo to a tile of barramundi.
A perfectly pink, moist duck breast props
on a rich patty of shredded duck leg hash
that deserves to be a dish in its own right.
A green salad is equally substantial, perhaps
overly complex. But a rich slab of chocolate
parfait with honeycomb shards competes in
the generosity stakes. This is pub dining as
it should be: relaxed yet highly professional,
and a very welcome treat.

Hours Lunch daily 12–3pm; Dinner Mon–Sat
6–10pm, Sun 6–9.30pm
Bill E $14.50–$17.50 **M** $21.50–$31.50
D $14.50–$21.50
Cards AE DC V MC Eftpos
Wine Strong, imaginative, varied list, very
competitively priced; 13 by the glass
Chef Graham Johns
Owner Damian Silk
Seats 120; outdoor seating
Child friendly Highchair
www.thewelcomehotel.com
And...the apricot chutney served with cheese
is worth bottling

The Wharf Restaurant

Pier 4, Hickson Road, Walsh Bay
Tel 9250 1761   Map 1

Contemporary   ♛
                                    Score 15/20

There's a sense of anticipation as you walk
the echoing length of Pier 4, home to the
Sydney Theatre Company, with its age-
old wooden boards and heavy overhead
beams. The reward is a wide-open dining
space with sensational harbour views that
somehow feels warm and intimate despite its
expansive industrial setting. Service is prompt,
efficient and wise, and the menu elegant in
its simplicity. Ever-so-lightly smoked ocean
trout with pickled beetroot and shiso is a
delicate pleasure. But not every dish was the
bravura performance we've come to expect.
A flavoursome escalivada – a jumble of
ratatouille-like aubergine and capsicum with
haloumi and ravigote dressing – appeared
a little monotonous. A fish "sausage" with
rosemary and white bean salad hits the
right notes, and braised pork shoulder with
kipfler potatoes, lifted by tart red cabbage,
is generous and more-ish. To finish, a creamy
goat's curd cheesecake with a sensational
nutty base and poached cherries on the side
deserves a standing ovation.

Hours Lunch Mon–Sat noon–3pm; Dinner
Mon–Sat 6–10pm
Bill E $19.50–$22.50 **M** $26.50–$37.50
D $13–$13.50; 5% surcharge on Sundays,
10% on public holidays
Cards AE DC V MC
Wine Neat, well-priced selection; 22 by the glass
Chefs/owners Aaron Ross & Tim Pak Poy
Seats 180; private rooms; wheelchair access;
outdoor seating
Vegetarian Varied and original dishes
www.thewharfrestaurant.com.au
And...arrive early for drinks on the deck

Whitewater

35 South Steyne, Manly
Tel 9977 0322   Map 7

Contemporary ♀
Score 13/20

Across the road from Manly's stately Norfolk pines, Whitewater is like an upmarket beach shack, right down to the friendly cabana-boy waiters in their denims and striped cotton shirts. Designer Michael McCann has a gift for creating visually striking spaces, and dim lighting, sandstone walls and massive, roughly hewn wooden columns add just enough warmth to this otherwise white space. The menu jumps around the world with a strong seafood focus, just as the location demands. An entree salad of smoked trout is a loosely assembled mix of avocado, baby beets and tangy horseradish cream. Peking duck, so popular it's been on the menu since day one, was, however, a little dry and one-dimensional. Deep-fried squid tubes in the lightest coating work better, stuffed with couscous and feisty chorizo, but grain-fed beef lacked the flavour and tender texture that slow roasting suggests. A chocolate tasting plate is a highlight: chocolate fondant with bittersweet chocolate ice-cream.

Hours Breakfast Sat–Sun 8–11am; Lunch Mon–Fri noon–3pm, Sat–Sun noon–4pm; Dinner daily 6–10pm

Bill E $18–$21 **M** $28–$36 **D** $12–$16; 10% surcharge on Sundays & public holidays

Cards AE DC V MC Eftpos

Wine Impressive selection of mainly new world with something for everyone; 23 by the glass

Chef Luke Cesare

Owner Allan Simpson

Seats 140; private room; outdoor seating

Child friendly Kids' menu

www.whitewaterrestaurant.com.au

And...have a drink and a nibble in the cosy bar

The Yellow Bistro

57–59 Macleay Street, Potts Point
Tel 9357 3400   Map 2

Contemporary
Score 13.5/20

Dining at Yellow is a more rustic and less sophisticated affair than at some of its more upmarket restaurant neighbours, but we wouldn't have it any other way. There are wooden chairs and floorboards, homely artworks, and tables extending onto the chicness of Macleay Street, while an open turbo gas fire provides extra cosiness. It's packed out daily for breakfast, lunch and dinner, which may explain why the otherwise friendly and knowledgeable waiters can seem slow at times. The diverse, well-priced and I-want-everything menu may feature chilli salt squid with the added intrigue of Korean pickled cabbage, lime and shallots or a joyously unpretentious roast chook with beans, chips and aioli. Kingfish on a lush potato puree, plus grated beetroot enhanced by herbs, garlic and onion, is a more elegant offering. Predictable we may be, but you must have a Lorraine Godsmark pudding or cake for dessert, especially her unbelievably light cheesecake. And if you're just too full, get a slice of something nice to take home.

Hours Breakfast Mon–Fri 8–11am; Brunch Sat–Sun 8am–3pm; Lunch Mon–Fri 11am–3pm; Dinner Mon–Fri 5–10pm

Bill E $17.50–$18.50 **M** $24.50–$34.50 **D** $8.50–$12; 15% brunch surcharge on weekends & public holidays

Cards AE V MC Eftpos

Wine Short, eclectic boutique list; 13 by the glass; BYO (corkage $10 per bottle)

Chefs/owners George Sinclair & Lorraine Godsmark

Seats 60; wheelchair access; outdoor seating

And...locals love the adjoining takeaway store

Ying's

270 Pacific Highway, Crows Nest
Tel 9966 9182   Map 5a

Chinese (Cantonese)/Seafood
Score 14/20

Cars zip along the Pacific Highway past the floor-to-ceiling windows at Ying's, but it's for the live barramundi darting to and fro in their large glass tanks that diners come – as well as the more sedate mud crab and lobster. Service at this traditional Chinese dining room can be abrupt, but hold out until the affable Ying himself makes his way round to your blue-clothed table and all your questions will be answered – from the day's seafood specials to menu planning, with bonus asides about his self-described "playboy" youth in Hong Kong. Classic Cantonese flavour profiles rule: tender baby salt-and-pepper squid is everything the imitators aspire to, while ginger and shallot sauce crowns a beautifully sweet mud crab from the tank. Back on dry land, flavours aren't quite so spectacular, but crisp-skinned san tung chicken and garlicky stir-fried yin choy greens would hold their own in Chinatown.

Hours Lunch daily 11am–3pm; Dinner daily 6–10.30pm
Bill E $6.60–$38.80 **M** $19.80–$38.80 **D** $5.50–$7.50; $3.50 pp surcharge on public holidays
Cards AE DC V MC
Wine An appropriate list, with a selection of aromatic whites and lighter reds; 9 by the glass; BYO (corkage $5 pp)
Chef Ken Yau
Owner Ying's Seafood Restaurant Pty Ltd
Seats 120; private rooms; wheelchair access
Child friendly Highchairs
Vegetarian Several options
And...give Ying your price range for a seasonal seafood banquet

Yoshii

115 Harrington Street, The Rocks
Tel 9247 2566   Map 1

Japanese
Score 16.5/20

Tracking down a bona-fide sushi master in Sydney, despite our endearing love for fish on rice, is astonishingly tricky. Of the few expert steel knife-wielders, Tokyo-trained Yoshii-san displays a delicacy and artistry rarely equalled locally, which is reason enough to brave the awkward silence of his dark-timbered restaurant temple. Perch, preferably, at the sushi counter to admire the man himself at work after choosing from a range of multiple-course menus of sushi, sashimi and omakase (chef's selections) dishes. The subdued, softly lit main room offers two menus of 11 tiny, kaiseki-style courses designed around taste, presentation and season. Each is a miniature work of art – an eggshell cup of quail egg yolk in rust-brown dashi, overlaid with trembling gold leaf; or white fish and nori wrapping caviar-like soba spears, soaking in a tannin-bitter stock. Not everything is immaculate. Service can be clumsy and hesitant, and some dishes, such as a fresh bamboo shoot trio, sacrificed flavour for looks. But a row of exquisite sashimi flowers – each petal a fishy wafer – with real wasabi, fine soy and a bowl of umami-laden red miso, reveals a true master.

Hours Lunch Tues–Fri noon–2.30pm; Dinner Mon–Sat 6–10pm
Bill Degustation menus from $120 pp
Cards AE DC V MC
Wine A complex global list; 11 by the glass
Chef Ryuichi Yoshii
Owner Saqura Investment & Consulting Pty Ltd
Seats 42; private room
Vegetarian Degustation
www.yoshii.com.au
And...lunch sets to sample Yoshii-san's touch

Zaaffran

Level 2, 345 Harbourside Shopping Centre,
Darling Harbour
Tel 9211 8900   Map 5b

Indian

Score 13/20

In 1998, Zaaffran led Sydney's new wave of upscale Indian restaurants, inviting diners to think beyond subcontinental cliches. Chef Vikrant Kapoor presents subtle, contemporary regional cooking. His refined reinterpretations can sometimes make the distinctive flavours of Punjab through Gujarat to Goa seem rather polite. But this popular Darling Harbour stalwart is undiminished, and the modern dining room with its city lights outlook is as busy as a Bangalore bus station. A chaat (starter snack) of crisp English spinach, potatoes and chickpeas is decorated with squirts of sweet yoghurt and date and tamarind chutney. A lobster stir-fry with idiyappam (rice noodles) was one-dimensional, but cauliflower and potato stir-fry with tomato–onion masala and ginger stands out. Friendly, energetic waiters weave their magic. So does a creamy, perfumed kulfi (saffron, pistachio, rose petal and more) and those endlessly twinkling lights.

Hours Lunch daily noon–2.30pm; Dinner Sun–Thurs 6–9.30pm, Fri–Sat 6–10.15pm

Bill E $10.50–$18.50 **M** $19–$39.50 **D** $6.90–$11.90; banquets from $39.90; $3 pp surcharge on Sundays & public holidays

Cards AE DC V MC Eftpos

Wine High-end commercial list; 11 by the glass

Chef Vikrant Kapoor

Owners Rush Dossa, Freddie Zulfiqar & Vikrant Kapoor

Seats 220; private room; wheelchair access; outdoor seating

Child friendly Highchairs; mild dishes

Vegetarian Starters, mains and banquet

www. zaaffran.com

And...ask for a window seat when you book

Zilver

Level 1, 477 Pitt Street, Haymarket
Tel 9211 2232   Map 3a

Chinese

Score 14/20

The decor is as different from Chinatown as the fusion-crossover touch at Zilvers, adding contemporary influences to a Cantonese-inclined menu. Yum cha arrives fresh and fast: dinky Peking duck pancakes and must-have custard tarts. The evening's a la carte food is subtle and well executed. Sugar snap peas are just that, contrasted with three varieties of plump, slippery mushrooms; big, fluffy balls of gently fried tofu are spiked with Chinese sausage; pork belly in dark soy sauce with preserved mustard greens is wonderfully rich, soft and sticky; outstanding noodles are bathed in a briny, savoury abalone sauce touched with shallots and ginger. In this big, low-ceilinged room, noise levels are agreeable, high-backed chairs padded, portions generous – make that huge – and desserts as cheerfully perfunctory as the service, although complimentary fruit more than suffices.

Hours Lunch Mon–Fri 10am–3.30pm, Sat–Sun 9am–3.30pm; Dinner daily 5.30–11pm; bookings essential

Bill E $8–$16.80 **M** $16.80–$128 **D** $4–$8.80; $2.50 pp lunch surcharge ($3 pp dinner surcharge) on public holidays

Cards AE DC V MC

Wine Good variety and names, fairly priced; 8 by the glass; BYO (corkage $10 per bottle)

Chef Lei Kuok Wa

Owner Henry Tang

Seats 550; private rooms

Child friendly Highchairs

Vegetarian Many options

www.zilver.com.au

And...the cold cucumber salad with chilli is a refreshing side dish

When at home do as the Romans do.

While you're sleeping, legions of coffee mad Italians will be using their Talea Touch to whip up a sublime espresso, cappuccino or latte.

Wake up to Italy's favourite coffee machine and join in.

Choose from Saeco Talea Touch (pictured), or any machine from the Primea, Talea and Odea range.

Ideas with Passion

⊘ **Saeco**

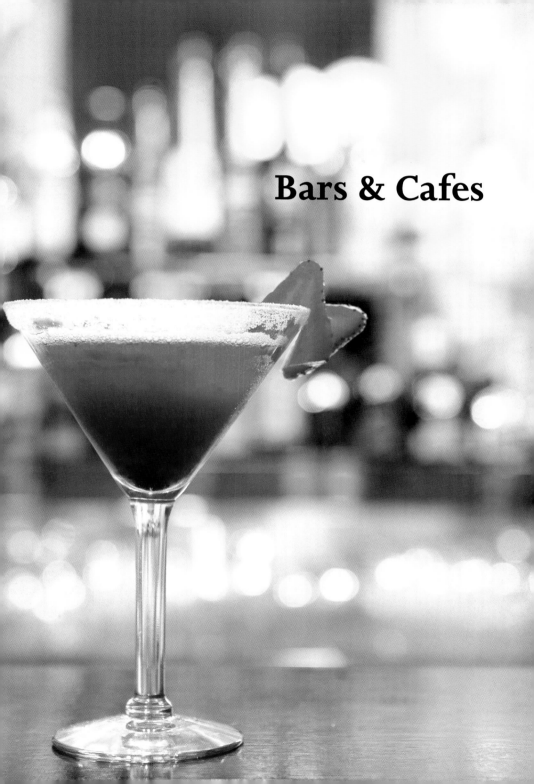

Bars & Cafes

Bars
By Paul Chai

Bambini Wine Room
185 Elizabeth Street, Sydney
Tel 9283 7098
The opulent, refined surrounds make the most of the elegant interiors of this treasure. Bambini is often referred to as "very Melbourne", much to local dismay. But with more quality wines than you can shake a chandelier at, knowledgeable staff and prompt service, it's simply very good.

Bayswater Brasserie
32 Bayswater Road, Kings Cross
Tel 9357 2177
Something about this cocktail bar speaks of an earlier era of sharp suits and sharper tongues. It could be the casual elegance of the dark wood interior, the vast array of quality bottles that commands the bar be taken seriously or its definition of classics, including a Corpse Reviver #2 and a Georgia Mint Julep, replacing the usual suspects.

Dean's
5 Kellett Street, Kings Cross
Tel 9368 0953
Dean's louche, 1950s-inspired decor – sagging couches, overhead surfboards, Robbie the Robot-style jukebox – feels like your wacky uncle's sunroom in a Kings Cross backstreet. Grab a monstrous serve of nachos and a frosty beer and resist the urge to clean the bar's murky fish tank.

Foveaux Restaurant + Bar
65–67 Foveaux Street, Surry Hills
Tel 9211 0664
Using vanilla in cocktails is always brave and too often misguided. Not so when it's the finely balanced La Chica (Havana Club rum, vanilla and citrus liqueur, kaffir lime leaves, hibiscus cordial and fresh lime juice). This welcoming, snug basement is equally well designed and never cloying.

Hugo's Lounge
33 Bayswater Road, Kings Cross
Tel 9332 1227
While it maintains its status as the Pied Piper for Sydney's comely set, Hugo's has done little to change its formula of sultry lighting, simple, chic furnishings, fresh and fruity concoctions and nightly visits from some of Sydney's top DJs who spin discs at a chat-friendly tempo. If it ain't broke…

Icebergs Dining Room and Bar
1 Notts Avenue, Bondi Beach
Tel 9365 9000
It's a pleasure to see that Icebergs' bird's-nest position at the southern end of Bondi Beach hasn't gone to its head. Fine cocktails, a solid selection of beers and, while the muted blue decor is showing some wear and tear, who's looking when there's rolling surf outside?

Ivy

320–330 George Street, Sydney
Tel 9240 3000
Justin Hemmes has added a few more slick bars to his panoply. Eighteen, to be precise, all under a single multimillion-dollar three-storey roof (or not, for recalcitrant smokers). Striving to be all things to all people, with designs to match, it feels a bit like the Ikea of drinking holes. Bring a map.

Kudu Lounge

225a Victoria Street, Darlinghurst
Tel 9331 8900
Vibrant young staff look pleased to be here. Laid-back live entertainment might see a trumpet player wandering around riffing off the DJ's sultry set. This new nocturnal nook with marvellous twists on the classics is on two floors next to the Darlo fire station.

Lotus

22 Challis Avenue, Potts Point
Tel 9326 9000
This dimly lit, elegant boite behind Lotus the restaurant has a New York-chic interior of plush wallpaper and artisan light fixtures as well as some of the best bartenders in town. Is Sydney's best margarita here among the perfectly created classics? The originals always hit the mark, too.

Madame Fling Flong

Level 1, 169 King Street, Newtown
Tel 9565 2471
King Street is the perfect place for this temple of op-shop cool, yet it's more than the sum of its St Vinnie's decor. Cocktails – chocolate-heavy Madam CoCo or lychee-inspired Madame's Passion – are first-rate.

Melt Lounge

12 Kellett Street, Kings Cross
Tel 9380 6060
A grown-up student bar with rows of cosy banquettes on entry, oversized sunken leather couches in the bar, walls slathered with vibrant murals and a crowd whose clothes are as fashionably distressed as the surroundings. Great live funk and soul bands on Thursdays.

Opera Bar

Lower Concourse Level, Sydney Opera House, Sydney
Tel 9247 1666
The only way the view could get any better is with a drink. Sunset is best as the white sails of Joern Utzon's masterpiece light up, the bar gets its groove on with up-and-coming bands, and the upbeat office crowd orders another bottle of bubbles to ease into the night.

Oxford Art Factory

38–46 Oxford Street, Darlinghurst
Tel 9332 3711
Part art gallery, part cocktail bar and part live performance space, the Factory takes its inspiration from Andy Warhol. The design is minimalist–industrial, a blank canvas for the acts and exhibitions. The vibe changes depending on who's performing. The one constant is a fascinating night out.

The Patio

Cnr Darlinghurst Road and Liverpool Street, Darlinghurst
Tel 9331 3672
A refreshingly kitsch take on the new-breed urban beer garden, with white metal chairs, faux grass and plenty of lattice work – like a Mad Hatter's Tea Party in Darlo. The vibe is friendly, the crowd casually funky, and while the furnishings may scream Pimm's and ginger ale, beer is the local currency.

Rambutan

96 Oxford Street, Darlinghurst
Tel 9360 7772
Tiki bars, like wild animals, shouldn't be too restrained but Rambutan's basement pulls it off with aplomb with an understated take on the South Pacific: bamboo wallpaper, floral-print couches, ample greenery. Drinks have an Asian flavour to complement the Thai menu.

Rose of Australia Hotel

1 Swanson Street, Erskineville
Tel 9565 1441
The Rose is a perfect blend of old and new: a restored but not ruined tiled front bar with a terrific, sympathetically decorated cocktail

bar out back. Drinks from the venerable bar whizzes may take a while, but they're worth it.

Ruby Rabbit/De Nom
231 Oxford Street, Darlinghurst
Tel 9326 0044
A dusky rock-and-roll den of iniquity packed to the rafters with hipsters, drawn to the drinks doled out from the fern-covered bar or to the regular live music. Upstairs is the French palace-themed De Nom, with decor so ludicrously over the top they should hand you a powdered wig on entry.

Sticky Bar
182 Campbell Street, Surry Hills
Tel 0416 096 916
Phone from Taggarts Lane, they say, to gain entry to this bare-brick temple of all things dessert wine (or slide in via Table for 20 restaurant downstairs). With a wall of elegantly tattered posters, regal, yet cosy ottomans, and exotic designer lamps, it's hip enough to overlook the gimmicks. Not a sauternes fan? Choose from an equally exhaustive list of wines, beers with a European bent and top-drawer cocktails.

Tonic Lounge
62–64 Kellett Street, Kings Cross
Tel 8354 1544
One of Tonic's big sells is the crowd; a relaxed and sociable collection of fellow travellers that feels like a rolling private party to dip in and out of each time you front up. The look is boho-chic with blood-red walls, quaint lamps and oil paintings you would laugh at if your parents owned them.

Trademark Hotel
1 Bayswater Road, Kings Cross
Tel 9357 5522
This slick venue tucked in under the Coke sign is a mix of retro–futuristic moulded plastic and eggcup chairs overseen by a wasps' nest of clustered lights. In the Piano Room, things are skewed towards the mature drinker with a broodier supper club feel, live music and an expansive outdoor terrace.

The Vanguard
42 King Street, Newtown
Tel 9557 7992
Built as a temple to the blues, this scarlet boudoir transports you to the French Quarter of New Orleans. Cocktails reflect the Southern vibe with monikers such as Muddy Waters and Lafayette Iced Tea, and when the live music isn't jazz or blues, it's bound to be good anyway.

The Victoria Room
Level 1, 235 Victoria Street, Darlinghurst
Tel 9357 4488
There's an intentional whiff of a venerable colonial hotel bar – verdant palms, discreet screens, gilt-edged sofas and high tea on weekends – but the ambience is anything but stuffy. The theme is reflected in the glass, with drinks such as a West Indies Yellowbird made with fresh-pressed sugar cane.

Water Bar
6 Cowper Wharf Road, Woolloomooloo
Tel 9331 9000
After a half-million-dollar facelift, the Blue Hotel's bar has emerged unscarred. Silver-grey and black couches flow like the moonlit harbour down the length of the industrial-chic hotel interior, while curtains of Swarovksi crystal rain down overhead, glinting in the candlelight. The bar team of Neil Littlewood and Nick Braun has created a rich list of very original mixes, but they still make a mean martini.

Zeta Bar
Level 4, Hilton Sydney, 488 George Street, Sydney
Tel 9265 6070
There are few more striking outdoor spaces than Zeta's terrace looking across to the cupola of the QVB. Frequent overseas jaunts by bar maestro Grant Collins make the drinks list so cutting edge that it's virtually molecular mixology. Find a swank nook and cranny to hole up in and watch the passing parade of somebodies, nobodies and everyone in between.

IN 1862 THEY DISCOVERED GOLD AT
THE BRAIDED RIVER.

IN 2008 WE FOUND IT AGAIN.

The alluvial deposits of the braided river are once again
yielding hidden treasures. The Sauvignon Blanc displays
a tropical fruit nose that dominates and sweetens the more
classic Marlborough herbaceousness. While the Pinot Noir
is enriched by bold toasty oak flavours. Enjoy these special
discoveries from world famous Marlborough.

Braided River. Replenish your soul.

Cafes

CITY

Bertoni Casalinga
262 Kent Street, Sydney
Tel 9262 5845
Also at 90 Vista Street, Mosman
Tel 9969 5845
281 Darling Street, Balmain
Tel 9818 5845
Authentic Italian–Australian exuberance and excellent coffee are all part of the Bertoni charm. Then there are the panini, the pasta, the minestrone (and several other soups in winter) and the much-loved ciambella alla Nutella, zuccherati and eggplant parmigiana.

Café Chicane
2/10 Bond Street, Sydney
Tel 9232 4456
It's as loud and buzzy as the trading floor, while everyone tucks into steak burgers, porcini risotto and salt-and-pepper squid, matched with recommended tipples. Solid breakfasts and decent Toby's Estate coffee are a morning heart-starter.

Caffe Cino
Ground Floor, Hilton Hotel,
488 George Street, Sydney
Tel 9266 2000
If fast-food joints can muscle into the market, why not posh hotels? Amid the smart, soaring glass-framed Hilton foyer, swing by the long counter with stool seating for a quick soup of the day, BLT, a real-deal "Hilton" caesar, swift, smiling service and good Single Origin coffee. Afternoon tea on one of the couches is a guilty pleasure – a loose-leaf brew and a mousse pyramid in three shades of chocolate, or perhaps a gold-leaf topped Opera slice.

Central Baking Depot
37–39 Erskine Street, Sydney
Tel 9290 2229
Now we can relax. The city has the perfect bakery. From the oven each morning – and you can breathe in the aroma a block away – come danishes, croissants and sourdough loaves. Legendary sausage rolls – chicken and fennel, lamb and harissa – and organic coffee.

Fioro Café
2/60 Pitt Street, Sydney
Tel 9241 6800
Blink and you'll miss it, right opposite Macquarie Bank. Blink and your macchiato is served. The speediest coffee delivery ever, and a great drop to boot. A big blackboard menu of sandwiches, salads and "open grills" – go the chorizo, haloumi, spinach, mushrooms – and more. If you want to hide away from it all, there's basement seating with table service.

Illy Cafe

8 Bent Street, Sydney
Tel 1300 366 303
Dr Ernesto Illy has departed for the big cafe in the sky, but his cult coffee lives on. This "concept cafe" sells beautiful French teas, pastries, panini and simple lunch dishes made with premium deli ingredients, such as organic olive oil and risotto rice. And then there's the expertly pulled coffee. Heaven on earth.

Plan B

204 Clarence Street, Sydney
Tel 9283 3450
This hole-in-the-wall cafe next to Becasse lets you eat Justin North's food for a fraction of the price. The wagyu burger is sublime, the sausage roll nothing like schooldays, and the Single Origin coffee lush. Grab a salad or pre-packed sandwich to go.

Toby's Estate

129 Cathedral Street, Woolloomooloo
Tel 9358 1196
Also at 32–36 City Road, Chippendale
Tel 9211 1459
cnr Manning & Macleay streets, Potts Point
Tel 8356 9264
Not just coffee – although there are umpteen blends including single origin, organic and Fair Trade brews. Toby also does tea – fine loose-leaf green, black, white and herbal infusions. Book in for a coffee or tea tasting class. Or just enjoy a barista brew and a pastry, biscuit or Spanish hot chocolate.

Velluto Nero Coffee Couture

3/259 Clarence Street, Sydney
Tel 9268 0755
This skinny, latte-coloured, almost-too-slick designer den for all matters coffee produces nigh-on the perfect espresso. The cafe knocks up basic breakfasts, salads and sandwiches, plus lots of sweet things. Decent loose-leaf teas, too.

NORTH

Avenue Road Cafe

185 Avenue Road, Mosman
Tel 9969 8999
Inside, under quirky dangling lights, or on the footpath, it's all-day breakfast with Rio coffee, fresh juices and smoothies. Lunch is full of flair: corn and zucchini fritters with speck, grilled haloumi and roasted tomatoes, excellent wraps and salads, plenty of pastries and chirpy service.

Bacino Kiosk

Clifton Gardens Beach Walkway, Clifton Gardens
Tel 0401 666 166
Also at Building 2, Chowder Bay Road, Chowder Bay
Tel 9960 4566
With just enough room in this former ammunition store to produce a worthy espresso, it's a miracle when banana bread and bircher muesli also emerge for breakfast, followed by panini, baguettes and antipasto for lunch. All outdoor seating, right at the water's edge, means it's closed on rainy days.

Barefoot Cafe

47a Sydney Road, Manly
Caffiends hide from the tourists in this hip ristretto-sized shop with its teal-blue tiled wall, eight tree stump seats and big open window seating. The seriously good coffee is Toby's Estate organic and the only edible offering is a hot, made-on-the-spot Belgian waffle. Who's complaining?

The Barn Café Headland Park

Building 3, 1100 Middle Head Road, Mosman
Tel 9968 2923
Surrounded by natural bushland and stunning harbour views, cyclists and bushwalkers refuel on the popular "Mosman brekkie" – eggs with the works on thick toast. At lunchtime, the courtyard is full of families tucking into antipasto, soups, salads and hearty lamb and chicken burgers.

Blue Water Cafe

28 South Steyne, Manly
Tel 9976 2051
The food's a little smarter than most at this popular, polished beachfront setting where the coffee's good and the breakfasts are big. Lunch means seafood: snapper with chilli fries or prawn curry; and dinner's as flash as a Portuguese beef espetada.

The Chelsea Tea House

2/48 Old Barrenjoey Road, Avalon
Tel 9918 6794
Well-coiffed grannies and barefoot beach babes sip wine by the glass in the sunny courtyard and exotic teas with names such as Dandy and Lover's Leap. The Chelsea's huevos rancheros – tortilla with black beans, fried eggs and salsa – are justifiably famous.

Forsyth Coffee and Tea

284 Willoughby Road, Naremburn
Tel 9906 7388
Rob Forsyth is a serious coffee man, which is why his shop and cafe are all about the beans – where they're from, how they're roasted, how to brew them and how to taste them in the cup. From single-origin beans from all over, try one of his 100 or so signature blends with something sweet. A northside coffee shrine.

Girdlers Grind

Shop 3C, 7 The Strand, Dee Why Beach
Tel 9972 2336
Inside every rugby league legend lurks a latte lover... Former Penrith and Kangaroo centre Ryan Girdler runs this small coffee and juice bar with beach views through the Norfolk Pines. A popular morning spot where you can chew the fat over the weekend footy results, with panini and sweet treats to nibble on.

Micalini Café

7/332 Military Road, Cremorne
Tel 9909 8282
Squint hard enough (no, harder) and this Military Road-side piazza with its outdoor tables could be Cremorne's answer to Rome's Via del Corso. There's Latin cosiness in nonna's pasta with beans in a napoli sauce. Start the day with big eggy brekkies and bowls of fruit-laden house-made muesli, unless of course your idea of a breakfast cornetto is one of the ever-changing choices of house-made sweets, such as the mini New York cheesecake.

Nor'easter Cafe

1093 Pittwater Road, Collaroy Beach
Tel 9984 1222
Sarah Wilmot comes from a long line of salty seadogs and is no slouch in the kitchen or a headwind. This nautically themed cafe serves hearty breakfast till 3pm, lamb pie with ratatouille for lunch, a good range of T2 teas and loads of ice-cream.

The Peppermill Café

30 Glen Street, The Colonnades, Milsons Point
Tel 9954 1444
Keep an eye on the daily blackboard specials at this cool blue, super-efficient spot, dishing out generous, lively tucker, such as chicken and mushroom pie, roast pumpkin gnocchi with goat's cheese, and scrummy buttermilk pancakes for breakfast. It's licensed too.

SOUTH

Adora Handmade Chocolates

10 Homer Street, Earlwood
Tel 9559 5948
Also at Wentworth Connection, 2 Bligh Street, Sydney
Tel 9323 6601
Down by the riverbend between Earlwood and Marrickville is a neat little cottage that's popular with cyclists (they've earned it) and everyone else as well. Coffee comes with a handmade chocolate from Greek–Australian sisters Tina Vamvoukakis and Katerina Stavropoulos. Then you buy a beautiful box of the same for someone you love.

Brasserie Bread
1731 Botany Road, Banksmeadow
Tel 9666 6845
We love this warehouse-style mix of bakery
and cafe for its fabulous sourdough and
Allpress coffee. Breakfast is brilliant: danishes
or sourdough pancakes and corned beef
hash. Lunch is smoked ocean trout on house-
baked bread, roast lamb on schiacciata, or a
croque monsieur.

Cordial Café
Shop 8, 130 Carillon Avenue, Newtown
Tel 9557 6066
The excellent Vertigo coffee at this chilled,
loud cafe is named after Hitchcock's movie.
The decor's a little rev-head, with communal
and outdoor tables. The breakfasts are just
swell, and the rest is fresh and fun.
Weekends are family time.

Edith and Rose
142 Malabar Road, South Coogee
Tel 9344 3255
An old-fashioned corner cakery where the
sponges and slices are made with real butter
and eggs. So too the lemon meringue pie,
and the remarkable vanilla milkshake cake.
Morgan's coffee and savoury pies full of
serious meat fillings give sweet tooths respite.

Kaimaki
Shop 4, 9 Montgomery Street, Kogarah
Tel 9553 0600
A name that means "crema" in Greek is a
promising sign. And they're referring to a
strong, well-made cup of coffee, of course.
In summer, try a Greek-style frappe – similar
to coffee granita. There's a full menu, too –
from simple breakfasts to salads, sandwiches,
grills and cakes.

Melonhead
256 Coogee Bay Road, Coogee
Tel 9664 3319
This juice bar also serves a decent Karmee
coffee and Turkish rolls, but most come for
the fruit salad, a fruit smoothie or fresh juice –
or in summer, ice-laden fruit crushes.

Pastizzi Café
523 King Street, Newtown
Tel 9519 1063
How many ways can you stuff pastizzi?
This cheery, whitewashed cafe is out to set
a record. Their large, flaky, pinched ovals
come both savoury and sweet, with ricotta,
pea and spinach, lentil, vegie curry and even
chocolate inside. Take a dozen home for later
or hang around for a plate of Maltese ravioli.

Saint Germain Patisserie
88 Rosehill Street, cnr Gibbons Street, Redfern
Tel 9319 7161
French boulanger Gwen Lecampion bakes a
mean croissant at this petite corner bakery
stacked with glorious cakes and tarts. Have
one filled with ham and brie for lunch, and
take home an almond croissant and pain au
chocolat for after. Just because you deserve it.

Single Origin ★
60–64 Reservoir Street, Surry Hills
Tel 9211 0665
FAVOURITE CAFE
The lads behind this corner hangout are
coffee's answer to computer geeks and
we're impressed. They care till it hurts, will
happily tell all and advise on getting the best
from the beans you take home. The aroma
from the roaster is as sexy as the crema on
your ristretto.

South End Cafe
644 King Street, St Peters
Tel 9517 1344
Two talented, personable young sisters run
this baby- and dog-friendly spot with its mod–
retro Newtown-hand-me-down ambience.
Robust coffee and hearty, thoughtful,
seasonal food, such as pea and haloumi
pancakes; penne with thyme, pumpkin and
bacon; and dried tomato-topped quiche.

Wall Café

80 Campbell Street, Surry Hills
Tel 9280 1980
This colourful corner cafe with its funky layout seems so very Melbourne because it is, with an older sibling down south. Toasted pide, great soups and lemon tart, but really, it's all about the Genovese coffee.

Zensation Teahouse

656 Bourke Street, Redfern
Tel 9319 2788
There's a splash of Asian bohemia about this cosy tea-drinkers' den with cushioned tables for tastings – and jewellery for sale, too. Come for tea appreciation classes, for a cuppa with your girlfriends or to stock up on Fujian oolong, pu'er and herbal teas for home.

WEST

Abla's Patisserie

6 Sherwood Road, Merrylands
9682 6638
Do the cafe thing the Middle Eastern way, with something flaky, sweet and nutty and a strong, thick, scented Lebanese coffee. A branch of the original Abla bakery family (there are several Abla shops around town), this take-home or sit-in pastry palace also sells sticky Lebanese ice-cream.

Bar Mattino

96 Abercrombie Street, Chippendale
Tel 9699 1442
The much-loved Sunday lunch roast sees most through till Monday breakfast at this small, colourful child-friendly English-style caff. Slide in for a generous roast beef sandwich, a chip butty or black pudding for breakfast.

Bar Passalacqua

128 Marion Street, Leichhardt
Tel 9572 8820
Trust a Little Italy hole-in-the-wall to feel just like downtown Rome with boys chattering in the mother tongue over great coffee and melts as they watch Italian sport on the telly.

Big Brekky

316 Stanmore Road, Petersham
Tel 9569 8588
A scrubbed, cheerful corner building with a big communal table has country farmhouse charm and lives up to its name. Start the day with a smoked salmon bagel, goat's fetta omelette, rhubarb and banana pancakes or, if you're that way inclined, scrambled tofu.

Espresso Galleria

84 Ramsay Street, Haberfield
Tel 9798 2112
If the ancient Greeks had a coffee god, he'd be something like barista Emanuel Patniotis: warm and welcoming, likeable and talented. With some of his mama's superb baklava, his smooth, full-bodied brew certainly tastes like the nectar of the gods.

Locantro Fine Foods

9 Catherine Street, Leichhardt
Tel 9568 3637
Two generations of the Locantro family combine in this blend of cafe, pasticceria and deli that bubbles with Italian charm. Shop up big on pasta and other Italian provisions, or settle in for a pizza slice, focaccia or arancino. Coffee combines nicely with a gorgeous house-baked pastry, especially a chocolate-filled cannolo or a mini tiramisu.

Love #3

27 Barr Street, Camperdown
Tel 9519 2727
Out front there's an old biscuit stamp from the Weston's factory. This small, cyclist-inspired espresso bar is run by upbeat barista Dieter Steinbusch (ex Escabar). A fresh, fun menu includes specials such as duck salad and lamb ragu pie plus lots of sweet treats. For nostalgia's sake, have a Wagon Wheel.

Plunge Cafe
46 Lackey Street, Summer Hill
Tel 9799 9666
The crisp white haunt of yummy mummies and their broods plates up an amalgam of Mediterranean- and Middle Eastern-influenced fare, such as mezze plates of felafel and lamb kofta, chermoula-crusted fish with fat, beer-battered chips, and Afghan pizza.

Sideways Deli Cafe
37 Constitution Road, Dulwich Hill
Tel 9560 1425
Two sisters serve breakfast – corn fritters, ricotta pancakes, kid's egg with baked beans and soldiers – till 1pm on weekends, plus strong Di Lorenzo coffee and good-value straightforward lunches, including a fab steak sarnie.

EAST

bills
433 Liverpool Street, Darlinghurst
Tel 9360 9631
Also at 359 Crown Street, Surry Hills
Tel 9360 4762
Queens Court, 118 Queen Street, Woollahra
Tel 9328 7997
The man who launched a thousand ricotta hotcakes still sets the pace for all-day breakfasts in this trinity of cheerful, classic bistro-style cafes. From noon, it's steak frites, fish cakes and duck and beetroot salad. Oh, and salted peanut brittle, thanks.

The Bunker
399 Liverpool Street, Darlinghurst
Tel 0404 407 349
Take your sunny morning seat on the footpath; there's not much room inside anyway. Good strong Campos coffee and a chorizo and egg muffin are eat-in or take-away for brekkie. Brasserie bread lunchtime sambos include smoked chicken, gorgonzola and chilli relish.

clodeli
210 Clovelly Road, Clovelly
Tel 9664 1885
Cafe rule number one: a long stretch of morning sunshine and lots of outdoor tables. Number two: good coffee. Three: house-made fruit bread toasted for breakfast; salads, wraps and spinach pie for lunch. Four: a constant crowd, all day, every day. Clodeli sticks to the rules.

Favoloso
43 Belgrave Street, Bronte
Tel 9389 8002
The name means "fabulous" in Italian and that's definitely how the locals see it – try getting a seat after week-day school drop-off time when it's packed with parents sipping a fortifying latte. The Italian owners do excellent coffee, bacon-and-egg breakfasts (Italian style) and homely meals, and they also stock some terrific deli items including bread, salami, gourmet ice-cream and more.

Flat White
98 Holdsworth Street, Woollahra
Tel 9328 9922
This snazzy white local goes off on the weekends with all-day breakfasts such as chorizo omelette, before dishing up seriously smart European-styled comfort food and strong coffee that helps frazzled parents cope with the Saturday sports run.

Selected by France's finest tables.

Heart of Europe Cafe
114 Bronte Road, Bondi Junction
Tel 9387 1677
The Central European in you comes for home cooking: speck and eggs or kolacky – farm-cheese filled pastries – for brekkie, then hearty goulash soup and chunky apple strudel. Others flock for the Junction's best and strongest coffee. And the roast duck with dumplings.

La Buvette
35 Challis Avenue, Potts Point
Tel 9358 5113
The local lads, plus the good and groovy, all recover from the previous night's excess with a latte, sunglasses and gossip on the footpath outside this skinny, busy home to reliable breakfasts, a cheerful welcome and comforting lunchtime faves.

Pasteleria Caravela
60 Bronte Road, Bondi Junction
Tel 9387 8456
The Ferreiras of Portuguese baking fame are back in Bondi with a long, skinny corner cafe and oven-warm custard tarts. Sugar-crusted vigilantes (croissants) crisp and tangy gila (melon jam) in puff pastry also make a sweet start to the day. Good coffee, fresh juices, egg 'n' bacon roll and salt cod fritters any time.

Peaberry Espresso
166 Riley Street, Darlinghurst
Tel 9331 3806
Connoisseurs claim the peaberry is the caviar of coffee. We reckon this little slip of a spot is a good excuse for a nostalgia hit of Coco Pops, fine banana bread, open grills, salads, sexy sarnies and a damn fine doppio espresso.

Ruby's Diner
173 Bronte Road, Waverley
Tel 9386 5964
Even a bland new building can look funky when a retro-styled cafe opens below. Stools on footpath, strong Single Origin coffee, fat raspberry muffins, eggs any way and Waverley's favourite burger and shakes – yay for Belgian chocolate!

Speedo's Cafe
126 Ramsgate Avenue, North Bondi
Tel 9365 3622
The lazy end of Bondi is where the locals hang, dragging sandy feet from the surf pool shallows into this sleepy sunshiny cafe for juices, coffee, Bondi eggs Benny or a chicken burger with roasted pumpkin.

Global Gems

CITY

Chat Thai
20 Campbell Street, Haymarket
Tel 9211 1808   Thai
The window theatre is fabulous – young women thread satay skewers, roll pandan-flavoured dumplings and sear prawns on the grill. It's Thai Town's most popular address and you may wait for ages unless you book. It's best to order daily specials and northern Thai-influenced dishes, such as super-spicy som dtum (green papaya salad) and grills with bitter nam jim jeaw (dipping sauce). Don't miss dessert – it's a specialty.

Din Tai Fung
Level 1, World Square, 644 George Street, Sydney
Tel 9264 6010   Taiwanese
This branch of a famous Taiwanese dumpling house is the beating heart of the new World Square eating hub. Buns and northern Chinese-style dumplings are stuffed, pinched and pleated before your eyes (watch through the window) then steamed in bamboo basket towers. The baskets are part of the clever décor too. Make sure you have the steamed pork soup dumplings (xiao long bao) as well as buns, noodles, soup and sweet bun desserts.

Heritage Belgian Beer Café
135 Harrington Street, The Rocks
Tel 9241 1775   Belgian
With soaring ceilings and mahogany panelling, a long stretch of marble-topped bar and gleaming beer taps, this repro Belgian brasserie looks like it's been here forever, and that's part of the charm. Its other salient attributes are Belgian beers, including some girlie, fruity ones, and weighty black enamel pots full of just-opened mussels. Good fries and house-made mayo on the side and you'll want this as your heritage, too.

La Mint
62–64 Riley Street, East Sydney
Tel 9331 1818   French/Vietnamese
Don't expect pho at this upmarket Vietnamese with its strong French accent. In a spacious room of white-clothed tables, you'll score tangy beef rolls wrapped in a vine leaf; snails with tomato, chilli, and mint; soft, peppery cubes of beef called bo luc lac (shaking beef); and a melting pavé of sweet and salty pork belly with a fiery chilli sauce. Rice and cocktails offer relief, along with a refreshingly minty pudding of bitter melon jelly with tapioca and coconut.

Lee's Malaysian
Pavillion food court, 580 George Street, Sydney
Tel 9262 7771
Also at Wintergarden, 1 O'Connell Street, Sydney
Tel 9241 2828   Malaysian
Good cooking runs in Kim Lee's family (his sister, Irene, was for many years the face of To's, North Sydney's premier laksa ladler). Lee's laksa is good, his noodles are great and his har mee is even better. Sambal-spicy and subtly prawny, it's a rusty-filmed broth, poured over a noodle base and topped with whole prawns, fried garlic, pork bits, kangkung and bean sprouts. Check out the food counter and his noodle store next door for hawker fare at its finest.

Mamak ★
15 Goulburn Street, Haymarket
Tel 9211 1668   Malaysian
FAVOURITE ASIAN
It's fast food, street-stall style, in a long, skinny room of hip young waiters and no-frills table settings. The theatre of the roti cooks entertains the nightly queue, waiting to sample irresistibly flaky roti chanai with spicy dhal and jammy sambal, waif-like chicken satays, a funky, soft, clove-scented lamb curry, and the sugar rush of jellies with condensed milk over shaved ice, washed down with a stretched tea. If you love bold, spicy flavours on the cheap, this is your place.

Seabay

372 Pitt Street, Sydney

Tel 9267 4855   Chinese (northern)

China's far north-west is famous for its handmade wheat-flour noodles (lian mian). Seabay is equally famous for the same thing. Have them in soup or stir-fried with lamb. Come with friends so you can order more – crisp-bottomed minced pork dumplings, lamb buns, shallot pancakes and peppery northern-style salads. Service is fabulous, and so is the cooking.

Sydney Madang

371a Pitt Street, Sydney

Tel 9264 7010   Korean

If you know that Korean is cool across Asia, you'll understand why this back-lane, lantern-hung tavern pulls in the World Square crowds. Alternatively, just try the food. The menu may be daunting, with so many choices, but there's chilli coding for the faint-hearted, and everything from steamboats to table barbecues comes with excellent side dishes (lots of kimchi and more). And everyone loves haemul panjon – a crisp, stuffed rice-flour pancake.

EAST

Azteca's

140 Avoca Street, Randwick

Tel 9398 1020   Mexican

Mexi-kitsch lines the walls and, in keeping with the surrounds, owner Jose Cruz plays infectious host, serenading birthday guests on his guitar. Snack on tortilla chips and a Dos Equis beer before an authentic ceviche of marinated raw fish, or the spice and chocolate flavours of chicken mole poblano. Then it's tender pork ribs, with a sticky ancho and guajillo chilli sauce and soft tortillas, and retro desserts such as choc mousse in a sundae glass, ensuring warm feelings towards this lively neighbourhood favourite.

Bay Bua

2 Springfield Avenue, Potts Point

Tel 9358 3234   Vietnamese

If you have a touch of deja vu about the menu in this cheerful purple setting with chandeliers and a black marble cocktail bar, it's because host Mai Tran is the granddaughter of Tinh Tran, founder of Marrickville's Bay Tinh. So expect good value bonfire beef and prawns, pork-stuffed calamari, addictively crisp quail, fragrant curries and bounteous egg and rice noodle stir-fries, all served with a gentle smile.

Churrasco

240 Coogee Bay Road, Coogee

Tel 9665 6535   Brazilian

We love all-you-can-eat, especially when you don't have to move from your table. It's even better on sword-like skewers. Coogee's very own Rio-style churrascaria, also known as rodizio, will raise your iron levels in minutes with a succession of chargrilled chorizo, rump steak, eye fillet, marinated chicken and more, slid from the skewers to your plate. There are salads and condiments, too. As if you care.

Gelbison

10 Lamrock Avenue, Bondi Beach

Tel 9130 4042   Pizzeria

There is nothing – repeat, nothing – fancy about Gelbison (named rather mysteriously for a holy mountain near Naples). And who'd have it any other way? There may be other things on the menu but, really, you just come for pizza in the oldie-but-goodie style. Try the potato version, Santa Lucia (tomato, garlic and mushrooms, no cheese) and Magic Boot with anchovies and oregano. Just remember you'll need to queue.

Heggies Vineyard Riesling is made exclusively from spoilt grapes.

Because our wines come from a single vineyard, we have to care for every single grape. We can't rely on a swathe of unknown growers to top up our juice if we fall short. In short, we indulge them so you can enjoy indulging in them.

Java
151 Avoca Street, Randwick
Tel 9398 6990   Indonesian
Time was when Randwick/Kingsford was
wall-to-wall warungs – low-key Indonesian
eateries offering a selection of dishes on rice,
nasi campur style. Java has survived, had a
makeover and ditched the once-ubiquitous
bain marie, but the food remains
authentically good. Beef rendang tops the
favourites list, along with satay, banana-leaf
fish (ikan pepes) and wok-tossed kangkung
with fresh chilli rings and shrimp paste.

Lebanon and Beyond
3/187 Alison Road, Randwick
Tel 9326 5347   Lebanese
It's home-style Beirut fare to satisfy any
hummus and felafel cravings. There's not
much room here, and passing traffic doesn't
make for the best ambient soundtrack, but
for dips, baked kibbeh, garlic chicken (with
gorgeous garlic sauce) and fine fattoush –
crunchy scraps of Lebanese bread mixed
through cucumber, iceberg lettuce, mint and
tomato and sprinkled with sumac – why
go anywhere beyond?

Sabbaba
82 Hall Street, Bondi Beach
Tel 9365 7500   Middle Eastern
Felafel nuggets? In a takeaway pack? Why
not, when they come with a choice of Israeli-
style dip and are sizzled to order from a neat
felafel-making machine? Otherwise it's grills
and salads, including some spicy dips and
spongy, baked-on-the-premises pitta. Try one
with Jerusalem chicken livers. It's a winning
formula for takeaway or for cramming into
one of the tables, preferably a sunny one.

Snakebean
95 Oxford Street, Darlinghurst
Tel 9380 8808   Vietnamese/Thai
It's not for lingering but definitely for good
eating. After closing their modern Asian fine-
diner RQ, owners Jeremy and Nhut have
poured their creative energies into this little
nook. Stop in for Vietnamese rice-paper

rolls with chicken and green mango (they
sell hundreds a day), salads of lotus root,
green papaya or banana blossom and rich
red duck curry or Vietnamese pork with
coconut juice.

Yong Jing's Kitchen Enlightenment
430 Anzac Parade, Kingsford
Tel 9697 0011   Chinese
Locals are spoiled for choice around here
when it comes to home-style Chinese eat-
and-run joints. But who can resist somewhere
with such a great name? The menu is
overwhelming – from soups to noodles, rice
dishes to Cantonese-style chef's specials. But
it helps to know the chef is from Beijing and
that he does good Peking dishes and hotpots.
Great value, too.

NORTH

Avalon Chinese
Level 1, 74 Old Barrenjoey Road, Avalon
Tel 9918 6319   Chinese (Cantonese)
Bonus points for the manager's smiling,
personal service and the crazy, cosy, den-like
room with its gilt-and-red wallpaper and its
blackboard specials. Of those, a Buddha pot
is a saucer-sized ring of fried yam filled with
a mix of seafood or vegetables in a light
Cantonese sauce. Prawns gow gee are
steamed to order, and gingery Emperor's
chicken is an easy pick. Ask for advice and
you'll get it, too.

BBQ One
181 Rowe Street, Eastwood
Tel 9874 5332   Chinese (Cantonese)
Simple pleasures: roasted meat, steaming,
nourishing house soup with a whisk of Chinese
greens and some rice on the side. Every local
seems to be here, whatever time of day you
drop by, but that's probably because of the
huge range of barbecued meats: flattened
pi-pah duck, roast pork, soy chicken, squid and
more, and the helpful, affable owner. Eat in for
a free house soup, or take away. They make
their own Chinese sausage (lap cheong), too,
in sweet and not-too-sweet versions.

Bhaji on the Beach

315A Barrenjoey Road, Newport

Tel 9979 4944   South Indian

Signature onion bhaji (chickpea-batter fritters) sit on a mixed snack platter, showing off south Indian shtick. That's what this well-above-average beachside Indian is about, despite crowd-pleasers such as mango and butter chicken and the odd Kashmiri korma. Head south for peppery chicken chettinad or a feisty beef Mangalore (with a sharp vinegar and chilli gravy). Masala dosa is fat and crisp, and there's a full vegetarian menu, from dhal to avial (vegetables in a coconut and curry leaf sauce).

Elkarim

126 Pacific Highway, Roseville

Tel 9416 4099   Lebanese

The name means "the generous", and this 30-year-old stalwart lives up to its moniker with colourful, fresh and vibrant dips, salads and more, with the decor refreshed by new owners. Slather lemony hummus, including a lamb version, and labna with garlic and mint, over Lebanese bread. Lamb with pomegranate and almonds on rice pilaf is a specialty; the fried kibbeh great; while barbecued octopus is one of the more unusual proteins to receive the lemon, garlic, parsley and olive oil treatment. There's baklava, of course, and Lebanese ice-creams, too, plus takeaway.

Goemon

161 Middle Head Road, Mosman

Tel 9968 4983   Japanese

Sorry to let out the secret but this youthful, cheery, sushi-and-more cafe on the quieter side of Mosman Junction does fresh, easy, tasty Japanese with a smile. The fact that it's a bit small and popular means you may have to come early, yet it's a fun place for all the usual tempura and teriyaki dishes plus a fine choice of "creative" sushi – big fat rolls with lots of yummy things inside. Try salmon and spicy leek or miso kaori kingfish with dried miso paste.

Grape Garden

52 Penshurst Street, Willoughby

Tel 9967 2001   Chinese (northern)

No prizes for decor here but Peking duck is a winner: glistening red-lacquered skin, meaty and fatty below, served with not-too-thin, not-too-thick pancakes and a choice of nourishing duck and cabbage soup or rich handmade noodles tossed with on-the-bone duck pieces to follow. A plate of greens – minced pork and stir-fried beans – is all you need to round it off. Oh, and their jiaozhi (pan-fried dumplings) are yummy, too. BYO, cash only.

Kaiserstub'n

Cnr Mona Vale & McCarrs Creek roads, Terrey Hills

Tel 9450 0300   Austrian

An authentic Austrian country inn next to Australian bushland comes complete with stags' heads, lace curtains, Germanic staff and huge serves of well-prepared hale-and-hearty fare. Roast pork dumplings and sauerkraut, bratwurst, schnitzel, goulash and spaetzle might just do it for you, washed down with Austrian beers and wines. Otherwise there are excellent cold cuts and soups plus house-made ice-cream and hot fruit desserts. You may need to leave some space for pancakes with apricots or quark cheese pockets.

Top BBQ

828C Pittwater Road, Dee Why

Tel 9982 8088   Chinese (Cantonese)

Barbecue is just one feature of this lantern-hung roadside Chinese, just shy of Dee Why's busy heart. Yes, there's crisp-skinned Shandong chicken and roast duck but it's worth unearthing some of the home-style pork and pickled vegetable braises and hot pots, or asking about weekend seafood specials. Service is friendly and obliging, with advice available. It'd be tops in your 'hood.

Toriciya

18 Cammeray Road, Cammeray

Tel 9904 2277 **Japanese**

An authentic izakaya (Japanese bar/eatery) in deepest Cammeray is something to be celebrated – if you're into sake and shochu and bar-food-sized dishes. Add hard-ish dark-wood chairs and a choice of counter or plain-table seating, an izakaya-obsessive owner and good little yakitori – classic izakaya food – and Toriciya is the whole package. Order a series of skewers, including tsukune (minced chicken patties) and maybe the finely sliced okra with squid, served in a pretty ceramic beaker.

SOUTH

Delhi O Delhi

1/3 Erskineville Road, Newtown

Tel 9557 4455 **Indian**

It may be off the King Street strip but curry-heads have had no trouble finding this modern Indian diner at the base of a new apartment block. That's probably because of the good service and carefully spiced regional (mostly northern) menu. Try goat aloo – flakily rich-sauced meat still on the bone and a zingy chicken chettinad, sparked with curry leaves.

Dong Ba

296 Chapel Road South, Bankstown

Tel 9708 0327 **Vietnamese**

Also at 40 Park Road, Cabramatta

Tel 9755 0727

It shares a name with the main market in the central Vietnamese town of Hue. That's probably why its specialty (most Vietnamese eateries have one) is Hue-style noodle soup, or bun bo Hue. Order a basinful, dump lettuce, sprouts, salad herbs and purple cabbage shreds into the strong, spicy, lemongrassy broth, season with lemon, and slurp.

Emon

432 Cleveland Street, Surry Hills

Tel 9698 0778 **Japanese**

Chef Koichiro Mizusawa has an impressive CV and an equally impressive approach to

Japanese cooking – a few prime ingredients, start-from-scratch stocks and market special dishes daily. Check the sashimi specials list for snapper skin or collar, or perhaps just a one-bowl serve of bakudan – where the sashimi offcuts land. Salmon, tuna, kingfish, sea urchin and snapper are piled on rice, with a just-set quail egg that's been slow-steamed in the onsen (hot spring) style.

Green Bamboo

159 Tower Street, Panania

Tel 9773 0262 **Modern Asian**

Add great service – and the prices – to your list of reasons for loving this family-friendly suburban gem with its bamboo-lined walls, majestic Buddha heads and temple engravings. The tasty, nourishing food weaves through traditional Vietnamese, Thai and Malaysian dishes where the chilli intensity is turned down and the coconut milk use restrained. Kway teow noodles are very good indeed. A red duck curry with pineapple and tomato is a masterful balance of hot, sweet, salty and sour.

Green Palace

182 King Street, Newtown

Tel 9550 5234 **Cambodian/Thai**

Meat eaters beware: protein here is gluten dressed as lamb, or chicken, or... Surrender to the talent of Kijja Silanuluck as he makes a religious vocation of feeding you (and your inner Buddhist) on tasty vegan Cambodian and Thai standards. Tempeh masquerades as brawn with chilli basil; soya wraps bob like mini croissants in a light five-spice broth.

Janani

32 Burlington Road, Homebush

Tel 9763 2314 **Sri Lankan**

Also at Shop 3/108 Station Street, Wentworthville

Tel 9636 5233

189 Missenden Road, Newtown

Tel 9519 0057

A mini Sri Lankan-spiced empire is coming soon to a suburb near you. Or that's how it seems as Janani spreads its wings. Lunchtime thalis are probably the key to its success but

be part of the scene

king street wharf

delve deeper with sambols (relishes such as pol sambol with fresh coconut), hoppers (pancake-style flat breads) and pittu (steamed rice cylinders). Goat curry, too, of course.

Kammadhenu
171 King Street, Newtown
Tel 9550 2611   **Asian**

Roaming through South and South-East Asia keeps the kitchen busy at this colourfully casual cheap'n'cheerful. You can order Malaysian laksa and an Asian beer, although a massive south Indian/Sri Lankan dosa or a thali tray of curries, rice and pickles is even better. Complete your regional tour with lampreis, a post-colonial blend of crusty yellow rice, clove-spiked curry gravy, pickles and fried fish balls baked in a banana leaf parcel.

Seri Nonya
561 Kingsway, Miranda
Tel 9525 0036   **Malaysian**

There's something so addictive about lemongrass and turmeric, coconut milk and chilli. A waft of Nonya aromas from this stalwart southern outpost will quickly satisfy any serious hankerings. Go for daily and seasonal specials, assam (tamarind) fish, popiah (fresh pancake rolls) when available, sambal eggplant and gula sago melaka (sago pearls in palm sugar syrup) for dessert. Chilli crab is a marvel, too – ring first to check that it's on or order ahead.

Taste Bakery
42 Foveaux Street, Surry Hills
Tel 9281 7228   **Thai/Vietnamese**

Co-owner Hieu Luong keeps the food coming. From a chicken shop in Bondi to a fine diner (see City review of Taste on Sussex), he has also found time to feed Surry Hills lunchtime crowds on tangy Thai and Vietnamese stir-fries plus classic banh mi – filled Vietnamese baguettes, and sandwiches. The three kinds of pork roll with pickles, fresh vegies and fresh chilli rings is all five food groups in one yummy package.

WEST

Al Aseel ★
Shop 4, 173 Waterloo Road, Greenacre
Tel 9758 6744   **Lebanese**
FAVOURITE GLOBAL GEM

Foule, fatteh, felafel and fattoush are just four reasons this canteen-style fast-foodery packs them in day and night. Then there's thick, airy hummus, even nicer with lamb mince and pine nuts on top, and more mezze than you could hope to consume in one sitting, as well as grills and tahini-baked fish (samke harra). No alcohol, no BYO, lots of fabulous food.

An
27 Greenfield Parade, Bankstown
Tel 9796 7826   **Vietnamese**

Pho as fast-food franchise? This large, efficient noodle-soup shop may feel a little clinical but the soup stock is comfort food in a bowl. A long-time favourite with a straightforward menu – beef (bo) or chicken (gai) pho (noodle soup) plus choices of added meat, right through to dac biet (house special) – An remains un-pho-gettable.

Bau Truong
250 Canley Vale Road, Canley Heights
Tel 9755 7099   **Vietnamese**
Also at 42 John Street, Cabramatta
Tel 9727 4492

They specialise in chargrilled meats, served on big white plates with steamed "broken rice" (a softer, second-quality grain), table salad (herbs and lettuce) and soup. Noodle soups are nourishingly good here, including the signature bun bo Hue (central-style chilli soup), bun rieu (a tomatoey snail and seafood soup) and bun moc (with pork loaf slices). Don't forget to dip your meat slices in the shrimpy, lemongrassy, chilli jam.

Frattini

122 Marion Street, Leichhardt

Tel 9569 2997   Italian

This 17-year-old landmark local is a fave for the friendly welcome, the classic Italian decor and spectacularly direct waiters. Sides and salads such as bruschetta and caprese are unfussy and fresh. The signature dish, spinach and ricotta dumplings with gorgonzola sauce, is fabulous, and spicy rigatoni with Italian sausage is perfectly satisfying. Pancakes with cooked strawberries, cream and mascarpone is something every local should serve.

Gelateria Caffé 2000

650 Darling Street, Rozelle

Tel 9555 6032   Italian

Rome in Rozelle. Italian breakfasts, focaccia, salads, rustic soups, pasta, risi e bisi (rice and peas), meat dishes, warm, gracious service, and the winter tradition of polentata – polenta with toppings served on a communal board. Then make sure you have the famous gelato (see Ten of the Best Ice-creams). Cash only.

Jasmin 1

224 The Boulevarde, Punchbowl

Tel 9740 7866   Lebanese

Word is their felafel are Sydney's best. We haven't tried every version but these fat, crunchy balls are pretty fine. Garlic chicken is another benchmark dish you should always sit down to here, in Jasmin's fanciful faux marble and mural-covered surrounds. Great hummus, babaghanoush and all the favourites. No frills, no alcohol. Who needs them?

La Boheme

332 Darling Street, Balmain

Tel 9810 0829   European

It's not a central European hunting lodge; it just feels like one. With its vaulted, wood-panelled ceiling, leadlight and dark wrought-iron light fittings, schnitzel, goulash, dumplings and roast duck with two kinds of cabbage (sweet, vinegary red and gentle sauerkraut), it'll quell your deepest comfort food cravings. We love the mushroom gravy that comes in a gravy boat with a chicken Jaeger. Make merry with a mug of Czech, German or Belgian beer.

Na Zdrowie

161 Glebe Point Road, Glebe

Tel 9660 1242   Polish

Barszcz is Polish for borscht. Just so you know. And the Poles have their own hearty version of this beef and beetroot-based soup, including a white (no beetroot) version. These and other soothing broths are just part of the show at Na Zdrowie (Polish for "cheers"). There are pierogi (savoury parcels) and platters of cold cuts. Pretty decor and BYO vodka. Na zdrowie!

Nostos

121 Norton Street, Leichhardt

Tel 9550 0144   Greek

Loud, late-night bouzouki parties are one way to test-drive this eatery. Or else put the excellent modern yet home-style menu through a quieter, weeknight workout. Oven-baked lamb topped with a half-roasted garlic head is so good you'll try to eat the bones, too. Baked fetta, fried haloumi, marvellous moussaka and a slice of yiayia's walnut cake and yoghurt will get you dancing the Zorba with the best of them.

Spicy Sichuan

1–9 Glebe Point Road, Glebe

Tel 9660 8200   Chinese

Instant word association: Sichuan cuisine and dried red chillies. There are heaps of them here, strewn over and under whole fish, swimming in hotpots and blended in very, very hot chilli oil. There's a chilli-red and lucky-yellow photo menu to assist but don't miss the soup-squirting Sichuan dumplings and cumin and Sichuan pepper-spiced beef. Expect to queue. And sweat a little.

Summerland

457 Chapel Road North, Bankstown

Tel 9708 5107   Lebanese

Take a trip to Tripoli at this no-frills diner. You can't beat the $30 banquet for a taste of almost everything, from creamy hummus to rich smooth labna, a tangy oregano salad and house-baked Lebanese bread. Love those mahanek – tiny pine nut-studded sausages, spicy kibbeh nayeh (minced lamb tartare with burghul) and fluffy felafel.